GW00759748

Racecourse Architecture

Paul Roberts and Isabelle Taylor

Turnberry Consulting and Acanthus Press

Contents

Preface

Two hundred and fifty years ago, a young architect by the name of John Carr began a glittering career by designing a grandstand at York Racecourse in England. This was not merely York's first grandstand, nor was it only the first grandstand of any thoroughbred racecourse, but – in the modern sense of the building type – it was the first grandstand at any sporting venue anywhere in the world. This is no mean pedigree. Nonetheless, in the world of sport architecture, racecourses have, for the most part, been overlooked. This book sets out to remedy that oversight.

I have been involved in the strategic planning and design of racecourses for a number of years. I have worked with racing clubs across the world and visited countless tracks in my professional capacity. What has never failed to strike me is the singular and special position that racecourses hold within the realm of sporting venues. They have a long, varied and fertile architectural heritage. It is not uncommon for a single site to boast great architectural diversity in terms of the ages, styles and shapes of their physical components. Saratoga Race Course, for instance, has stables from the 1840s, a grandstand from the 1890s, clubhouse from the 1920s, a stand extension from the 1960s and entrance buildings from the 2000s. Few other sports venues, if any, possess this breath of physical evolution.

By stadium standards, racecourses boast impressive lineages. The earliest extant cricket ground, Lord's, opened on its present London site in 1814; Fenway Park in Boston, the oldest continuously-used baseball stadium, dates to 1912. The third oldest baseball arena – Dodger Stadium in Los Angeles – was built as recently as 1962. Chester Racecourse, in comparison, has been holding races on the same land since 1539. Admittedly, Chester is a precocious example, but as Newmarket (founded in the seventeenth century), Ascot (founded 1711), or nineteenth-century examples such as Flemington, Randwick and Saratoga illustrate, racecourses have maintained a pattern, albeit not without exception, of continuing on the same location upon which they began life. They may undergo radical redevelopments, but rarely are they moved. A cursory survey of sporting history shows how often the major stadia of other sports undergo wholesale demolition, relocation and rebuilding.

What is the reason for this difference in approach? Put simply, building a racecourse is an enormously challenging task, more so than other stadium types. To begin with, they are large in scale, which often prohibits finding a new site. Secondly, compared to the typical stadium, a racecourse requires a wider range of facilities. A racecourse environment encompasses many different elements: various stands, parade ring, sometimes pre-parade ring, temporary and permanent stabling, betting facilities, refreshment facilities and the track itself. Furthermore, these facilities are spread out over the site; it is not possible to have the condensed arrangement of other stadium types. Racecourses must cater for the very specific requirements of the horses, jockeys and trainers, not to mention the spectators. Unlike many other sporting events, racegoers do not remain fixed to a ticketed seat. They wander from pre-parade ring, to parade ring, to betting window to grandstand, and want the passage between each to be smooth and swift. They want at all times good views of the horses, jockeys, track and, often, other spectators. Moreover, relative to other sports, the period of sporting action is very short in terms of the time attendees spend at the venue. With all these components to consider, racecourses are amongst the most complex of sports facilities. Their design, therefore, requires prudent consideration.

The following chapters, documenting the evolution of this specialised form of architecture, will outline that over the centuries racecourses have grown progressively more and more composite in nature. With technology increasing apace and society becoming ever more demanding, this pattern will continue. As racing clubs face escalating competition from other forms of leisure, the function of racecourses transcends being purely a place for racing. They must be places to drink, dine, host conferences and more. The factors to be considered when running or designing a course are mounting, and achieving a venue of long-term success has and is becoming a matter of increasing complexity.

For any racecourse, success must be measured by the ability to stage the best racing over the long term in an economically sustainable way. Lasting success and high-quality physical environments are mutual bedfellows; the former is contingent on both the standard of its racing and the standard of its spectator experience. 'Selling an "experience" is the core business of any stadium, and will remain so for many years to come,' wrote architect Rod Sheard of stadium design. Although applicable to almost all sports, it is especially true in the case of thoroughbred racing that spectator experience is unconditionally linked to physical environment.

The most cursory of glances through the history of racecourse architecture suggests that, in the western world at least, attractive environments are chief constituents of permanence and renown. Saratoga, for instance, is the oldest surviving sports venue in North America and ranks amongst its most high-attended tracks. It is celebrated for the charm of its historic buildings and landscape. Compare this to Garden State Park in New Jersey. Opening initially in 1942, Garden State Park hosted some of the finest thoroughbreds and richest purses of the day. It was rebuilt in 1985 (following a fire in 1977) as a soulless, glass and steel stacked monolith. The course never regained its earlier status and, only 16 years later, it closed down permanently.

Design is key to creating the raceday experience that draws racegoers, jockeys, owners and trainers to the world's best racecourses again and again. The combined environment of grandstand, parade ring, entrances and stalls is the stage on which the racing spectacle is played out. It provides the setting for what should be a theatrical experience of colour, excitement and celebration. Physical environments matter at racecourses. The best-designed racecourse in the world would struggle to attract spectators if it failed to host good racing, but physical setting can make or break a racegoer's experience.

Racecourses are fragile enterprises, vulnerable to economic downturns and in particular to the vagaries of gambling legislation. Having a well-designed plan or impressive architectural ensemble is no absolute safeguard against these factors – the dashing Agua Caliente in Mexico, for example, withered after a volte-face of US betting laws reignited neighbouring California's racing industry. Yet, they can significantly improve a racecourse's chances of longevity. Carefully-orchestrated planning and inspiring architecture can distinguish functional destinations, place to watch racing and wager, from theatres of sport, spirit and memory. In the dynamic world of racing, it is the latter which will endure.

Paul Roberts, October 2012

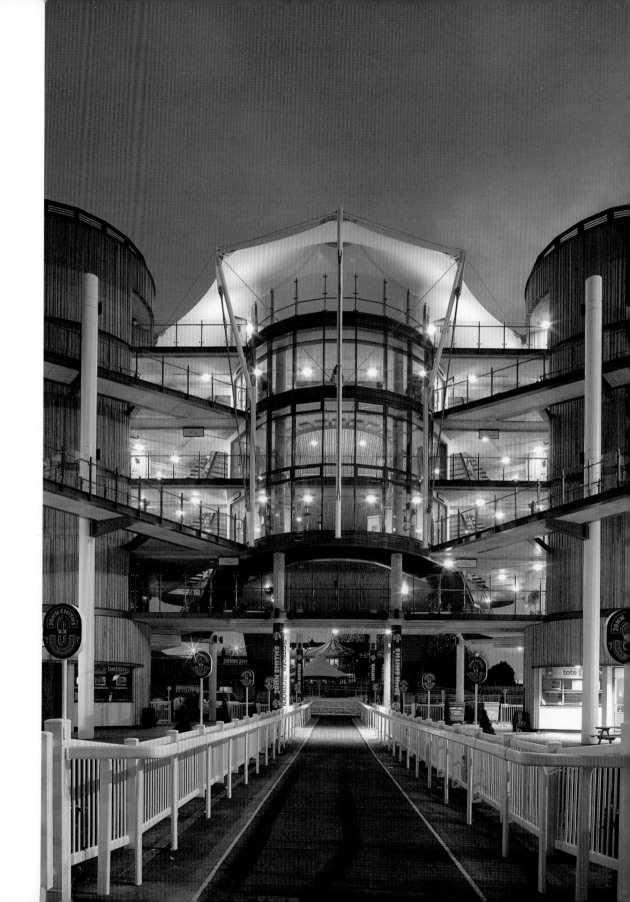

Introduction

'Panem et circenses', bread and circuses, were, according to Roman satirist Juvenal, the driving forces of society. Bread may be needed to feed the body, but spectacle sustains the soul. Few events in sport can rival the visceral pleasure of a day at the races. Few can parallel the spellbinding moment when the horses step majestically onto the track before the Kentucky Derby, or the breakneck dash as the starting tape lifts at Aintree's Grand National. But what have these mesmerising moments to do with architecture? What heed does the racing enthusiast pay to a racecourse's aesthetic so long as their favourite horse is in the lead?

Racecourses are the stage upon which the drama of the thoroughbred is played out, and their buildings are the scenery. Architecture is vital. Yes, its practical dimension in providing shelter is indispensible, but its value transcends this. The buildings of thoroughbred racecourses are crucial ingredients in creating the pageantry and theatre that are integral to the popularity of the sport. The grandstands, clubhouses, totalisators and other structures that make up a racecourse ensemble tell the story of the sport through their physical fabric, making visible in physical form the social, political and economic evolution of thoroughbred racing. Amidst the abundant body of literature on the thoroughbred, however, this subject has been largely overlooked. This book seeks to redress this omission. It charts the hitherto untold story of thoroughbred racecourse architecture from across the world.

The book is divided into two sections. Part I is a chronology that recounts the history of thoroughbred racecourse architecture as a condensed narrative of the most defining phases of the genre. Its pages will chart the dramatic shifts in the nature of racecourse environments over the sport's lifetime, from the ramshackle wooden viewing huts of early Newmarket to the enormous Meydan complex (2010) in Dubai housing a hotel, museum and cinema as well as racing facilities. Within this design evolution common themes have emerged. Six factors stand out as conditioning forces which have wielded the greatest impact upon racing architecture: architectural fashions, technology, scale, betting patterns and laws, competition and globalisation.

- Architectural Fashions: Outwardly, the appearance of racecourse buildings has radically evolved thanks to changing stylistic fashions. Each age has cloaked their grandstands to suit the tastes of the day. Some of these fashions have proved enduring whilst some have not.

- Technology: Technological advances have altered construction patterns of all building types, and racecourses have been no exception. Of new construction techniques, the most palpable impact upon grandstand design was the development of reinforced concrete in the early decades of the twentieth century. This made possible large, cantilevered canopies and obviated the need for obstructive supporting columns.

  Moreover, throughout the sport's history, advancing technology has changed the nature of racing and racegoers. Such changes have had implications on the design of its buildings. Chapter III, for instance, will explain how the advent of the railways in mid-nineteenth-century Europe made courses more accessible, thus more popular, prompting the building of bigger grandstands with higher capacities.

- Scale: The scale of racecourse buildings has grown continuously. They have increased in dimensions, capacity and number. John Carr's grandstand at York, holding two hundred or so patrons, has evolved into the stands of Tokyo Racecourse, with a capacity of 200,000.

Betting: No other single factor has impacted more upon the fortunes of the racing industry than gambling patterns. These patterns have been, in turn, expressed in its architecture. Chapter VII will describe the prodigious impact exerted by the legalisation of pari-mutuel wagering in 1930s America, for example. It triggered the construction of a spate of new courses, such as Santa Anita Park (opened 1934) and Del Mar Turf Club (founded 1937), which dramatically altered the nation's approach to racecourse design, not least by introducing comprehensive master planning and an *au courant* architectural aesthetic to the field.

Competition: York Racecourse pioneered the grandstand concept in the 1750s in what was, in effect, a marketing exercise. Its dazzling new building was intended to present the course as the cynosure of York society. The concept remains influential throughout racing's history. New or impressive structures have always been a means for racecourses to distinguish themselves and gain the edge over their competitors. In the competitive context of recent decades, this methodology has played an increasing role in shaping racecourse design.

Globalisation: The first transatlantic thoroughbred race was the DC International in 1952. Since that date the Sport of Kings has grown slowly but surely more and more international in scope. The escalating ease of international travel and communication has facilitated major worldwide competitions such as the Breeders' Cup and Dubai World Cup. Major competitions require large-scale facilities.

In Part II, the book profiles eight individual courses in a series of case studies. Out of the thousands of racecourses across the world, the book's scope can hope to include but a small proportion. The selection of case studies makes no claims to be a comprehensive survey of the building type but has been compiled with the aim of providing a representative sample of the history of this architectural milieu around the world, from the Sussex Downs to Singapore. The case studies aim to provide an analysis of thoroughbred racing venues which have made particularly original, influential, handsome or representative contributions to this realm. Unavoidably, myriad historic or venerated courses have been omitted from the list, not because they lack merit but rather that the philosophies that informed their design have been illustrated elsewhere. For instance, of the wave of racecourses built in America after the repeal of anti-gambling laws in the 1930s, only Santa Anita Park has been featured as a case study. Of this era, Santa Anita is the course in which the original design vision of its architect and owners survives most intact today. Formulated to complement the chronology, the case studies proffer a deeper look at some of the most important eras and racecourses in the long and varied trajectory of racing architecture.

Part I

A Chronology of Racecourse Architecture

Chapter I

Racing Begins

Antiquity

Horse racing ranks amongst the most ancient of sports. Since the days when nomadic tribesmen raced the earliest domesticated horses across the plains of central Asia, pitting the speed and endurance of horses has gripped the imagination of mankind. By 648 BC mounted horse racing held in hippodromes had established itself on the schedule of the Olympic games, while Plato tells of a 'torch race' ridden upon horseback to venerate the Thracian goddess Bendis. Under the Roman Empire, equestrianism became a passion. Throughout the Empire, ridden horse races were a significant event within Greek-style games whilst chariot racing attracted the greatest crowds of all the Roman sporting events. The hippodromes, or circuses, where these races were held were the mass entertainment centres of the day, acting as nerve centres for social and political life. They were, moreover, amongst the most recognisable and largest building types of the Roman world.

It was under the Romans that the hippodrome became a recognisable building type.[1] The circus at Lepcis Magna in Libya, built in the second century AD, is one of the best preserved examples (Figure 1.1). As typified circus construction, it consisted of two parallel sides with one end enclosed in a semicircle and the other end terminated by starting gates. The sides were formed of tiers of seats, built either against sloping hillside or atop robust stone substructures and topped by a colonnaded limestone gallery. The gates comprised a series of 12 individual stalls, formed by cut stone arches upon piers. Their façade was

lavishly decorated with mosaics and sculpted busts, and, almost certainly, over its centre was placed a box for the presiding magistrate.[2] This general formula was used across the Empire, and it derived its form from the greatest circus of them all, the Circus Maximus in Rome (Figure 1.3).

By the early second century, following remodellings by Julius Caesar (100–44 BC), Augustus (27 BC–AD 14) and Trajan (98–117 AD), the celebrated Circus Maximus had achieved its canonical format. The Circus Maximus was the largest and oldest of Rome's four racing courses, built in a valley between the Palatine and the Aventine. Primarily designed for chariot racing, it also hosted gladiatorial combats, wild animal hunts and processions. The circus measured 620 metres long by 120

Page 12 **1.1** Lepcis Magna in Libya, one of the best preserved Roman circuses

Above **1.2** The Roman circus in Tyre, Lebanon (second century AD), reportedly seated 20,000

Opposite **1.3** Reconstruction of the Circus Maximus, the Roman Empire's most celebrated circus

CIRCVS MAXIMVS

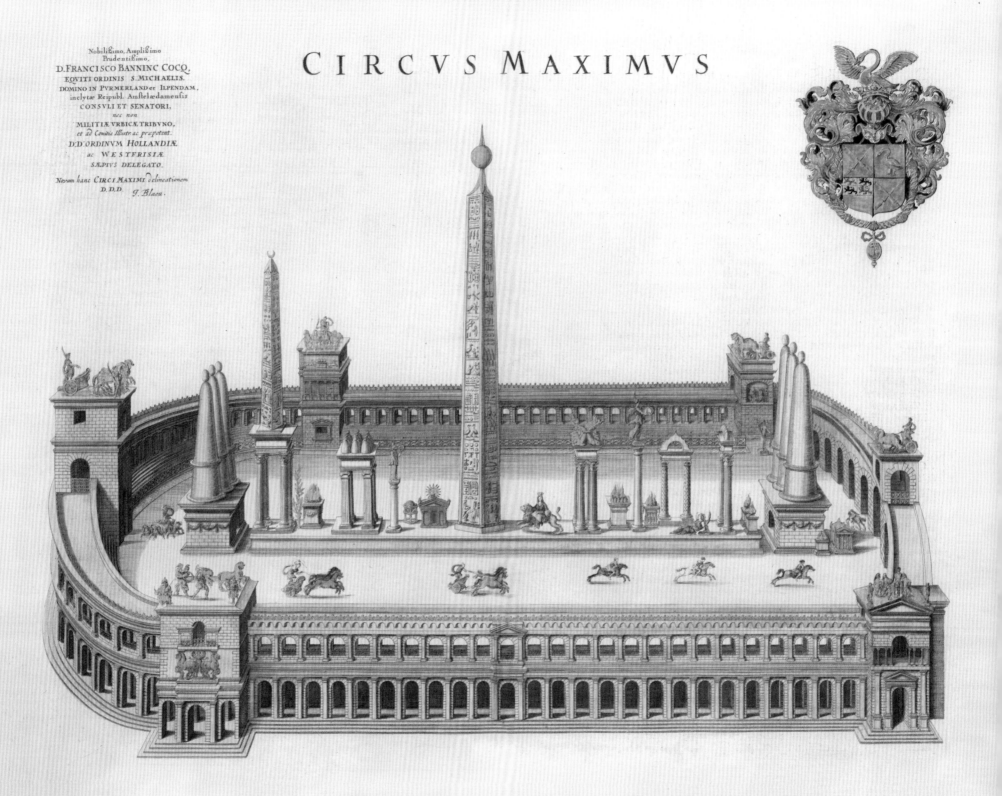

metres wide (over 2,000 by 460 feet), and accommodated at least 150,000 spectators on tiered seating which framed both long sides and the curved eastern end of the arena. The curved end is the only section of the ancient circus that can be seen today, after the substructure of its seating was uncovered in the 1930s. The three tiers of seating were divided by aisles, with marble seats reserved for senators and *equites* and wooden stands for the masses. A raised shrine for the images of the gods served as an imperial box. After fires in 103 AD, Emperor Trajan replaced the wooden stands with brick-faced concrete structures.[3]

Today, to the disappointment of modern visitors, all that remains is the broad outline of the circus yet in its heyday it was considered one of Rome's greatest buildings, which rivalled, according to Pliny the Younger, even the beauty of the temples (Figure 1.4). Its vast dimensions can still be appreciated, however. The Circus Maximus, and other Roman circuses, were colossal, permanent structures capable of holding congregations in the tens or even hundreds of thousands. After the fall of the Empire, though, this building art was lost. For 1,300 years the discipline of racecourse architecture lay dormant, constituting little more than wooden shacks.

1.4 The Circus Maximus today, set against the backdrop of the Palatine Hill

Opposite **1.5** The Hippodrome at Jerash in Jordan (second century AD) typifies the formula of the Roman circuses. The starting gates can be seen in the background

British Beginnings

It seems that the Romans carried with them an appetite for horse sports to the lands they conquered, for horse racing was established in Britain by the Middle Ages. The eighth-century monk-scholar Bede wrote of horsemen contending the mettle and speed of their steeds upon a plain ideally 'adapted to a horse-course', whilst in the Anglo-Saxon poem *Beowulf* racing was featured as an aristocratic pastime.[4] In the twelfth century, public holidays are recorded as being celebrated with informal races in London and Chester.

In the sixteenth century, the sport began to take on a more organised mantle. Horse races became regular events, typically accompanying local fairs, known to have taken place at Doncaster, Carlisle, York, Black Hambleton and Chester. The Roodee course in Chester survives to this day (Figure 1.6). Here, on Shrove Tuesday 1539[5] the Saddlers' Company donated a silver bell 'to be given to him who shall run best and furthest on horseback', marking the earliest racing held at the Roodee where it has been held almost continuously ever since. It is Britain's, indeed the world's, oldest extant racecourse. The nature of the racing that took place upon its track was, however, far removed from the sport known today.

It was not until the seventeenth century that the roots of modern, organised horse racing first took hold, under the fashionable impetus of the Stuart kings. James I (1603-1625) was far from being a natural horseman himself; indeed, one historian has described him as the 'worst rider in the world' who 'once went head-first into a frozen pond'.[6] But he and his court sparked a new aristocratic zeal for racing in England. He

instituted meetings at Richmond in Yorkshire and Enfield Chase in Middlesex; at Chester he reorganised the races; and, from 1619, at a small Suffolk market town he patronised a royal course, which has ever since been the unchallenged headquarters of racing the world across. This market town was, of course, Newmarket. Newmarket's flat heath offered the perfect setting for James's favourite pastimes of hunting, deercoursing and hawking, and the king, never slow to forsake scenes of business and employment for amusement, made the place a special object of benefaction. History has it that in 1621, parliament dispatched a contingency of its members to Newmarket to petition the king to return to London.[7] His first recorded attendance at a race there was in March 1619.

James's patronage kindled a light at Newmarket which was flamed by his son, Charles I (1625-1649) and, after the interval of the Commonwealth, by his grandson, Charles II (1660-1685). The contribution of Charles II to the history of horse racing was decisive. Just eight days after his restoration, he engaged a Master of the Royal Stud; in 1665 he instituted by Act of Parliament the first race to be conducted in Britain under written rules; and in the same year transported the sport to the Americas. The king was not content to merely watch racing but also took part himself, winning no mean share of contests. Royal interest enhanced the prestige of the sport in general, and Newmarket in particular. By 1669, it was established custom that the whole court would take up residence there twice yearly for long stretches of time. The poet Alexander Pope acerbically noted that 'Newmarket's

1.6 In this map of Chester from 1611, the 'Roode Eye' course is marked to the south west of the city centre where it remains to this day

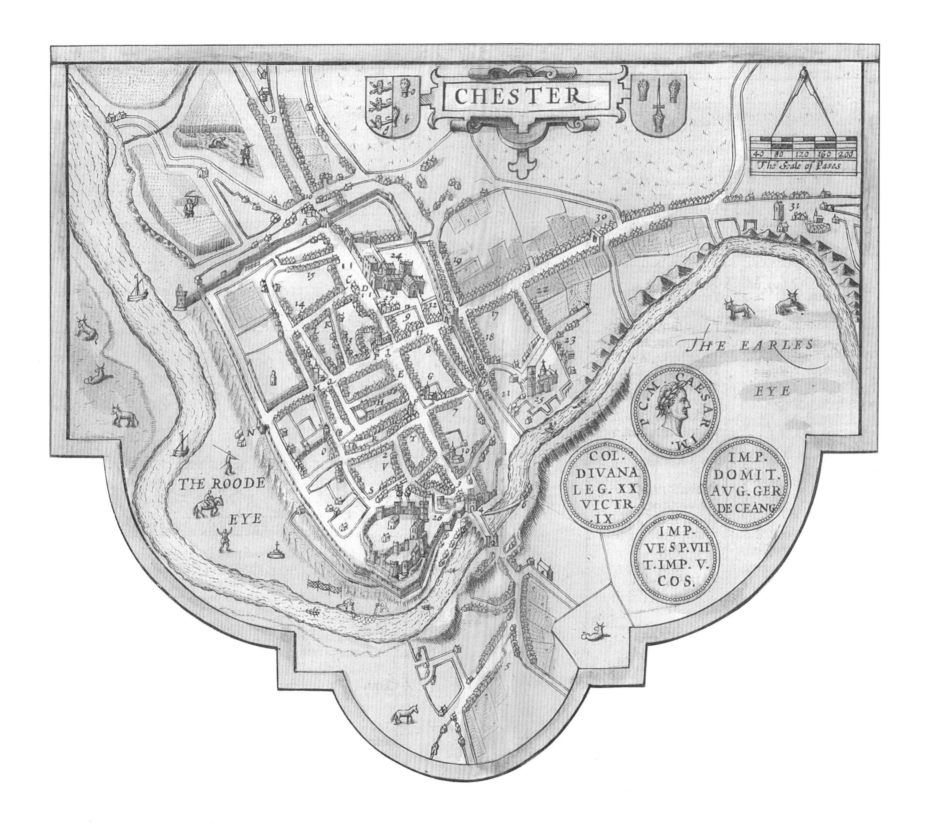

CHESTER

The Scale of Pases

THE EARLES
EYE

THE ROODE
EYE

P.C.M. CAESAR VLI.

COL. DIVANA LEG. XX VICTR IX

IMP. DOMIT. AVG. GER DE CEANG

IMP. VESP. VII T. IMP. V. COS.

glory rose as Britain's fell'. Charles's legacy at Newmarket remains to this day – it was he that established its racing stables, the Town Plate and the tradition of Spring and Autumn meetings.[8]

Its windswept heath was the birthplace of the modern sport, its importance measured not only by the quality of its racing but also by its long association with the Jockey Club, which made Newmarket its permanent home shortly after its foundation in the 1750s. No other venue is so synonymous with the history of thoroughbred racing. Yet despite its royal patronage, the racecourse was, in architectural terms,

thoroughly undistinguished. Newmarket's races were not a mass spectator sport; indeed, every effort was made to deter the crowds. The heath was not a public venue, but rather the playground of the nobility where little division was made between the rider and onlookers. Spectators on horseback charged alongside the racing horses in a cacophony of cheers, trampling hooves, and cracking whips (Figure 1.7).

It has been alleged that the first grandstand at Newmarket was constructed during the reign of Charles I. No contemporary sources survive to confirm this, but had such a structure existed it would have been far removed from the

1.7 Newmarket as it looked in the 1720s. Note the basic viewing stand on the right (Peter Tillemanns, *View of the Heath*, circa 1723)

modern-day idea of a grandstand, little more than a timber shed in fact, with a simple viewing platform offering some shelter from the elements.[9] A painting by Peter Tillemans documents that by circa 1723 Newmarket possessed a square, two-storey, masonry viewing tower with shuttered openings on the upper floor.[10] Perhaps, it has been mooted, this was the King's Stand commissioned by Charles II. Its form was a simplified version of the hunting towers erected within country estates, such as the Elizabethan example at Lyme Park in Cheshire.[11] Basic in appearance, it claimed few architectural pretensions. Accommodation within permanent buildings was, simply, not yet a part of the racing culture.

The racing culture was nonetheless to progress in leaps and bounds thanks to Charles II's enthusiasm. It catalysed the rapid development of racecourses throughout the British Isles. By the opening of the eighteenth century, meetings up and down the country prospered. Epsom, Salisbury, and Windsor all staged meetings, with Newmarket at the vanguard. From ovals to triangles and pear shapes to figures of eight, the tracks abounded in eccentricity. The ground could be emphatically flat or steeply inclined, or somewhere in between. Indeed, the only common feature of the host of courses was that the races were always run on turf. Racedays were arranged typically by local gentry on country estates or on common land alongside market towns that were keen to capitalise on the economic advantages horse racing could bring. As the century wore on, they became increasingly subject to formal organisation. Legislation passed in 1740 restricted the number of permitted horse races, with the effect of consolidating the organisation of the sport. A coordinated calendar of events took shape on an array of established courses, regulated by the newly-established Jockey Club. During the reign of George III (1760-1820), the five 'Classic' races were instituted: the St Leger, founded at Doncaster (1776); the Oaks (1779) and Derby (1780) at Epsom; and the 2000 Guineas (1809) and 1000 Guineas (1814) at Newmarket. Quickly lionised, these races both contributed to and reflected the growing excitement and cachet of racing.

Meetings were not only sporting events, but also great social ones, comparable to concerts, supper parties, and balls in the newly fashionable Assembly Rooms. The social facet was fundamental to the character of horse racing, and was to have a formative influence upon the architecture that accompanied it. Permanent buildings upon racecourses were, however, slow to appear. The aristocracy and gentry watched early thoroughbred racing from their carriages or horseback, while the less fortunate stood in the open, perhaps under canvas tents or upon raised wooden platforms akin to the earliest Newmarket stand. By the second half of the eighteenth century, though, the idea of a permanent structure offering more exclusive and sheltered surroundings from which to view the spectacle became increasingly attractive following the ground-breaking precedent set by York Racecourse in the 1750s. [12]

Chapter II

York: The First Grandstand

Page 22 **1.8** York Racecourse grandstand opened in 1756. Designed by architect John Carr, it was the first instance of the building typology and prompted numerous imitators

Opposite **1.9** Lodge Park, a seventeenth-century hunting lodge in Gloucestershire, possibly served as a model for York's first grandstand

In the eighteenth century, York held a covetable position as the economic and social centre of northern England. The city's corporation and private entrepreneurs capitalised on its burgeoning leisure industry, chartering a thorough development of the city's facilities from the 1730s onwards, beginning with the relocation of its racecourse to Knavesmire Common in 1730. The Palladian Assembly Rooms were completed in 1732, the New Walk was set out 1733-40 and a theatre was opened in 1744, having the combined effect of securing York's position as the fashionable metropolis of the North. Pivotal to this reputation was its racecourse. Visitors swarmed to the course, drawn both by the racing and the abundance of ancillary activities – refreshment stalls, cock and prize fighting, travelling players – which obliged spectators wishing to watch the action of the turf to vie with the throngs unless they sat in carriages or upon horseback. This scramble of racegoers, and suspension of the social hierarchy, was often the cause of much chagrin to the patricians of Georgian England.[1] There was distinct need for a building which would both physically and metaphorically elevate spectators.[2]

On 7 December 1753, York Corporation authorised a 99-year lease to build a stand on the Knavesmire racecourse (Figure 1.8). The ringleader of the project was the second Marquess of Rockingham. Young, rich, a future Prime Minister, Rockingham was racing's leading champion in the county and alongside fellow turfites and local citizens, he oversaw the construction of a grandstand intended to aggrandise York's course. It was a ground breaking moment for horse racing. The building unintentionally became the paragon for an ensuing skein of racecourse

architecture. As yet, however, there were no precedents for such a grandstand. The few buildings that existed on racecourses were crude, wooden dais with no architectural ambition, as those at Newmarket demonstrated. Thus the Knavesmire grandstand necessitated a completely new invention of type. A model suggested itself in the form of the hunting lodge, structures built as observation posts for the earlier recreation of deer coursing on country estates. Horse racing held several points of similarity with deer-coursing, which entailed releasing deer onto an enclosed track to be pursued by hounds. A structure was often constructed to afford a view over the finishing line, with the appellation 'grandstand' being coined circa 1615. A particularly fine example is that of Lodge Park in Gloucestershire, in use from 1634 (Figure 1.9). It displays all the fundamental components of later grandstand design – a hall or reception room on the ground floor, a large banqueting room on the first floor with large windows overlooking the course and a viewing platform on the roof. Drawings of Lodge Park were made by Rockingham's personal architect, Henry Flitcroft, which, it has been surmised, directly influenced the York commission.[3]

John Carr (1723-1807) was selected as the architect of York's grandstand. In 1753, Carr was a promising architect, having already completed several domestic buildings. It was with the York stand, though, that he made his name. His proposal was elegantly simple. A two-storey structure, seven bays across with standing accommodation on the roof, its appearance is known from a 1755 engraving by Fourdrinier.[4] In terms of style, the building's Palladian treatment demonstrated Carr's fluent grasp of the classical vocabulary. He created a symmetrical building of classical modular proportions. In both its plan and Italianate architectural features, it appears to have taken its cue from Lodge Park (Figure 1.10). Akin to the hunting lodge, it contained two substantial rooms. Its arcaded and rusticated ground floor with pedimented entrance sat below a first-floor reception room extending the length and breadth of the building where the racegoers could assemble to watch the racing and socialise. Again echoing the arrangement at Lodge Park, the assembly spilled out onto a balcony which extended from this room and wrapped around the sides of the building. The balcony was stepped to ensure those at the rear of the balcony and within the reception room a good view of the track. It was a dignified, comfortable building, uniting form with function.

The enormity of this commission in terms of the history of sports architecture cannot be overstated. Carr's structure vaulted the built environment of horse racing from makeshift shelters to elegant neo-classical edifice. The jump was spectacular. No other modern sport could boast any sort of architecture for another century.

Carr had formulated a new building-type deftly fit for purpose. It provided a space in which to view the races and socialise, and, through its sophisticated architectural vocabulary, enunciated the éclat of the sport and its patrons. While entry to the racecourse was free of charge, a fee was charged to gain admittance to the grandstand, making its commodious environment a foremost status symbol within York society. Carr, furthermore, underscored social hierarchies and activities

inside the building. The first-floor space was conceived akin to the fashionable assembly rooms. It was designed to appeal foremost to female racegoers, while the roof was undoubtedly a male preserve. The latter was a viewing platform from which the gentlemen could indulge their passion for the sport at hand, and the less salubrious pursuit of betting, without disturbing the sensibilities of the ladies below. The grandstand's form reveals its dual functions – sporting and social. These two factors have remained intrinsic to British racing ever since.[5] Since the inauguration of Carr's stand, successful grandstand design has entailed an intimate understanding and awareness of the social and cultural interests of the patrons.[6]

Upon opening in 1756, York's stand enjoyed a warm reception. In sharp contrast to the utilitarian and makeshift viewing stands of Newmarket, it quickly came to be emblematic of the meeting itself. A silver token bearing a reproduction of the building was given to each subscriber to the stand, while Fourdrinier's engraving and a perspective drawing made circa 1760 by William Lindley did much to publicise Carr's design. The design was reported throughout the country, and it was immediately established as the paradigm for the building type. For the first time, horse racing had an architectural identity, and York's superiority as a racing venue made Carr's stand a frequent subject of emulation as other courses across the country strove to imitate its success.[7]

Over the following decades, a series of grandstands was built in Britain which drew direct inspiration from the Knavesmire stand and firmly codified the nature of grandstand

1.10 John Carr's plans for the York Racecourse grandstand. The building still partly survives to this day as the façade of its ground-floor veranda, which was transplanted in 1908 to its present location in the paddock. Only one other grandstand thought to be designed by Carr survives, that at Kelso Racecourse in Scotland

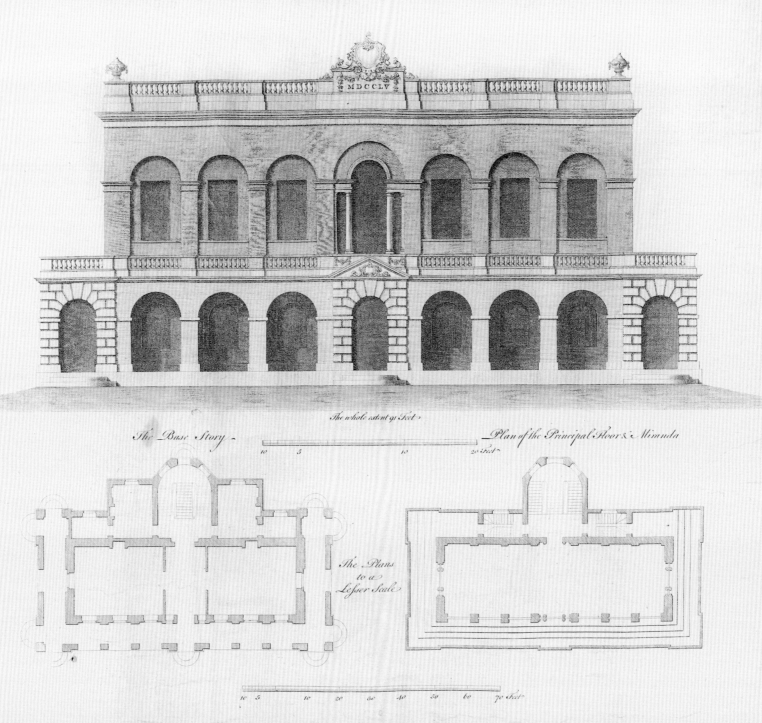

The whole extent 91 Feet

The Base Story   Plan of the Principal Floor & Mimuda

10   5   10   20 Feet

The Plans
to a
Lesser Scale

10   5   10   20   30   40   50   60   70 Feet

The Grand stand erected at York, for the conveniency of seeing the Horse Races.

A similar device was known to have existed at Stamford. The grandstands were in themselves sophisticated works and places of fashion in their locality, serving not only as venues to watch racing, but also for card parties, concerts and watching cricket, for instance. (The pliable, multi-purpose nature of the grandstand typology is, in fact, particularly valued today, as the final chapter of this chronology discusses.) Richmond's grandstand was an especially distinguished example. Built of ashlared stone, a sweeping staircase opened onto the grand reception room which gave views onto the course through five large windows. Its elegant fabric was made the more pronounced by its solitary setting on a low moor. Contemporary newspaper articles praised such stands as 'commodious and elegant' (Richmond), 'proper and commodious' (Beverley) and 'elegant and well-contrived' (Stamford).[8]

Carr's Knavesmire grandstand set his personal career upon a successful trajectory, and he received several other grandstand commissions. In 1776, a triad of racing enthusiasts, including Rockingham, approached Carr to design a grandstand as part of an extensive programme for a new racecourse at Doncaster. A year later, he was appointed by Nottingham Racecourse to design a stand. The stand built at Nottingham was, in all essentials, a replica of that at York (Figure 1.12). Although twenty years had elapsed since the erection of the York stand, that it was still held as practical and popular is in evidence from the buildings Carr produced for Nottingham and Doncaster, whose forms clearly echoed the Knavesmire prototype. Differences between the Nottingham and Doncaster stands, though, indicated

building. Examples include those at Stamford (1766), Beverley (1767), Richmond (circa 1775) (Figure 1.11) and Kelso (designed 1778, built 1822). The grandstand on Beverley Racecourse in Yorkshire typified the form that they assumed. It was rectangular in shape, two-storeys, with large arched openings overlooking the course and it adopted the classical architectural idiom. Offices and refreshments were housed on the lower floor, while, as at York, a large salon occupied the first floor topped by a viewing platform on the roof. Those watching proceedings from the rooftop were protected from the elements by a covering, possibly a timber frame covered in copper, canvas or paper.

Race Stand.

1.12 Nottingham grandstand by John Carr, built circa 1777. It was almost identical to the York grandstand

how the original blueprint could be modified to meet with the specific demands of the patrons. The Doncaster stand adopted the traditional two-storey, flat-roof format with a Tuscan arcade on the lower level supporting a balcony above. However, in terms of size and sophistication, it was far more ambitious than either York or Nottingham. It afforded two further bays of accommodation and a curved balcony opened out from the first floor on its eastern side to afford better views over the finishing line. The alterations reflected both the growing popularity of the sport and increasing crowds, and the heightened aspirations of the clients, who sought to create a premier racing venue on the virgin site.[9]

From the 1750s to 1800, Carr's designs established the grandstand as a specialised building type. In attaching a social and protean dimension to the building type, they set a model which applies to grandstand design in the twenty-first century. The fundamental template they had established was enormously successful. It was so successful, in fact, that it endured into the nineteenth century. It provided the bones upon which the next era of grandstand designers were to build, as they formulated the newest generation of racecourse buildings to answer the changing demands of the sport and society.

Chapter III

The Nineteenth Century

Britain

Horse-racing is no doubt strongly identified with the habits of an English-man. He must go to the Derby, and in so doing believes he is contributing to the support of a great national institution... He witnesses with intensest interest the struggles of the noble animals as they career along the turf with the fleetness of the eagle, and while his spirits become excited amid the general enthusiasm, he believes he is indulging feelings which are common to every Englishman, and which are about as essential to patriotism as loyalty itself.

(John Churchill, *The West of England Miscellany*, 1844)

In nineteenth-century Britain, horse racing became a national institution. Attendance figures at fixtures soared and surging numbers clamoured for admittance to grandstands. Meetings grew in numbers, organisation and commercialism. Races grew shorter, horses running in them became younger; and the results commanded increasing press coverage. Furthermore, the Jockey Club formalised its influence as its codified rules of racing were taken up across the country. In terms of its architecture, however, evolution was somewhat less fervent.

In the first half of the nineteenth century, no better model for grandstand construction could be devised than the 1756 York grandstand prototype. Its template of a two-storey elevation plus rooftop, housing a mixture of socialising and viewing spaces garbed in classical livery, continued to provide the blueprint for the building type. That is not to say, though, that the grandstands of the 1800s were identical to those of the preceding century. John Carr's pattern stood as the kernel to which the new generation added to accord with changing architectural tastes and, more importantly, advances within the sport itself.

The Carr-style stands, with their generous reception rooms built for the recreation of fashionable society, were simply too small to contain the growing crowds. Furthermore, these crowds were taking increased interest in watching the events of the Turf rather than the events of the social arena, and a growing need was perceived for more spectating seats and fewer for card-playing and polite conversation. The Carr template was adapted in response.

In the first instance, existing eighteenth-century stands were extended by the building of loggias, verandas and balconies. Raked seating was added internally, to roofs and to balconies to augment viewing. Doncaster's grandstand, which had been built in 1776, for example, underwent two remodelling campaigns circa 1804 and 1824 (Figure 1.13). To its flat viewing platform on the roof was added tiered standing and an additional balcony between the first floor and the roof was affixed to three of the building's sides. The Tuscan columns of the new balcony related it to the original, but their construction from cast iron signalled the introduction of a new material that would become enormously popular in nineteenth-century grandstand construction. Moreover, the social elements of the building were rendered increasingly subordinate to its viewing function. The stand's first-floor salon was degraded in importance as emphasis was given to enlarging the outside viewing capacity. The new balcony, in fact, blocked light from the interior.[1]

Adding tiered seating and extra balconies made for practicable adaptations to answer calls for enhanced capacity and vision. These modifications were not only deemed judicious and effective for existing stands but were, moreover, also applied to the Carr template to create a formula for new stands. The 1830s were important years in the crystallisation of new grandstand design, beginning with that built at Epsom Racecourse in 1829-30 (Figure 1.14).

Page 30 **1.13** Doncaster grandstand, built 1776. This image, dating to 1826, shows the alterations made to the building in the early nineteenth century to accommodate growing crowds

Opposite **1.14** The grandstand at Epsom, built 1829-30, marked a new phase of grandstand design in Britain

London Lithog Bermondsey Square.

THE NEW GRAND STAND,

ERECTING ON THE DOWNS AT EPSOM.

Architect
M! E W. Trendall.
Builder
M! W. Chadwick.

An Association has been formed for the purpose of building this Magnificent Stand, capable of accommodating nearly 5000 Spectators being 156 f! long & 70 f! wide. Capital £20,000 to be subscribed for in 1000 Shares of £20 each.

Office 9 Wellington Street, Strand

E. Sanford, Sec!y

Epsom Downs had staged organised race meetings since the 1770s, most notably the celebrated Derby, which today still ranks amongst the greatest international sporting spectacles. Its closeness to London made the course increasingly popular and by the 1820s crowds of 80,000 reputedly flocked there on Derby Day.[2] Yet despite its popularity, it had no permanent buildings. The 1830 stand, as designed by architect E. W. Trendall, was Epsom's first permanent grandstand. Reported to be the biggest grandstand in Europe, it was a large building, stately in aspect. Measuring 48 metres by 18 metres (156 feet by 60 feet), it was two storeys tall plus a rooftop viewing platform. Like Carr's stand at York, its architecture followed the classical tradition. Majestic Doric columns spanned the length of its ground-floor façade, while a classical balustrade railed both the ground-floor veranda and the tiered steppings upon the roof. Extending 33 metres in length by 10 metres in width (108 by 34 feet), the large proportions of its first-floor salon answered to Epsom's popularity. It was also elegantly appointed. The room was split into three sections by ornamental columns and pilasters shouldering an ornately panelled ceiling. Its viewing spaces were just as commodious. In addition to the panoramic view provided by the rooftop platform, large balconies extended from the first floor and raised ground floor and the building's trackside façade was almost wholly given over to floor-to-ceiling windows. It revolutionised the course's facilities and, consequently, its appeal.

Goodwood Racecourse, high on the Sussex Downs, quickly followed Epsom's example. The course had been established by the third Duke of Richmond in 1801, with the extent of its accommodation consisting of five or six pitched tents and later a small wooden stand. During the 1830s, Goodwood embarked upon a significant phase of development, beginning with the erection of a permanent stand in 1830 (Figure 1.15).

The substantial grandstand, designed by local architect George Draper, brought the course into line with the era's most sophisticated racecourses. Accommodating 3,000, it was similar in format and scale although less architecturally sophisticated than Trendall's stand at Epsom. It was a two-storey building, of simple outline and detailing. Internally it comprised refreshment rooms, retiring rooms, betting rooms, and a salon, plus a steeply-raked bench terrace on the rooftop open to the elements. An open, classical-colonnaded veranda on the ground floor with projecting end bays supported an uncovered first-floor balcony (added 1834) which enwrapped the building's elevation and provided space for over three hundred people. The first floor contained a large salon with tiered benches, whose main elevation was given entirely over to a parade of round-arched windows proffering good visibility over the course.[3] The building's form had much in common with other contemporary examples such as that at Bath Racecourse – a three-storey colonnaded structure built in 1831 which, although radically altered, still stands today.[4]

Another coeval example was that of Ascot, built in 1839. Ascot Racecourse had been founded in 1711 by England's corpulent but sport-loving monarch Queen Anne (1702-1714) upon open heath in Windsor Forest and, like Newmarket, its royal connections markedly influenced the nature of its physical fabric. Despite the steadily growing success of Ascot's races from the mid-eighteenth century, few provisions were made for spectators. Onlookers on foot and horseback jostled with carriages on the inner and outer sides of the track or found refuge within moveable wooden galleries which were erected specially for each meeting. Even the royal family used a wooden stand that could be moved around the course to allow multiple viewing points. It was not until 1793 that the course gained its first permanent stand, the Slingsby Stand. In 1826, this was altered by the introduction of raked seating on its upper level to increase its capacity to 1,650 spectators.[5]

Catering for the growing numbers of spectators became a mounting priority at Ascot as the century progressed. In June 1829 *The Times* reported of the annual Royal meeting:

> The spectacle was such as no words of ours can describe. The betting stand was crowded with rows of heads, tier above tier. The sides of the course were lined with double and triple tiers of spectators on foot; behind whom, on the side opposite to the royal stand were ranged carriages, ...human beings standing on and clinging from every part of them. So dense was the crowd that it was impossible for three-fourths of the persons present to obtain a view of the running , or know any thing of the results of the races, except by report.

By the mid-1830s complaints were levelled at its viewing provisions. 'Unless something be done towards [the races'] improvement,' *The Times* lamented on 4 June 1836, 'they will come to nothing.' The article continued,

> The want of accommodation for the ladies at Ascot has suggested the idea of a Grandstand, on the same lines as that of Goodwood; if placed between the Royal and betting stands, it could not fail to answer.

In 1836 Ascot's personnel was overhauled, holes on the track were filled in and turf was relayed, and in 1838 the

1.15 Goodwood's grandstand, built 1830, characterised the pattern of stand design in the 1830s and 40s

decision was made to erect a spacious grandstand between the Royal Stand, which had been built in 1822 for George IV, and the Slingsby Stand. The grandstand was erected to serve two functions. Firstly, to offer enlarged surroundings improved in quality 'for the purpose of affording additional accommodation to all classes of Her Majesty's Subjects attending the Races'; and secondly, to generate extra revenue to raise the standard of Ascot's racing. A well-appointed grandstand, it was anticipated, would allow the Ascot authorities to charge higher admittance prices. Designed by William Higgins and measuring 30 metres long, 16 metres deep and 17 metres tall (97 by 52 by 55 feet), the structure had a capacity of 3,000 (Figure 1.16). Internally, tiered benches lined its principal rooms, while externally the leaded roof afforded space for 800 spectators. Corinthian columns rose up to the first floor balcony, which sheltered a paved colonnade.

Shortly after its opening in 1839, the well-known sporting artist and architect, George Tattersall, bemoaned of the grandstand that,

> The great purpose for which it was built, that of seeing a Race well either from the one pair floor or from the roof, remains to be accomplished... As an example of a good Race Stand it is a signal failure.[6]

In general, however, the grandstand received warm welcomes. On 8 June 1839, the *Mirror* enthused,

> It has long been a subject of surprise and regret, that while Epsom, and almost every other provincial race-course in the kingdom, was provided with a grand stand, Ascot should have been until now without one. However, 'better late than never' the Stand is now erected, and a very handsome and commodious building it is.

Racing historian J. C. Whyte commended its selection of refreshment, retiring and play rooms. 'In fact', he praised, 'the conveniences are more numerous than at any other building of the kind in England.' He continued, 'judging from the attendance of company at the recent meeting, there can be no doubt that, the Grand Stand at Ascot is highly acceptable to the public, and will fully answer the objects sought by its projectors.' The grandstand and its enclosure wielded an important impact upon the reputation of the course. No longer lagging behind the nation's other racecourses, it had become the vanguard. In 1846, the *Illustrated London News* described Ascot as 'a little city of Olympian palaces' and in the 1850s, The Druid recalled the 'primitive days' preceding the grandstand's construction.[7]

The prestige that a modern grandstand rendered to a course continued to be recognised as the century progressed, as, for example, at Brighton, on the Sussex coast. Designed by the town surveyor Allan Stickney and built in 1851, Brighton's new grandstand was raised to resuscitate the venue's floundering reputation (Figure 1.17). It was a smaller structure than those of Epsom or Goodwood but borrowed their form and classical vocabulary. It did not, though, incorporate the raked rooftop seating of these earlier buildings; rather it had a hipped tiled roof akin to the 1831 precursor at Bath.

Just as the eighteenth-century stands of York, Doncaster, Richmond and others shared an homogenous vocabulary, so too did the mid-nineteenth-century generation of stands at Brighton, Epsom, Goodwood and others. They were uniformly larger in scale than those of the previous century, but their configuration was a fluid evolution of that earlier type. In essence, these were robust, enclosed buildings typically with rooftop platforms, tiered external and internal seating and a classicist architectonic. This was not a pioneering new typology, but rather one that modified the eighteenth century prototype with specific adaptations that reflected the nineteenth-century context. As Tessa Gibson has succinctly worded it,

> Whilst the demands made on the structure had changed, the form of the grandstand had not been comprehensively rethought. This period of the grandstand's history is not characterised by the creative application of ideas which had distinguished the emergence of the form.[8]

1.17 Brighton Racecourse grandstand, built 1851. The illustration shows the southern wing added in 1866 and northern wing added by 1871

comfort. Luncheon rooms were annexed to the rear of stands and specific areas within the buildings were allocated to their use alone while there were occasions in which dedicated ladies' stands were erected, as at Doncaster Racecourse in 1859. Meanwhile, the industrialisation and urbanisation of the Victorian working classes, plus a rise in real-term wages, also bolstered working-class numbers at racing fixtures.

The single most influential factor in the development of the grandstand typology was, however, the arrival of the railway. From the 1830s and 1840s, the expansion of the railway network introduced swarms of passengers to the thrills of travel – and to the thrills of organised spectator sports. For horse racing in particular, the railways vaulted it to commercial success on a national scale. As getting to race meetings became quicker, cheaper and easier, the numbers of racegoers swelled.[9] Even medium-sized courses, such as Southampton, Brighton, Newcastle or Liverpool, drew 30,000 or more.[10]

To accommodate the growing numbers, grandstands necessarily grew larger. In fact, during the Victorian age grandstands were ranked amongst the biggest buildings in which crowds amassed. The roof alone of the grandstand built at Epsom in 1829-30 held 2,500 spectators. A spur to this development was that the new stands were chiefly the venture of private companies, which, by their nature, intended to generate a profit. Epsom's new stand, for instance, was the achievement of the Epsom Grand Stand Association, founded in 1828 specifically to fund a new stand. Similarly, the Brighton Stand was commissioned by the Race Stand Trustees,

Social change was a prime catalyst for the evolution that the building type was experiencing. The opening years of the nineteenth century had brought a tremendous surge in the numbers and economic power of the middle classes, accompanied by increased opportunity for the pursuit of leisure. Horse racing had long drawn a large following, but its costly nature had hitherto restricted its traditional audience to the leisured aristocracy; now racecourses became an increasing destination for the middle classes seeking entertainment. In particular, middle-class ladies became a new presence at racecourses across the country, and racecourse managers promptly set about ministering to their

which had been formed in 1849-50 to rescue the course from financial difficulties. To achieve a good economic return, bigger, higher-capacity buildings were essential.

The 1830s grandstand was thus a scaled-up version of its predecessors complete with middle-class luncheon rooms, spacious balconies and tiered benches. The design innovations affected the physical appearance of the building typology but they also revealed changes in their patterns of use. Foremost, the tiered seats within the first-floor salons of the Ascot and Goodwood stands indicated its predominant function was shifting from a social to a viewing one. This trend was to augment as the Victorian era progressed. New stands evolved further and further along this route until their external appearance exhibited few parallels with their forebears. By the high Victorian period, grandstands had developed into being open structures with tiered terrace seating over either two storeys or, more typically, one. The stands built at York Racecourse in 1865 (Figure 1.18), Doncaster in 1881 and Lincoln in 1896 were exponents of this new generation. Recreation and circulation areas were relegated to the rear and ground floor. Rooftop seating fell out of favour, replaced by hipped roofs; sturdy stone Orders were supplanted by slender cast iron columns with florid capitals and bases.[11]

This late nineteenth-century evolution of the grandstand building typology in Britain was not an isolated happening. Since the days of the Stuart kings in the seventeenth century, Britain had held a near monopoly

on horse racing. However, in the mid-nineteenth century this began to change. Slowly but surely, the sport's popularity began to sweep beyond its shores to Europe, the Americas, Australasia, and beyond. Almost without exception, the British organisational model was adopted as the accepted template by the new turfites; its architectural model, however, did not receive the same unequivocal acceptance. New formulas evolved which, overwhelmingly, were of a simpler, more open creed. Arguably, their forms influenced the changes evinced in the stands of High Victorian British racecourses. It is to a discussion of the new forms developed in foreign lands that we now turn, beginning with France.

1.18 The County Stand (foreground) at York, built 1865. The upper storey was added in 1887

France

In the late eighteenth century, an aberrant symptom was sweeping through France. Its leisured classes were overtaken by a wave of 'anglomanie'. 'England is our model and our rival, our guiding light and our enemy', opined the Marquis de Luchet in 1790.[12] The nation's bloody revolution did not put a stop to the mania and it continued unabated into the nineteenth century. Ranging from a passing infatuation with Byron's poetry and a fashion for the 'milord' style of dress to more pregnant considerations of an alternative political system, the vogue for all things English included an adoption of the Sport of Kings.[13]

Horse racing as a formal sport began to take place in France at the end of the 1700s. In 1775 the first horse races were held on the Plaine des Sablons near Paris, and in 1833 the imperiously-titled Comité de la Société d'Encouragement pour l'Amélioration des Races de Cheveaux en France, France's equivalent of the Jockey Club, was established. The Société had a vital influence upon the growth and prominence of the sport, organising meetings in and around Paris. In 1834, it organised its first race meeting in the grounds of the Château de Chantilly, 40 kilometres (25 miles) north of Paris. The story of horse racing at Chantilly began, in fact, as the result of a bet. Then owned by the duc d'Aumale, the Chantilly estate was a popular venue for hunting. In 1833, several of its visitors challenged each other to a race on the grass sward between Chantilly's forest and the château's grandiose stables. They were so full of enthusiasm for the perfection of the turf that they persuaded the duc and the Société that a racecourse must be built there. The following year this was done, and the first race was watched in admiration by 30,000 spectators set against undoubtedly the most monumental backdrop in racing history – the *Grandes Écuries* (Figure 1.19).

Though literally translated as 'big stables', the *Grandes Écuries* were no mere stalls. Completed in 1736 to designs by architect Jean Aubert, the building embodied the eccentric but fervent conviction of the seventh Prince de Condé (1692-1740), the owner of the estate, that he was going to be reincarnated as a horse. The prince created a set of stables unparalleled in their architectural splendour. The vast, neo-classical building was festooned with ornamentation, from bas reliefs to cartouches, urns to stand-alone sculptures. And its 186-metre (610-feet) south façade has been the spectacular setting for racing at Chantilly since that inaugural meeting on 15 May 1834.

The first meeting was successful enough to merit a second the following year and, for this, lightweight, interim stands were erected by the architect Morin under the direction of the Société and the municipality of Chantilly. In 1847, permanent replacements were built following instructions by the duc d'Aumale to designs by the architect Jean-Louis Grisard (1797-1877). These were the first fixed racecourse stands in France and they established an immediate template for the first generation of racing architecture there (Figure 1.20).

Racing in France may have sprung from a burst of anglomania, but when it came to their grandstands the French assumed a remarkably different attitude to that of their neighbours across the Channel. The generation of grandstands that had been built in 1830s England – at Epsom, Goodwood and Ascot notably – were large, robust structures in classical garb. Grisard's grandstands were, in the first instance, smaller in size. Compared to the 100,000-strong crowds who attended

the St Leger or Epsom Derby in England, racing in France was still a nascent pursuit in the hands of an elite aristocratic circle. The design of Chantilly's new buildings reflected this. In total, they accommodated only 700 spectators. Moreover, whilst British racecourses had been developed upon an incremental basis with single-unit schemes, Chantilly was conceived as a set-piece ensemble with multiple buildings forming a unified whole. Grisard designed a tripartite ensemble: two covered stands, one each side of a small but stately pavilion dedicated to the duc's use known as the *Pavillon du Prince*. It was arguably the first instance in which an overarching, architectural vision was applied to the creation of an ensemble of racecourse buildings. Chantilly's repertoire of scale, layout and multi-building approach set a model which was to prove an enduring rubric for racecourse architecture in France and, indeed, across the whole of Europe.

Opposite **1.19** The Grandes Écuries have provided the monumental backdrop for the Hippodrome de Chantilly since racing began there in 1834

Above **1.20** *Les tribunes de l'hippodrome de Chantilly:* Chantilly's first permanent stands, built in 1847 by the architect Jean-Louis Grisard

Stylistically and spatially, the stands had evolved conspicuously from those of England a decade earlier. The grandstands of Epsom, Goodwood and Ascot were formulated upon an eighteenth-century inheritance of double-storey elevation plus tiered rooftop viewing space, with spacious internal rooms leading out to balconies or colonnaded verandas. Chantilly's two larger stands – and other European examples that followed – simplified this model. They provided a single tier of benches overlooking the track, roofed but unenclosed to the sides and front. Fusing a timber and iron frame with a brick base, the stands employed a lightweight building type similar to some contemporary industrial buildings. On the rear elevation, timber-railed balconies gave views over the paddock. It was a simpler, more open and less burly type of architecture; stylistically, it eschewed the staid classicism of its English predecessors and embraced instead the architecture of leisure in mid-century France, the *pittoresque* style. This style, based on that of Swiss chalets, was popular within the holiday resorts that surrounded Paris. The grandstands' timber fabric, hipped roof and carved wooden corbels were typical ingredients of the *pittoresque*. Following Chantilly's example, it was adopted at the Parisian courses of Longchamp (1857), Vincennes (1863), Maisons-Laffitte (1878) and Enghien (1879); indeed, it was employed almost ubiquitously for France's first generation of racecourse architecture. Chantilly's 1847 complex also established a template for another feature of nineteenth-century French racecourse architecture, the *Pavillon du Prince*.

The *Pavillon du Prince* was the central building of Grisard's trio, and it was also the pinnacle of the scheme. It was a petite yet distinguished edifice, encompassing a crowning glazed tower and glazed polygonal salon overlooking the track. The provision of a separate pavilion for regal or state use came to be a distinctive and idiosyncratic characteristic of French racecourses, which spread beyond France to Germany and Austria. Known variously as the imperial pavilion, *tribune du prince*, *tribune présidentielle* and *kaiserloge*, examples existed, amongst others, at the Parisian hippodromes of Longchamp and Auteuil (1873) and the German course at Baden-Baden (1858). Royal boxes, by which is meant an area of a stand reserved for royal spectators and their guests, were a common sight on English racecourses but the concept of an imperial pavilion was a European phenomenon.[14] They were, in simple terms, tokens of gratitude or obligation. At Chantilly, the *Pavillon du Prince* reflected the benefaction of the duc d'Aumale in erecting the course, and at the subsequent Hippodrome de Longchamp its equivalent structure expressed the patronage of the emperor.[15] The specialised building type was a development of the English concept of royal boxes, but elevated to a higher, more resplendent plane; in fact, they recall the imperial boxes of the ancient hippodromes, of which the Hippodrome of Constantinople (second century AD) had a particularly distinctive example. Its imperial box, known as the Kathisma, has been described as a small palace. At the front was the emperor's box, and behind were rooms for his accommodation.[16] Whilst not on a palatial scale, Chantilly's *Pavillon du Prince* nonetheless provided a commodious and elegant space for its aristocratic patron.

Built by the elite for the elite, the buildings of Chantilly were a sphere of exclusivity. This was equally, if not more, the case when the celebrated Hippodrome de Longchamp was constructed, during the reign of Napoleon III (1851-70). Louis-Napoléon Bonaparte

had spent several impressionable years of exile in England, and the Société d'Encouragement had little trouble persuading him of the merits of endowing Paris with a new racecourse on the large plain at the west of the Bois de Boulogne, the city's newly-created park. In 1856, the city granted the Société a 50-year lease for the land and it set about building a set of tribunes (Figure 1.21).

The nature of the Société d'Encouragement had a direct bearing on the tribunes that it constructed. The Société was not merely a sporting body, it was an elite and luxurious social club, probably the most exclusive of all of Paris's many clubs. It was a world of privilege, distinction and hierarchy, and the buildings that it commissioned at Longchamp were designed to articulate and uphold this.

The lead architect of the city of Paris, Gabriel Davioud (1824-81), was selected as their designer, alongside Antoine-Nicolas Bailly (1810-92). Their plan followed the stylistic and spatial pattern of those at Chantilly, but enacted upon a larger and grander scale. As at Chantilly, a 'whole-cloth' or set-piece plan was employed. Davioud and Bailly provided five separate stands, rigidly hierarchical in their siting and style. Together they totalled an elevation of 250 metres (820 feet) and hosted nearly 5,000 spectators.

At the centre of the ensemble was the *Loge d'Empereur*, the imperial pavilion. It was the tallest, grandest of the structures. Rising five storeys in height with a central belvedere tower, the lavishness of its fittings left little doubt as to the importance of its intended occupant. Internally, its walls were wainscoted and hung with red silk damask, ceilings were adorned with stucco mouldings and doors were made of polished, hand-carved ebony. To either side of this stood a pair of identical stands – the *Tribunes Reservées* – one for Société members and the other intended for the imperial family, ministers of state and army leaders. Seven rows of finely upholstered chairs looked onto the track covered by a carved wooden canopy supported by cast iron columns. Its formula was very similar to that espoused at Chantilly. At each end, tall, hipped-roof stair towers gave access to a flat rooftop deck (Figure 1.22). A restaurant and concierge desk were housed in their tall basements. All amenities were 'entirely first class'. For the general public, appointments were less lavish. The two public tribunes completed the ensemble, flanking the *Tribunes Reservées*. Measuring 40 metres long and 13 metres high (130 by 40 feet), the timber stands provided a single storey of seating beneath a roof upheld by iron columns and decorated with *bois decoupé*. They were the simplest of the architectural grouping. No upholstered seating was to be found here; racegoers were provided with basic tiered wooden benches.[17]

COUPE   FAÇADE LATÉRALE

1.22 Cross section of
Longchamp's *Tribune Reservée*,
which accommodated the
imperial family, ministers of
state and army leaders

All the buildings shared a *pittoresque* vocabulary of brick, half-timbering and denticulated wood, which became progressively less elaborate from the climax of the *Loge d'Empereur* down to the public stands. This visual distinction was emphasised by a physical barrier in the shape of a low, iron fence which divided the public stands from the select realm between them, and separate entrance drives to ensure that the general public was always kept apart from their more privileged fellow racegoers.[18] To the Société, Longchamp was to be a place of exclusivity and its physical environment was manifestly designed to reflect this. The arrangement, architecture and amenities of its five viewing stands were a cogent demonstration of its ambitions and of the strict observation of the hierarchical order of wider nineteenth-century society.

Longchamp's inauguration on 26 April 1857, attended by the Emperor himself, was a triumph. In addition to the 3,000 people that crowded into the paddock enclosure, there were 700 carriages, 4,000 on foot, 250 on horseback, and 5,000 accommodated in the stands.[19] In the years that followed, Longchamp became the epicentre of Paris society. 'I have never seen in France so numerous and so *choisi* a gathering,' observed one visitor there in 1862. 'Not a fine name in France but was there represented by some bearer of it.'[20] Its proximity to central Paris and setting within the sylvan Bois de Boulogne quickly established its place as France's premier racing venue. The races became a climax of the florid social arabesque of the Parisian haut monde and its buildings became a manifestation of an elite vision of France, in which Société members were on an equal footing with the most powerful legates in French government.[21]

With Longchamp as its centrepiece, racing in France enjoyed a golden age. A succession of set-piece courses opened, particularly around Paris, such as Fontainebleau (1862), Porchefontaine (1864),

Vincennes and Auteuil. These examples and many more modelled their tribunes on those of Longchamp, both in terms of style and plan: a *pittoresque* vocabulary of single-storey, tiered wooden benches sheltered by a wide canopy supported upon cast iron columns, and a plan with an imperial pavilion as its centrepiece. Vincennes, for example, situated on the edge of Paris's Bois de Vincennes and designed by architect Saint-Germain, possessed two tiered stands of 100 metres (330 feet) each either side of an imperial pavilion.

The courses were products of a comprehensive design vision. At Auteuil, wrote British onlooker Eustace Reynolds-Ball in 1900, 'the whole of the course is swept, garnished, and trimmed like the lawn of a well-kept garden'. The discrepancy between the very distinct set-piece building approach that shaped France's racecourses and the incremental, unsystematic patterns of growth of their British counterparts may have much to do with French attitudes towards the Turf. French racecourses were playgrounds of pleasure, as much about fashion as sport. 'The sport is fashionable,' explained American magazine *The Outing* in 1903. 'It is an appanage of good society. Smart folk go to the races, just as they do to the opera.'[22] 'A walk through the paddock and Pesage with the crowds of smartly dressed women, would suggest a fashionable bazaar or garden party rather than a race-meeting,' Reynolds-Ball continued of Auteuil.[23] With this mindset, appearances mattered and racecourse environments were conceived to be as well groomed as their patrons. A holistic approach to layout and architecture was the natural outcome of this.

As horse racing spread beyond France's borders across Europe and racecourses were built there, this attitude spread too, notably in the case of Austria and Germany.

Germany and Austria

It is, in fact, to France that we owe the foundation of Germany's most celebrated racecourse, Baden-Baden. Baden-Baden was a popular spa town nestled between the Rhine and the Black Forest. By the mid-nineteenth century, however, it was renowned less for its curative hot springs than for its status as a gambling haven where the crowned heads, nobility and epicurean industrialists of Europe came in the pursuit of pleasure. A more congenial situation for a racecourse would have been hard to find. This, at least, was probably the thought that struck Frenchman Edouard Bénazet, already owner of Baden-Baden's casino, when in 1858 he set about building a racecourse there. The propitious opening of Longchamp, only a year earlier, was at the forefront of his mind.[24]

No suitable site for a racecourse could be found in Baden-Baden itself, so a site was selected approximately 13 kilometres (eight miles) west of the town centre near the village of Iffezheim. It was bounded by the village to the south, the Mühlbach river to the east and woodland to the north, with the Rhine in the western distance. Construction was begun immediately and Bénazet spent unstintingly.[25] On 5 September 1858, the first race was held, under the aegis of the French Société Sportive d'Encouragement.

Not only was Baden-Baden's racecourse founded under French auspices, but its architecture drew on French precedents too. It comprised plural stands that enforced a definite social hierarchy. Its plan consisted of a small Prince's Stand and small Club Stand for officials, plus a larger patrons' stand (Figure 1.23). Akin to the 1840s and 50s stands of Chantilly and Longchamp, tall stair towers were prominent features; in the case of the Prince's and Club Stands, one rose from the centre of the rear elevation whilst the main grandstand possessed a pair of towers, one at either end of its length. Nevertheless, in other respects, the Baden-Baden racecourse showed definite Anglo tendencies in its architecture. Its buildings were greatly indebted to the grandstand model of 1830s England, characterised by the stands of Goodwood and Epsom. Baden-Baden adopted a double-storey elevation, plus additional level of tiered seating on its roof. The main stand comprised a ground floor which opened onto a veranda, above which was a large first-floor salon with large glazed windows leading to a balcony. Compared to the recent Longchamp and Chantilly, this was a retrospective approach.

Notwithstanding its English influences, Baden-Baden is illustrative of a distinct current of European racecourse architecture that had evolved in France. It was characterised by a pattern of multiple viewing stands which firmly articulated social hierarchies, at the apex of which was the imperial stand. It was by no means the only idiom visible at racecourses in Europe, but it was an important pattern. The Viennese racecourse of Freudenau was perhaps its most handsome example (Figure 1.24).

Races were first run at Freudenau in 1839 on a site within the Prater, Vienna's large public park. In 1869, the construction began of stands on the present site, completed in

1.23 Galopprennbahn Baden-Baden in Iffezheim, opened in 1858

1870 to designs by Austrian architect Karl von Hasenauer (1833-94). Hasenauer was one of the city's most important architects. A key exponent of the historicist school, he worked in partnership with Gottfried Semper to create some of the most prestigious monuments of the day, including the Burgtheatre and Neue Burg. Following a fire at Freudenau, Hasenauer's buildings were remodelled and enlarged by brothers Anton (1858-1940) and Josef Drexler (1850-1922) from 1885-7. Like Hasenauer, the Drexlers ranked amongst Vienna's most successful architects. The focus of their partnership was residential work, but their portfolio included public works such as the City Hall in Feldberg (1888) and Vienna's Palais des Beaux Arts (1909); Anton had in

1880 served as architect for Budapest's racecourse and the pair went on to design Vienna's trotting course, Krieau, in 1910.

The Drexlers's remodelling preserved the layout and form of Hasenauer's buildings, the apogee of which was the *Kaiserloge*, or imperial pavilion (Figure 1.25). It was a cruciform-shaped building with a copper dome at its centre. The tall onion dome roof made for an elegantly striking silhouette; indeed, everything about this small building was elegant. Cast-iron filigree work of ornate foliate scrolls filled the spandrels of its front elevation, while large arched windows saturated the double-height salon inside with light. The salon opened onto a semi-

circular balcony, around which a double set of stairs curved
to lead to the track apron. The building was at the cusp of the
late nineteenth-century transition between historicism and the
emerging Jugendstil. The curvilinear sweep of the steps hinted
at the coming of the new aesthetic. Not only was the Kaiserloge
and its fellow stands one of the most graceful illustrations of
racecourse architecture in its day, it survives as perhaps the
finest nineteenth-century racecourse complex preserved today.

By the time the Drexler brothers had built Freudenau,
European racecourse architecture had developed a distinct
blueprint. There were similarities with the British formula of
the first half of the nineteenth century. Yet, the importation
of racing into Europe resulted in marked changes for its
physical fabric. Beginning with the model of Chantilly in
1847, grandstands were more open, lightweight and less
structural than their British antecedents and they comprised
a single storey of raked seating, rather than two or three. It
was not only the buildings themselves that differed though;
the whole approach to racecourse design had been rethought.
European racecourses were set-piece ensembles, made up
of a number of buildings conceived as a harmonious entity,
which enforced the strict social hierarchy of the day. The
construction of such complexes as Chantilly, Longchamp
and Freudenau pushed the building type forward in leaps and
bounds; their scale of planning and design had no precedent
within the British racing industry. Likewise, when racing
was exported across the Atlantic, British conventions were
quickly supplanted there too.

USA

1.26 Jerome Park in New York, built in 1866 by millionaire businessman Leonard W. Jerome

When the British colonialists arrived in North America, they brought thoroughbred horses and racing with them. As early as the eighteenth century, racing clubs had been founded in the United States and rules laid down. The sport was, as yet, unplanned in nature and modest in scale, but it flourished in the Southern colonies where the 'Cavalier Colonialists' engendered a passion for the turf. Racing was so synonymous with Virginia that the best jockeys were known simply as 'Virginia boys'. Maryland had its own jockey club by 1743, and, notwithstanding that its population was less than 15,000, the District of Columbia too had founded a jockey club by 1798.[26] It was, however, in the North that the country's first regular racecourse was laid out. Concerned about the dearth of good horses, in 1665 Richard Nicholls, the British governor of the New York colony, built a large, oval turf track on the open flatlands of Long Island known as Hempstead Plain (present-day Jamaica). Christened Newmarket after the celebrated British forerunner, for over 100 years all New York society, from governors, to gentry to farmers, flocked to this course.[27] It gave rise to many imitators.

Despite the pull of English racing traditions, quickly American racing began to look very different to its British parent. America was yet an untamed country, thick with dense forests that could only be cleared with backbreaking toil and at tremendous cost. The young (and hungry) nation needed every inch of cleared land for agriculture and recreating the park-like courses of Britain with their meandering turf tracks was simply impractical. Regular oval tracks came to be the standard model and, from 1819 following the celebrated example of Union Course in Long Island, Americans raced on dirt tracks rather than turf. No less distinct from the British model was the fact that US racing was, from the outset, closely tied to urban life; in other words, to towns and cities. The

American social hierarchy lacked the aristocratic stratum for whom the sport largely existed as a leisurely pursuit in Europe. The effect of this was that racing in the US was imbibed with a commercial or mercantile nature and its very survival was predicated upon drawing large crowds. And these were only to be had in propinquity with cities.[28]

The Civil War had a decisive impact upon horse racing. The bitter North-South conflict engendered its near collapse in nearly all Southern states, whilst in the North it became a flourishing industry. The hitherto ad hoc, localised sport became regional, even national, in scope; and at its centre was New York. Fundamental to this was the emergence of a new breed of tremendously rich capitalists. The Civil War, wrote one sporting magazine,

> had loosened the volume of money, inflated values and created a fictitious prosperity and its twin brother, extravagance. A change had come over the manners of the people. Many had made money, and now they began to seek pleasure.[29]

Into the racing milieu stepped millionaires such as August Belmont, Leonard W. Jerome and D. D. Withers, who poured vast sums into building top-class stables and, importantly, a spate of new racecourses.[30]

Jerome Park was the most important of these new courses (demolished 1894). Laid out on 100 hectares (250 acres) in Fordham just north of Manhattan, it opened its doors in 1866 as the brainchild of Leonard W. Jerome. Jerome, the maternal grandfather of Winston Churchill, was born to a farming family in upstate New York, but cultivated a talent for speculating on stocks that earned (and lost) him several fortunes. He was also an avid horseman with a passion for racing. In Jerome's eyes, thoroughbred racing was shamefully underrated within American society; indeed it had something of an ignominious reputation in many quarters. And, to use his words, ennobling the pursuit from a 'rowdies' outing' into a 'royal sport' became a lifelong resolution. Jerome Park was the result (Figure 1.26).

Compared to the courses built hitherto in the US, it was certainly designed upon a royal scale. By the mid-nineteenth century, modest grandstands had come to feature on courses, but their rusticity meant many racegoers eschewed these in favour of watching the races from carriages and coaches positioned alongside the course fence.[31] The contemporary Saratoga Race Course in upstate New York exemplified this. Built in 1864 to seat 2,000, Saratoga's grandstand was a single-storey timber building whose only decorative relief came from the trefoil-shaped 'gingerbread' cut-outs on its gable ends (Figure 2.27). Juxtaposed with this and like examples, Jerome Park's appointments represented unprecedented lavishness. 'As a mere matter of aesthetics the course is singularly beautiful,' wrote the *New York Times* before its opening.[32]

Its design was a profound departure from models in Britain. Jerome Park's grandstand was a two-storey building, 140 metres (450 feet) long and holding 8,000 spectators, and thus much larger in size than the typical British template. Notwithstanding the praise it earned from the contemporary press and its superiority compared to other American stands, it was nevertheless of relatively modest architectural bearing when pitted against the stands of Britain's major courses. It had none of their neo-classical elegance or masonry construction; it was a long, simple building chiefly built of timber. Timber's abundant supply in nineteenth-century America and new tools like the steam-powered scroll saw made wooden construction a habitual choice for most grandstand builders. Racegoers were furnished with covered, raked

Course	Dates of Operation
Union Course, Queens	1821–1870s
Saratoga, Saratoga Springs	1863–
Jerome Park, Westchester County, now Bronx	1866–1894
Brighton Beach, Brooklyn	1879–1908
Sheepshead Bay, Brooklyn	1880–1910
Gravesend, Brooklyn	1886–1910
Morris Park, Westchester County, now Bronx	1889–1904
Aqueduct, Queens	1894–
Jamaica Race Course, Jamaica	1903–1959
Belmont Park, Long Island	1905–

Table showing major New York tracks founded before the shutdown of the New York racing industry in 1911 following anti-gambling legislation

seating on two tiers which overlooked the track from an open colonnade of ornamental iron columns. At its centrepoint and at either end, the stand was capped with a plain gable. Bands of wooden cross bracing provided the only other decorative feature of the façade.

Stylistically, the grandstand bore greatest resemblance to the early European stands of Longchamp (1857) or Baden-Baden (1858). Like these examples also, Jerome Park adopted a set-piece architectural approach. In one key aspect of its plan, though, Jerome Park diverged palpably from both European and British precedents.

On a large hill opposite the grandstand stood a spacious building known as the clubhouse. The clubhouse was not a feature of European or British courses, but came to be a customary one of their North American counterparts. Its presence was indicative of the different attitude towards racing and racecourses in the two continents.

The clubhouse 'soon became the great society rendezvous', wrote the *Outing* magazine of Jerome Park. Comparable to a luxury hotel, it included a ballroom, dining room and even an art gallery:

> Driving and sleighing parties, trap shooting, skating and polo playing rendered the place a favourite tryst. Sleeping accommodations were plenty and it became quite the thing for an owner to take a party of friends to dinner, stop overnight and be up betimes to see the morning gallops.[33]

Whilst racing in Britain and France, for instance, was an unmissable entry in the social season, Jerome Park vaulted this to a different level. 'Jerome Park on a raceday became a Mecca of fashion.'[34] Its principal raison d'être was not the cultivation of the sport, but the cultivation of society and, in turn, commerce. Its admission policies were exclusive; especially compared to most British courses where infield admittance was free, entrance tickets were expensive, since, together with pool privileges and concessions, they provided the bulk of the revenue which enabled the racecourse to sustain itself without large audiences.[35] This rationale gave rise to the set-piece design approach and also the genesis of the clubhouse building type.

From the outset, Jerome Park was a success and legendary for its opulence. An estimated 30,000 clamoured to its opening day on 25 September 1866; carriages three abreast blocked the 30-metre (100-feet) wide road leading to the course.[36] 'As an event in the progress of the sport,' commented the *New York Times* on its inauguration, 'it opens

an era'.[37] And it certainly opened an era in the progress of racecourse design in the US.

By the 1890s, the racing industry had grown in the US to such an extent that 300 courses were in operation. New York remained the hub, with six courses running in and around New York City alone, each possessing an individual persona and ambiance. Such proximity inevitably bred competition, and the life expectancy of each course was not long.[38] Securing the attention and patronage of the race-going public was imperative.

The means that one New York course employed to achieve this was by giving the city the most elegant setting and buildings heretofore seen on a racecourse. The course was Morris Park, and it opened to a flurry of expectation on 20 August 1889[39]:

1.27 The palatial Morris Park Clubhouse, built 1889, demonstrates the growing pretentions of racecourse design in America

When Jerome Park was opened there was the greatest room for doubt whether the better classes of society would countenance the sport in any degree, yet long after all ground for hesitation on this score had been removed and the number of race-horses had increased—not ten-fold, but a hundred-fold—...the accommodation for the public, and the pattern of race-course remained much the same as it had been even in antebellum days. Had it not been for the foresight and liberal-mindedness of one man, Mr. John A. Morris, who grasped the fact that the race-going public had reached a point when they were bound to get better accommodation for their money and would show their appreciation of it, it is not at all unlikely that things might yet have been in the same old groove.[40]

Morris Park represented the apotheosis of the design approach pioneered at Jerome Park. It was perhaps the first example in America of a consummately planned, architect-designed racecourse whose architecture and landscape was deliberately intended as a vantage over its competitors. Its owner, John A. Morris, was a New Jersey businessman known widely as the 'Lottery King' for his majority share in the Louisiana State Lottery. His chief ambition, it was said, was to own the finest thoroughbred course in the world and in 1888 he purchased 125 hectares (307 acres) in an area now part of the Bronx to make this a reality.[41] The architect responsible for the buildings and track was Thomas R. Jackson (1826-1901). Jackson was an English-born American architect who rose to prominence as head draftsman in the office of Richard Upjohn, one of New York's most respected architects. Jackson's commissions included the New York Times building on Park Row (1851), Wallack's Theatre on Broadway (1861) and the New York Mercantile Exchange (1886). Notwithstanding Jackson's experience, though, Morris ensured that all plans were approved by him personally before construction. This lasted 12 months and amounted to $1.5 million (approximately $37 million in today's money).[42]

Using a palette of iron, red brick and stone, Jackson designed a long grandstand and, connected to it by means of an enclosed walkway from its south elevation, a spacious clubhouse, fitted with every modern convenience. Throughout, 'Pompeian richness in colour and decoration has been the idea of the architect,' enthused the New York Times.[43] The Outing extolled:

> At Morris Park the race-goer has every chance to the greatest enjoyment from the 'sport of kings,' for all possible accommodations for his comfort are provided. The club-house is not the mere cottage which generally answers the purpose, but a magnificent building, fitted throughout not with consummate luxury and good only money, but taste, every feature, from the ball-room down, being elaborated regardless of expense.[44]

The clubhouse was the centre of the racecourse and a centre of fashion. The brick structure was a towering five storeys tall and reminiscent of Manhattan's domestic palaces in style and scale (Figure 1.27). Its rear, or entrance, façade was the most imposing. This was a symmetrical, tripartite elevation with lower flanking wings and a central sculpted pediment. The lower floors were lit by round arched windows with prominent brick voussoirs, loosely evocative of Florentine Renaissance palaces such as the Palazzi Strozzi, Medici and Pitti, while its columned portico, engaged pilasters, and balustraded roof terrace were classicist motifs typical of New York's most eloquent architectural vocabulary.

The grandstand was longer and lower than the clubhouse, seating 8,000 on a single tier accessed from the lawn apron via nine broad stairways. It was a wooden structure built on a base of supporting stone, iron and brick arches. The arches gave access to a betting room, restaurants and retiring rooms housed in the interstice below the tiered seating. It was a much simpler, less stately edifice than the clubhouse

1.28 The clubhouse and grandstand of Saratoga, redesigned in 1892 by Boston architect Herbert Langford Warren

yet still incited popular praise. 'On opening day the public will find seats on a stand which surpasses those of Flemington, Ascot, Longchamps, or Buenos Ayres [sic], which have had, until this palatial structure came into being, the best in the world,' rhapsodised the *New York Times*.[45] Its correspondent is unlikely to have been so well travelled, but this conceit of establishing international comparisons between racecourses was growing progressively more common.

The size of Morris Park's buildings and its comprehensive scale was demonstrative of the nature of American racecourses. Whereas racing in its mother country, Britain, at this time was not a profit-maximising pursuit, the situation in North America was otherwise.[46] Run by financiers and businessmen like John A. Morris, its racecourses were commercial enterprises which needed to turn a profit. They were executed to be fashionable venues, whose clubhouses bustled with New York society. This had direct effect upon the physical forms they assumed.

The approach to planning taken at Morris Park was at complete odds with the incremental growth of the typical British racecourse, belonging instead to the 'set piece' attitude pioneered in France. Jackson gave such thought to the completeness of the ensemble that red-tinted concrete was used for sidewalks and pathways to harmonise with the hues of the architecture. Supported by its new breed of millionaires, the notion that racecourses should have aesthetically appealing physical settings slowly gained ground in the US. While never a ubiquitous concept, Morris Park embodied a racecourse trend in which public stands, clubhouses and surrounding landscape were conceived together as a designed ensemble and a sense of architectural style was injected into what had previously been a sober and utilitarian building typology.

Amongst the most dynamic example of this current of thinking was the redevelopment of Saratoga Race Course in the 1890s. Situated 50 kilometres (30 miles) north of Albany in New York, Saratoga is the oldest continuously-operating course in the country; indeed, it is the nation's oldest surviving sports venue. Its first grandstand succumbed to the wrecker's ball in 1892 and Saratoga's architectural ambitions rocketed. Architect Herbert Langford Warren (1857-1917) transformed the site with a state-of-the-art racing complex comprising betting ring, saddling shed, clubhouse and grandstand, the latter surviving as the nucleus of today's stand (Figure 1.28). Warren was a renowned figure in Boston's Arts and Crafts movement. He had studied under one of the nineteenth century's most celebrated architects, H. H. Richardson, and by the time of his death in 1917 he was dean of Harvard's School of Architecture. By commissioning him to design its new buildings, the Saratoga Association identified itself as a sophisticated architectural patron. For the Saratoga Race Course, it seemed, no mere utilitarian shelter would do; it wanted to make an architectural splash. Indeed, Warren transformed the face of the Race Course, creating a powerful architectural presence that has dominated the site since its opening day on 25 July 1892.[47]

Saratoga's new grandstand was a single-storey building, 60 metres (200 feet) long. Akin to the grandstands of Morris and Jerome Parks, its chief construction material was timber. The basic structure of Saratoga's grandstand was functional and spartan, but it was crowned with a strikingly unique feature – a vast slate roof supported by a timber trusswork system. The sweeping slate roof with clusters of sloping turrets at its centre and ends continues to dominate the character of the course to this day. Eccentric roof forms were at the time symptomatic of the widespread popularity of the Queen Anne

1.29 Churchill Downs grandstand was built in 1895 to rejuvenate the course's failing fortunes

Kentucky Derby since 1895. It is almost unfathomable to think that they were once an afterthought.

Churchill Downs had been founded in 1875, but by the early 1890s it was verging on bankruptcy. It had earned a reputation as a gambling hall, profits were low and management issues plagued the course, when, in 1894, a syndicate led by horseman and bookmaker William F. Schulte, purchased the site. Spending a reported $100,000, the new ownership sought to resuscitate the course's fortunes by transforming its architectural setting. Its early structures were torn down and replaced, most notably by a new grandstand (Figure 1.29).[48] Alongside Saratoga's 1892 stand, it prevails as a rare survivor of the nineteenth-century architectural heritage of American racing.

Designed by a 24-year old draughtsman named Joseph Dominic Baldez, working at prominent local firm D. X. Murphy and Brother, it was a 1,500-seat stand built upon a red brick base. The rectangular building had a single storey of raked seating sheltered by a gabled slate roof, intersected laterally by two gable projections. Each gable end was filled with an arcade of shallow-relief pilasters, a motif continued on the brick base of the rear elevation. The rear façade was dominated by a horizontal parade of wide, round arches with prominent brick voussoirs, and decorated with roundels bearing horse head reliefs.

It was not until the end of the design process neared, as Baldez brooded over his drawings in quest of something that would give his stand that extra panache, that the iconic spires were added to its roofline. The two octagonal cupolas, capped with tapering slate spires, measured three-and-a-half metres (12 feet) wide and soared 17 metres (55 feet) above the top of the building. Each face of the cupolas was pierced with a round-arched opening with a fleur-de-lis at its peak. Flanking rosettes added further decoration. Spires were a recurrent feature of late nineteenth-century American

architectural style across the US, of which steeply inclined roofs were a key feature. The style also informed the silhouette of the two structures which flanked the grandstand, the betting ring to its east (demolished 1963) and the clubhouse to its west (demolished 1928). The clubhouse was built smaller, lower and at an angle to the grandstand, but it shared its timber frame, shingle cladding and, moreover, was topped by a dramatic slate roof with deep overhanging eaves and conical peaks capped by golden finials.

Saratoga's sweeping rooflines became an emblem of the course, something that occurred even more potently at Churchill Downs in Louisville, Kentucky. There is undoubtedly no other image more compellingly associated with American racing than that of Churchill Downs' twin spires. Gracing the top of the course's historic grandstand, now sandwiched between subsequent monolithic expansions, the two octagonal towers have presided over the venerable architecture. Perhaps Baldez took inspiration from the twin turrets of Louisville's Central Kentucky Asylum (1869) or indeed from Churchill Downs's original grandstand (1875), which had two end towers plus central spire (Figure 1.30). The twin spires added instant distinction to Baldez's grandstand. As at Saratoga Race Course, the distinctive roofline became a motif of the racecourse as a whole and these two courses stand as early examples of architectural branding within the racing world (Figure 1.31).

Precious little survives of America's nineteenth-century racecourse architecture, in part a corollary of the tradition of building in timber. What does remain, therefore, has been elevated to emblematic status. Racecourses of the era chiefly followed a template of roofed timber grandstand with raked benches typically one-storey tall, though sometimes two as in the case of Jerome Park, plus a smaller clubhouse for members. This general make-up warranted comparison with the early European stands of Longchamp, for instance. However, the evolution of racecourse design in North America also brought a new feature, not seen before on the courses of Europe or Britain – the clubhouse. This was more than a members-only stand; as the case of Jerome and Morris Parks evince, they could be designed in the likeness of deluxe hotels replete with ballrooms and they commanded high admittance fees. American courses were money-making ventures, and thus the most ambitious examples launched themselves as venues of fashion, using architecture as a tool to do so.

The majority of courses were modest in their architectural ambitions, but as the decades advanced, the increasing social and economic prominence of racing within the national culture was reflected in the growing sophistication of its architecture. This reached its height in the palazzo clubhouse of Morris Park and the soaring turrets of Saratoga's grandstand.

Australia

Victoria Park grandstand (1882), illustrates the Australian fervour for decorative cast iron

Whilst by the close of the nineteenth century racing in America had grown in prominence, this was nothing compared to the enthusiasm with which the new colony of Australia immediately embraced the sport. Horse racing was adopted there on a singular scale. 'The first care of the pioneers is to mark out the site of the cemetery, the second to plan a racecourse,' recorded one journalist and writer.[49]

When the First Fleet docked in Sydney in 1788 its cargo included one stallion, one colt, three mares and two fillies – most of which reportedly escaped – but a mere 22 years later, the fledgling colony hosted its first official race meeting. It was held in Sydney's Hyde Park and such enthusiasm surrounded its staging that a grandstand was erected especially for the occasion. It was but a humble structure: a simple wooden viewing stand to accommodate some 60 onlookers, not dissimilar to those of England a century earlier.[50] The sport was not slow to grow, though.

In 1861, Australia saw the launch of what remains its most venerable race of all, the Melbourne Cup. This was the height of the gold rush, and over 4,000 spectators flocked to watch, their pockets teeming with gold sovereigns and tiny nuggets direct from the goldfields. This was a tremendous crowd for the fledgling colony. Year after year, its popularity grew exponentially. By 1897, Mark Twain was calling it 'the Mecca of Australasia':

> Cup Day, and Cup Day only, commands an attention, an interest, and an enthusiasm which are universal – and spontaneous, not perfunctory. Cup Day is supreme – it has no rival. I can call to mind no specialised annual day, in any country, which can be named by that large name – Supreme. I can call to mind no specialised annual day, in any country, whose approach fires the whole land with a conflagration of conversation and preparation and anticipation and jubilation. No day save this one; but this one does it.[51]

Cup Day was held at Melbourne's Flemington Racecourse. Racing had been held on that site since 1840, yet by the inauguration of the Cup in the 1860s, its physical fabric was still humble, limited and lacklustre. This typified the nature of Australian racing. For the first half of the nineteenth century, most racecourses were modest affairs, typically open paddocks with posts loosely marking the circuit and wagons serving as grandstands. Few, if any, amenities were afforded to attendees. The 1860s saw this begin to alter. The gold rush of the 1850s engendered a surge in prosperity and racing metamorphosed from a rustic sport into a flourishing industry. The Victoria Racing Club and Queensland Turf Club were formed, important races were instituted, and Australian courses grew increasingly sophisticated. Tracks were railed, more facilities were offered and comfortable grandstands were built which rivalled, albeit usually on a smaller scale, those of Britain, Europe and America.[52]

Perhaps the earliest example of aesthetically sophisticated racecourse architecture was the grandstand at the country racecourse of Hamilton in Victoria; it is certainly the earliest surviving example. Races had been run at the site for 15 years when, in 1873, the Hamilton Racing Club laid down a new course and commissioned a grandstand. Reflecting the

1.33 Hamilton Racecourse
grandstand (1873) was typical of
the physiognomy of stand design
in late-nineteenth century Australia

were enclosed within this base, whilst the tiered seating above was accessed by a double staircase at the front (stairs replaced at a later date). This simple formula was repeated time and again across the country.

As Hamilton Racing Club demonstrated, however, Australian racecourses did not follow the American/European template for large-scale, set-piece racecourses. Racing was beloved by the nation but the populace was small and sparsely distributed; there was simply no call for large-capacity stands or multiple buildings as at Longchamp for instance. The country's racecourses operated, therefore, on a pattern of incremental, single-building schemes; it was a pattern shared by Britain.

This was a golden age for Australian racing, and the Hamilton grandstand expresses the great changes that were reshaping the sport. With its new building in place, Hamilton Racing Club now boasted what a regional newspaper deemed 'the finest grand stand to be seen on any course in the Western district'.[53] Racecourses up and down the land were awakening to the value of building commodious facilities to attract racegoers, particularly female racegoers. Local press wrote of the Hamilton stand that:

> On the ground-floor is a spacious hotel-bar, and luncheon-room, one side of which is formed of moveable panels, so that the whole can be thrown open for ventilation, if desired. There is also on this floor a stewards' room, retiring room for ladies, and a room for the jocks... the place cannot fail to be a favourite resort with the ladies, who will now be able to take a greater interest in the various events than has hitherto been possible.[54]

size of the Hamilton township, it was a small structure but one that encapsulated the physiognomy of late nineteenth-century Australian racecourse design (Figure 1.33).

The Australian racecourse, in many respects, drew together the planning and architectural trends which shaped the courses of nineteenth-century Britain, continental Europe and the US. Akin to the American and European grandstand blueprint, Hamilton's grandstand was a single-storey structure with raked seating overlooking the track open to the front and sides. It was a timber-framed building with cast-iron columns, built upon a bluestone ashlar base. Service and recreation spaces

The provision of better amenities, in particular to encourage women, was a trend pioneered by the stand's designer, Robert Cooper Bagot (circa 1828-81). A British-born civil engineer, Bagot ranked amongst the chief figures of Victorian horse racing. As the first secretary of the Victoria Racing Club (1864-81), he transformed Flemington Racecourse by relaying its track and creating popular viewing areas, notably the unfortunately-named Bagot's Cowshed grandstand (1873) (Figure 1.34). He not only boosted the fortunes of Flemington and established the Melbourne Cup as the country's leading horse race, but played a key part in establishing racing's populist, egalitarian nature in colonial Australia. Working alongside him in the design of Hamilton's stand was architect William Smith (1838-1909), who had settled in Hamilton from London. Bagot and Smith's grandstand was not only commodious and functional, it was also unexpectedly ornate. Its roof was shaped as a graceful double curve with overhanging eaves supported by curving iron brackets attached to the cast-iron columns. A pair of octagonal timber turrets capped by an ogee roof and tall spires stood at each end of the roof ridge, giving a distinctly exotic flavour. Extensive cast iron lace work further embellished its architecture. A cast-iron lattice roof plate extended around its perimeter and a cast-iron lace balustrade stretched across its front.

Introduced to Australia in the 1840s, decorative cast iron was a hallmark of the Victorian era. From bandstands to balconies, fountains to shop fronts, no structure however

humble escaped embellishment in nineteenth-century Australia. The cast-iron ornamentation was often so delicate that it was popularly likened to lace. Most of the towns and cities of the infant colony developed at the height of its popularity. The city of Adelaide was a conspicuous instance of this.[55] It was a cornucopia of rich, graceful cast-iron decoration and its racecourse, Victoria Park, was no exception.

The first 'Adelaide Races' had taken place a year after the town's settlement and by the 1840s horse racing was conducted on the site of Victoria Park. Refreshment booths and dancing facilities were initially the only amenities

1.34 Flemington Racecourse in 1877. The grandstand – the unfortunately-christened Bagot's Cowshed - was built in 1873

offered but by 1850 a temporary stand was in existence.[56] Notwithstanding the highs and lows of the pioneering years, racing there flourished. By the 1870s, the racecourse drew crowds of several thousands, prompting the building of a new grandstand in 1882 (Figure 1.32). This was a peak of prosperity for Adelaide and the city was expanding accordingly. Coeval building projects such as the Art Gallery of South Australia and the zoological gardens were manifestations of the township's expanding cultural and recreational purview which resulted from its burgeoning stability and fortune. This equally came to be expressed in the projects' architectural ambitions. The Victoria Park grandstand should be contemplated in the same light.

The grandstand was designed by architectural partnership Bayer and Withall and it followed much the same formula as at Hamilton. A single tier of seating was located above an undercroft housing bars, retiring rooms, a dining room, plus stewards', secretary and jockeys' accommodation, accessed by stairs leading from the trackside apron. It was a timber and cast-iron frame structure, built upon a bluestone base arranged symmetrically about a gabled porch at the midpoint of the building's façade.[57] This porch formed the centre-point of a repertoire of delicate surface decoration. The porch's gable roof projected forward, laterally intersecting the length of the building. A turned wooden pendant dropped from its centre, a spired flagpole rose from its apex, and it was upheld by slender, fluted cast-iron columns replete

with Corinthian-esque cast capitals. These were just a taster of the decorative cast iron work which enriched the building's façades.

The grandstand was a significant example of the use of cast-iron ornamentation in a non-domestic setting. On each surface, elegant detailing enriched the building. A parade of cast-iron columns supported its roof, framed by finespun, florid lacework brackets. Cast-iron baluster panels railed the front of the stand and extended down its curving stairways. Ornate cresting ran along the roof ridge whilst cast rosettes adorned the fascia board. The work throughout, judged one reporter, afforded 'a light and elegant appearance'.[58]

Grandstands were not the only building type to grace Australian racecourses in the late nineteenth century, however. Behind Victoria Park's new grandstand, a totalisator building was erected.[59] As the racing industry developed and racecourses grew, small subsidiary structures were called for. This trend was to be most prolific in the early decades of the next century, but it had its roots in the final years of the nineteenth. During Victoria's gilded age in the 1880s, Flemington Racecourse was increasingly aggrandised by new construction including a pagoda, weighing room, jockeys' room, and oyster house, which provided both improved sporting and public facilities. The 1880s likewise also brought a boom for Eagle Farm Racecourse in Brisbane, Queensland. Since holding its first meeting in August 1865, Eagle Farm had become the most popular course in the north and in 1887 considerable improvements were undertaken which demonstrate the accumulating register of buildings at racecourses during this period. The programme of works included the construction of a steward's booth, a low masonry building with hipped gable roofs (Figure 1.35). Its light-coloured stone quoins, thick cornice and window and door surrounds made for a striking contrast with its red brick elevations. Whilst not a seating stand, a central veranda was added to its roof in 1891 from which to watch the racing.[60] A tote building followed in the late 1890s.[61] The single-storey brick building with deep overhanging eaves made an elegant addition to the racecourse. The stately cupola which rose from the ridgeline of its tiled roof and projecting gable below epitomised the Federation Free Style, an architectural style which dominated Australian architecture circa 1890 to 1920.[62] By the close of the century, the *Brisbane Courier* commended that 'Eagle Farm never looked better'.[63]

It was no rare thing for an Australian racecourse to sport the latest architectural fashions. These were modest buildings but they could be embellished with turrets, cupolas, cornices and, above all, cast iron. Australian racecourses were prolific in the use of ornate cast iron, skilfully worked into intricate lacework railings or slender columns ending in florid capitals. Such embellishments were applied to the familiar grandstand template of a timber, single-storey building with tiered cross-section. It was a template prevalent in North America, albeit Australian grandstands were typically built

to smaller sizes. Australian racecourses were, though, far more akin to their British parents in their approach to small-scale, cumulative building patterns. Their ensemble of grandstands and, later, totalisator buildings, weighing rooms and others, grew in piecemeal fashion as necessity arose and funds permitted. The gradual accumulation of small, secondary buildings not designed for mass spectator seating was indicative of the growing popularity and organisation of the sport. It was a trend which was to prove increasingly important in Australia and across the world in the early decades of the following century.

1.35 The Steward's Stand at Eagle Farm, built 1887. The central viewing platform was added in 1891

Chapter IV

The Gilded Age

Antipodes

The first two decades of the twentieth century, excepting the four years of World War I, were a golden age for horse racing. Almost the world across, the Sport of Kings grew in popularity in leaps and bounds. In Edwardian England, no other pastime matched its appeal; in Latin America, racing was a byword for elegance and urbanity; and in France, the celebrated Parisian course of Longchamp ranked amongst the most fashionable public venues in the country, drawing Sunday crowds of 40,000.[1] Often as much places of fashion and society as sport and betting, racecourses the world across were patronised with vigour.

Society's greater enthusiasm for racing bred greater crowds; greater crowds in turn bred a need for bigger racecourses. Existing courses remodelled and replaced their old stands with larger successors, whilst new courses were also built from scratch.

The basic structural formula of these Belle Époque grandstands remained based on the pattern honed during the Victorian era: covered tiered structures of raked seating built atop stone or brick bases. However, racecourse architectonics did not remain static; the nature of racecourse buildings was evolving. Firstly, new construction materials and technologies gained sway, notably reinforced concrete and steel frames. Secondly, architectural styles reflected the tastes of the new era; French neo-classicism was particularly conspicuous. Thirdly, subsidiary buildings for eating, drinking and betting increasingly appeared upon racecourses. The latter was particularly visible on the courses of Australia and New Zealand.

All men are born free and equal; and each man is entitled to life, liberty and the pursuit of horse racing.

(Andrew 'Banjo' Paterson, *Racehorses and Racing*, 1914[2])

Across the world, the opening of the twentieth century saw the fervour for racing steadily increase. The demands for viewing accommodation mounted and racecourse design was impelled to evolve to keep pace with them. The grandstand template underwent an inexorable shift further towards the provision of fixed seating, whilst social spaces for refreshment or betting were further pushed to the rear of stands. Particularly in Australia and New Zealand, they were also progressively pushed into completely separate buildings.

The Tea House at Riccarton Park Racecourse in Christchurch, New Zealand, was a charmingly Antipodean manifestation of the proliferation of supplementary buildings on racecourses (Figure 1.36). Recently brought back to life by an extensive restoration campaign,[3] the Tea House was built in 1903 at a time when racing in the young colony was at its height. Racecourses teemed with men, women and even children. Only men though were permitted to enter the grandstand refreshment rooms on the grounds that alcohol was served there. Hence, tea kiosks to cater primarily for female racegoers and families became a regular feature of racecourses across the country. The Riccarton Park example formed part of a programme of improvements at the course to celebrate the Golden Jubilee of the Canterbury Jockey Club in 1904. It was designed by influential local architects, the Luttrell brothers, specialists

Page 66 **1.36** Riccarton Park Tea House (1903). Tea houses were a common sight on early twentieth-century racecourses

Opposite **1.37** Feilding Racecourse Tea Kiosk (1906) was set on its own landscaped island

in the design of racecourse buildings; in fact, they had lately designed a grandstand at the course as well. Their tea house was a stylistically unpretentious but elegant Edwardian building. Of timber construction, it was a long, low structure with a deep veranda running along its front sheltered by broad eaves. A central gable porch marked its entrance and two large peaked turrets crowned either end of its length, giving a festal, pavilion quality to the building.

The pavilion was situated to the west of the grandstands in a meticulously contrived landscape. The Canterbury Jockey Club clearly placed emphasis on creating a beautiful natural setting for its patrons, for it set the tea house on what was effectively its own landscaped island surrounded by a moat and accessed via a bridge.[4] The *Press* reported on 4 November 1903,

> The artificial waters encircling the island upon which this new structure
> stands surrounded by a belt of fir trees and pretty borders, so planted
> that there shall be a constant succession of bloom, present a scene such
> as cannot be surpassed for beauty by any Australasian race course.

Another example existed at Feilding Racecourse, on New Zealand's north island. Built in 1906 to designs by local architect Alex James, the Feilding Tea Kiosk was perhaps set in an even more picturesque setting than its Riccarton counterpart (Figure 1.37). 'The ladies' tea kiosk is a special source of attraction,' wrote the *Wairarapa Daily Times*. 'It is surrounded by water, crossed by two handsome bridges, with a fountain playing in the centre, with swans and other birds on the water, also a tame deer in an enclosure.'[5] It was a small octagonal building, built of timber, cast iron and glass with a veranda over three metres (11 feet) deep,

below which refreshments were dispensed. 'The kiosk is a handsome structure, and was greatly admired by all,' decreed the *Feilding Star* upon its opening.[6]

The tea kiosk no longer survives. In fact, the Riccarton Park tea house is now the only known extant building of its type in New Zealand. While once a common building typology on racecourses, its original function has been superseded and the building is a dying breed. The epitome of this is the tea house at Royal Randwick Racecourse in Sydney, demolished in 2012 (Figure 1.38). Racing begun in earnest at Randwick in 1860 and for the rest of the century the course steadily flourished. By the early twentieth century, the popularity of horse racing as a spectator sport had proved so profuse that Randwick embarked upon an extensive flurry of construction to keep apace with the demands of the racing community and public. It is to this period that the tea house belongs. From 1906 to 1917, Randwick was transformed. Additions to the original grandstand and Members' Stand between 1907 and 1914 rendered them unrecognisable; brand new Ladies' (1910) and St Leger (1911) Stands added further accommodation; and a large tea pavilion built in 1914 provided spacious refreshment rooms.[7]

'Having provided ample seating accommodation for the great crowds that visit Randwick by the completion of the grand and official stands,' reported the *Sydney Morning Herald* on 8 April 1914,

> the A.J.C. [Australian Jockey Club] has appropriately followed up
> that essential work by the erection of an up-to-date and commodious
> two-storeyed building, to be known as the 'Tea House', and capable of
> seating between 1,200 and 1,300 persons.

Constructed in the saddling paddock behind the stands, Randwick's new tea house replaced the members' tea room and public tea room which had both been sited at the rear of the grandstand. Large, robust and perfectly proportioned, it made for one of the most impressive examples of its type. Running 50 metres in length by 27 metres in width (158 by 90 feet), it was a cream-painted, textured rendered brick structure rising two storeys. Loosely inspired by Indian Colonial architecture, a deep, arched veranda encircled its front and side elevations on the ground floor, which was balanced on the upper storey by an open balcony. Each corner of the building was anchored by a square pavilion whose hipped roof added variation to the tea house's silhouette. At the centre of its principal façade extended a prominent double-storey entrance porch with a barrel vault and tall arched openings on both floors. Although built less than a decade after the Feilding tea house, its design signalled the encroaching modern age. Its lines were simple and geometric and its forms were spare and symmetrical, yet these were enlivened by variations in massing and planes and a deft understanding of proportion.

The architects responsible for this design were leading Sydney practice, Robertson and Marks. Founding partner Theodore Marks (1865-1941) was likely responsible for most of these commissions.[8] He was an enthusiastic turfite and longstanding member of the Australian Jockey Club, which no doubt worked to the firm's advantage in procuring these projects. Indeed, Robertson and Marks were responsible for not only the tea house but all the building projects at Randwick in these years. The firm's long running relationship with the racecourse resulted in a comprehensive and harmonious ensemble of buildings at the racecourse.

In 1917, this ensemble was joined by two automatic totalisator buildings behind the St Leger and members' stands.[9] One still stands today. Like the tea house, they illustrate the growing proliferation of subsidiary yet substantial buildings upon racecourse grounds. In fact, their presence marks Randwick as something of a trailblazer; they were the fourth in the world to be installed. Automatic totalisators were a very recent invention. Devised by Sir George Julius, they allowed a system of machine betting in which the total number of 'unit bets' made on each horse entered for a race and the grand total of all such bets were displayed in large readable figures in real time, as bets were being placed. First installed in 1913 at Ellerslie Racecourse in New Zealand, the introduction of automatic totalisators had a prodigious impact upon the nature of racecourses

1.38 Randwick's Tea House (designed 1914) was part of an extensive expansion campaign for the racecourse by Sydney architects Robertson and Marks

the world across. Their net spread widely, from Caracas to Colombo. They were systematically legalised amongst horse racing nations, predominantly in the 1920s and 30s, appearing first in France at Longchamp in 1928, in Britain at Ascot and York in 1930, and in America at Hialeah Park in 1932. The system had quickly and readily taken hold across the Antipodes by 1920, however.

The new technology not only changed the ritual of betting, but it also necessitated large-scale structures and called upon architects to formulate a new building type. For the most part, this took the form of a big, rectangular building with a vast indicator board displaying betting figures above ticket windows or booths.

The Randwick totalisators, though, were housed in highly unusual structures, both attractive and inventive.

To house Randwick's first automatic totalisators, Robertson and Marks designed two identical buildings. Each building was tripartite in ground plan. At each end was an unusual octagon crowned by an elegant domed lantern (Figure 1.39). Louvered dormer vents projected from the lantern's slate roof with a cantilevered overhang to shelter patrons at the ticket vending windows which lined its sides. The two octagons, measuring 23 metres (75 feet) in diameter, were the banking chambers and linking them both was an imposing, double-storey central administration block. Here,

1.39 Elevation drawings of the new totalisator building at Randwick Racecourse (1917) by Robertson and Marks

Opposite **1.40** One of two identical totalisator buildings at Randwick, photographed in the 1950s. In the foreground is the betting ring with bookmakers' stalls

Robertson and Marks combined a stripped classical vocabulary – domed cupola, engaged pilasters, Doric columns – with the demands of this new building type – a first-floor display board of betting figures on its eastern elevation (Figure 1.40). [10]

Following their work at Randwick, Robertson and Marks developed something of a specialism in the racing world. The racecourses of Warwick Farm, Rosehill Gardens and Canterbury Park in Sydney and the West India Turf Club in far-flung Mumbai featured in their portfolio, as did Flemington in Melbourne. The Victoria Racing Club engaged the firm to mastermind a grand redevelopment at Flemington. From 1922-4, the course was completely transformed with the construction of a new complex to the east of its earlier buildings, comprising a new Members' Stand, betting ring and paddock (Figure 1.41). The Members' Stand (1924) was a 90-metre (300-feet) long, reinforced-concrete building, three storeys tall. Its simplicity of line within the context of classical structural forms was indicative of the stripped classicism that characterised interwar architecture. It was a bold new architectonic for Flemington, in tune was the bold scale of Robertson and Mark's master plan.

Their master plan, however, was controversial. Much to the chagrin of Victoria Racing Club members, it involved the radical solution of relocating the nucleus of its facilities away from the finishing post where they had been since the 1860s, to the eastern portion of the site. The scale of the project and its total cost was prodigious in terms of Australian precedents. At a time when the Melbourne Cup prize money was around £10,000, the estimated expenditure was over a quarter of a million pounds.[11] The scale was nonetheless justified by the magnitude of Flemington's popularity. In 1919 and 1920 Melbourne Cup crowds exceeded 100,000.[12]

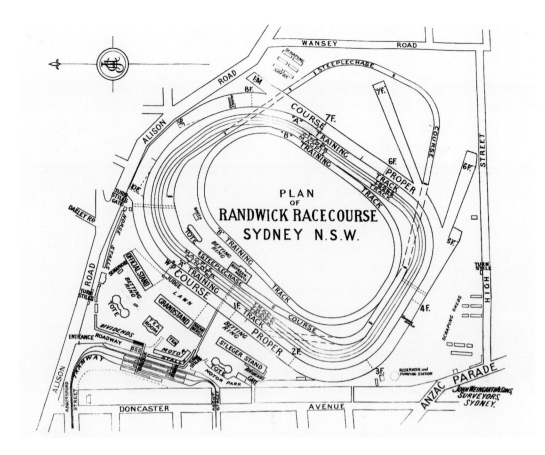

With the completion of the 1924 master plan, Flemington possessed a disparate series of buildings varying in age, style and size alongside its track. Robertson and Marks's redevelopment of Flemington and Randwick are illustrative of the type of incremental growth that had shaped Australian and New Zealand racecourses in the Victorian age and continued to do so in the early twentieth century. Contrasting with the 'whole-cloth' approach practiced notably in France, this method yielded racecourses with structures of all shapes and sizes, built over decades. This additive approach often did not make for the most lucid, navigable layouts (Figure 1.42). This characteristic was not one evinced by Antipodean racecourses alone; it equally defined British racecourses of the era as well.

Opposite **1.41** Aerial view of Flemington showing new parade ring and Members' Stand (1924) built to the east of the original nineteenth-century buildings

Above **1.42** Plan of Randwick circa 1921. The incremental addition of subsidiary buildings such as tea houses and totalisators in the opening decades of the twentieth century tended to produce a congested, haphazard layout

Britain

Notwithstanding the lustre of Australia's Melbourne Cup, nowhere was racing more popular than in Edwardian England. Basking in the prestige of King Edward VII's patronage, it was the national pastime. The Derby and Oaks at Epsom, St Leger at Doncaster, Goodwood's summer meeting and, most notably, Royal Ascot were unmissable entries on the society calendar. In 1902, the year of Edward's coronation, Royal Ascot enjoyed its largest ever attendance.[13] This was a foretoken of the decade to come. Under the auspices of the new monarch, Ascot emerged as one of the most stylish events of the year, encouraged in no little part by a fashionable remodelling of its most socially exclusive arena.

Following the death of his mother in January, in the summer of 1901 Edward indulged his passion for Ascot by ordering the rebuilding of the entire Royal Enclosure. The project was executed with astonishing speed. By June the following year, three spacious and well-appointed new stands had been erected (Figure 1.43). Each differed in style and size. Running from east to west, they comprised the Jockey Club Stand, the Royal Stand and, the largest of the three, the Royal Enclosure Stand. On the front elevations, stacked tiers of seating overlooked the track, whilst balconies, ornately railed with cast iron, projected from the rear façade (Figure 1.44). This feature of balconies on the rear elevation had its precedents in France, at Chantilly and Longchamp in the mid-nineteenth century. In their tiered configuration with cast iron details, these stands diverged little from the established Victorian model, but they were nevertheless enthusiastically received. The *Horse and Hounds* commended the new structures as 'excellent, and put at an angle which enables one to see all the races perfectly'. The *Times* praised that 'everywhere are to be

seen signs of a desire to move with the times, and to make Ascot as attractive socially as it is interesting from the racing point of view'.[14]

Located opposite the winning post and adjacent to the parade ring and paddock, these three stands offered Ascot's best view of the action of the turf. They also offered the best view of Ascot's elite. As the buildings of the Royal Enclosure, they were accessed by personal invitation only and these invitations were governed by strict rules.[15] The Edwardian age did, however, also see attempts to popularise Ascot. Conscious that 'not quite enough was done for the comfort of the ordinary public at Ascot', the King was reportedly influential in the erection of the Five Shilling Stand – later called the Silver Ring Stand – in 1908.[16] Constructed at the eastern end of Ascot's row of stands, the Five Shilling Stand provided lower priced admissions for those unable to afford grandstand rates.[17] It was indicative of the additive attitude towards buildings which had always characterised Ascot. A further spate of additions which began in 1911 added bars and luncheon rooms to the Silver Ring, grandstand enclosure and paddock to cater for the expanding crowds. The 'much-felt want of a luncheon room in the paddock', for example, was addressed in 1911 with the construction of a 120-seater luncheon room with adjoining champagne bar in the saddling paddock.[18] These buildings belonged to the trend for specialised subsidiary structures which was born of the demand for more and more fixed seating within grandstands. Increasingly, as Ascot's crowds grew larger, ancillary facilities were transposed from its grandstands into dedicated buildings.

Ascot was not alone in this. Epsom saw similar additions, notably a large luncheon annexe in 1914 (Figure 1.45). It was a singularly idiosyncratic structure appended to the rear of the 1830 grandstand,

which now struggled to keep apace with demands for refreshment and viewing spaces. 'The building runs parallel to the back of the Grand Stand, and the connexion between them is by means of a bridge,' described the *Times*.

> It is from the designs of Albert Charles Williams and is in the Renaissance style, the materials used being brick and cement. There are four floors, which include public and private luncheon rooms and rooms for stewards, ambulance cases, and doctors.[19]

It was a restrained yet refined example of early twentieth-century classicism. Within the context of racecourse design, the luncheon annexe and the changes at Ascot reveal not only the amplifying of subsidiary structures upon racecourses in general, but also the demands for social entertainments felt by racegoers of the period.

Opposite above **1.43** Royal Ascot 1909. King Edward VII processes before the Royal Enclosure, built 1902

Opposite below **1.44** Royal Enclosure at Ascot. The rear façade was domestic in appearance

Above **1.45** Epsom Racecourse luncheon annexe, built 1914, was joined via a bridge to the 1829-30 grandstand

France

'On Grand Prix Day one would imagine that all Paris and half of London were in attendance,' wrote one commentator of the scene at the Hippodrome de Longchamp in 1901.[20] If, compared with England, France came to the Sport of Kings late, it certainly came to it with gusto. From Parisian aristocracy and haute-bourgeoisie to merchants, students and clerks, Belle Époque France embraced racegoing – especially its social and gambling aspects – wholeheartedly. The turn of the century saw a veritable explosion in its racing industry, catalysed in no small measure by a trailblazing law of 1891 which banned bookmakers and instituted the pari-mutuel upon the nation's courses. With the passing of this edict, came the democratisation of the Turf. Progressively, its appeal widened beyond its traditional blue-blooded circle to encompass all levels of society. Between 1890 and 1900, the annual number of thoroughbred meetings in France had soared from 1,871 to 2,463, whilst the number of active racehorses rocketed from 1,234 to 2,242.[21]

The growth of the industry is best illustrated by the flurry of construction at racecourses old and new during the first decade of the twentieth century. Existing hippodromes procured bigger grandstands and whole new courses were founded, especially in suburban areas. This was the second generation of racecourse architecture in France. Almost invariably, new developments adopted the 'whole-cloth' approach to design which had moulded the nineteenth-century wave of French racecourses. Modern technologies and materials slowly began to be embraced, specifically reinforced concrete, but these were almost always hidden beneath veneers of traditionalist architectural styles. Amongst the most popular of these styles was the Anglo-Normand.

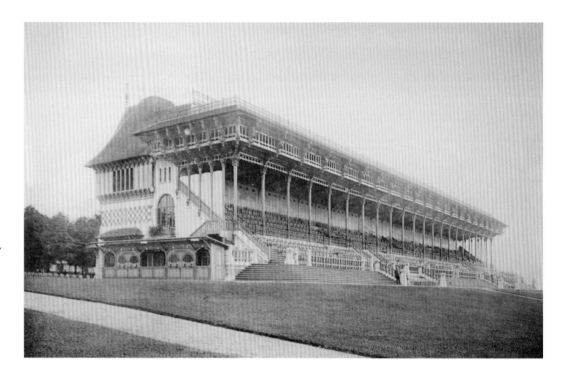

The Anglo-Normand was the idiom employed by architect Berthault Léon when he was engaged to design the new Hippodrome de Saint-Cloud, near Paris, built between 1898 and 1902 (Figure 1.46). The Anglo-Normand had already been used at the seaside course of Deauville for a weighing house (1890) (Figure 1.47). Based upon the vernacular architectural tradition of Normandy, it was an eclectic style characterised by a jamboree of half timbering, overhanging eaves, dormers and gables. At Saint-Cloud, it was put to use upon a large scale.

Saint-Cloud did not use the nineteenth-century layout of the Chantilly-Longchamp type, based upon a line of hierarchical stands with an imperial pavilion at its apex. This had much to do with its origins. Unlike Chantilly and Longchamp, which were run by the Société d'Encouragement on land owned by the duc d'Aumale and the State respectively, Saint-Cloud was the private enterprise

1.46 Hippodrome de Saint-Cloud (1898-1902) epitomised a trend for new suburban racecourses around Paris at the turn of the century

Opposite **1.47** The *Pavillon des Balances* or weighing room at Deauville (1890), built in the Anglo-Normand style

of wealthy thoroughbred breeder, Edmond Blanc. It belonged to the new breed of suburban racecourses. No rationale existed, therefore, to build an honorific imperial tribune or hierarchical members-only club stand and its ground plan reflected this.

Saint-Cloud had no imperial pavilion, but a single vast grandstand complemented by a host of subsidiary structures – pari-mutuel building, weighing house, and stabling – all dressed in the picturesque Anglo-Normand dialect. The great wealth of Blanc was reflected in an impressive architectural panorama. The grandstand was a deep building. It housed a single tier of raked seating, with an expansive set of ancillary rooms below and to the rear. Although large in scale, its architecture took its cue from the traditional forms of rural farmsteads, giving the stand, and indeed the whole complex, a contrived mien of the country manor house, very different to Paris's other racecourses. Its rear façade was an ensemble of half-timbering, chequered red and white bricks, gables and finials. The three gabled pavilions which projected from the elevation – one at the centre and either end – were perhaps an Anglo-Normand take on the stair towers of nineteenth-century Chantilly and Longchamp. Exaggerated timber rafters supported the building's overhanging eaves, with consoles fancifully sculpted as dragons in a nod towards the late nineteenth-century taste for orientalism. The grandstand no longer exists – it was replaced in 1954 – but Léon's lively intonation of the Anglo-Normand survives in the extant old farriery workshop and caretaker's lodge (Figure 1.48).

The vernacular Anglo-Normand was likewise the style preferred when the racecourse of Maisons-Laffitte on the outskirts of Paris replaced its buildings in 1904. The racecourse had been opened in 1878 by the inventor of the Pari-Mutuel, Joseph Oller, but in the 1890s it was bought by the Société Sportive d'Encouragement (founded 1887). The democratisation of the sport in the 1890s together with the arrival of the railway to the racecourse in 1898 resulted in a surge in crowds attending Maisons-Laffitte. By the turn of the new century, its small grandstand was overcrowded and inadequate. A new complex was planned. In 1904, its old grandstand was pulled down and in its stead rose a larger stand (Figure 1.49) and companion weighing pavilion (neither extant). Their architect was André Raimbert (1865-1927), who had recently designed the hippodrome of Saint-Ouen (1903), another suburban course on the outskirts of Paris.[22]

The new Maisons-Laffitte may not have compared to Longchamp or Auteuil in scale or glamour, but Raimbert endowed this modestly-sized, suburban venue with a charmingly picturesque architectural ensemble. The weighing room was an almost direct copy of the cottage-esque weighing pavilion of Deauville, sporting a jamboree of half-timbering, overhanging eaves and thick timber bracing and topped by ornamental finials and red and white chequered brick chimney stacks. Likewise, its grandstand made great play with a profuse Anglo-Normand repertoire of half-timbering, red tiles, half-hip steeply-pitched roofs, gablets and ornately carved balustrades.

The capricious medley of steep roofs, dormers, gables, herringbone brick and half-timbering which characterised Saint-Cloud and Maisons-Laffitte was not the sole architectural

idiom employed upon France's racecourses at this date, however. Likewise, the nineteenth-century pattern of multiple stands and imperial tribune had not been rendered obsolete. In 1904, the same year that Maisons-Laffitte's stand was built, Paris's most famous racecourse replaced its collection of old stands with a gleaming new ensemble (Figure 1.50). By the early 1900s, Longchamp's position at the vanguard of the French beau monde was unassailable. Its stands, however, were acknowledged as antiquated. Since Longchamp's inauguration in 1857, its stands had undergone several remodellings; they were repaired after extensive damage during the 1870-1 siege of Paris and renovated and extended in multiple campaigns in the 1880s and 1890s.[23] By 1904, the Société d'Encouragement determined to erect a set of stands as resplendent as its fashionable clientele.

They opted for a bold course of action. Its exiting fabric was swept away and replaced by a long line of new stands. The new tribunes echoed the layout of the 1850s complex: a row

Opposite **1.48** Saint-Cloud's caretaker's lodge (1898). The racecourse was rebuilt in 1954 and its Anglo-Normand grandstand replaced, but this lodge from the original scheme survives today

Above **1.49** The Hippodrome de Maisons-Laffitte on the outskirts of Paris was rebuilt in 1904 in Anglo-Normand style

of stands with a small, stand-alone *Tribune Présidentielle* as its
centrepiece. Furthermore, they shared common architectural
features with their predecessors, notably stair towers and balconies
on the rear façade. However, they were realised on a far larger,
more commodious and majestic scale. Built in stone, they were
designed by architect Charles Girault (1851-1932). There were
two grandstands. Each possessed two tiers of raked steppings
overlooking the course (Figure 1.51), whilst the rear elevation
was built three storeys tall in a rhythmical parade of arcades
punctuated by stair towers. From its arcaded galleries, patrons
could survey the horses, or more likely their fellow racegoers,
promenading in the paddock.

Longchamp's renown as a centre of French racing and
fashion, combined with the elegant, classical vocabulary and
near-perfect proportions of the buildings made them immediate
models of emulation. The influence of their architecture upon the
immediate generation of grandstand construction was enormous. It
stretched across France, across Europe and across the globe, as shall
soon be seen.

For now though, the scene remains in the French capital.
Not long after the unveiling of Longchamp's new range of
buildings, yet another new racecourse was opening in the Parisian
suburbs. The Hippodrome du Tremblay opened to great fanfare
in 1906, built to designs by Octave Raquin (Figure 1.52).[24] Whilst

Longchamp and Chantilly replaced their grandstands with greater luxury and comfort, wrote *Construction Moderne* in 1906, other parts of the courses were left unmodernised. Tremblay, conversely, catered for all the needs of the racing public and professionals; it was saluted as being completely equipped for the modern age.[25] Racquin designed a comprehensive series of buildings comprising a grandstand, weighing pavilion, pari-mutuel buildings and stables, united by a palette of pink-coloured bricks and white stone trim.

The weighing pavilion was a lively, assymetrical medley of pitched gables, chimneys, terraces and arched windows of distinct domestic character, that was sited alongside the grandstand. Contemporary commentators made much of the heed given to improving sightlines within the building, something which was to increasingly preoccupy grandstand designers in the forthcoming decades. 'The columns which ordinarily uphold the roof,' wrote the *Architectural Record*, 'have been replaced by an iron veranda the span of which is 10 metres, or just inside of 33 feet. It is a very daring and ingenious innovation. Until now, verandas of such large span have not been attempted in France.'[26]

Tremblay's grandstand also drew attention for its construction method. It was a steel-framed construction, filled in with bricks (Figure 1.53). It was a frank and simple building, whose underlying form was not concealed but rather formed the basis of its aesthetic. This aesthetic was to become increasingly widespread, as the stand built in 1919 at Deauville illustrates.

The Hippodrome de Deauville had been France's premier seaside racing resort since its construction in 1864 by the devoted horseman, the Duc de Morny, as a summertime rival to Baden-Baden. In 1913, as part of a wider remodelling, the architects Louis Lefranc and Alfred Pigny were charged with designing a new stand to replace those that had stood since the 1860s. The First World War interrupted the realisation of the stand until 1919. The new grandstand melded the prototype of Longchamp with that of Tremblay. Its rear façade, in its stair towers, balconies and arches, recalled the rhythm and proportions of Longchamp (Figure 1.54). Its palette of materials and construction, on the other hand, shared a similar mindset to that of Tremblay. The Deauville grandstand had a red brick and white-trim skin covering a reinforced concrete frame. This most modern of materials was put to use in creating a cantilevered canopy on its trackside, enabling the column-free structure that won such plaudits at Tremblay (Figure 1.55). No other material or construction technique yielded such an influence upon grandstand design not only in France, but across Europe.

Reinforced concrete was pivotal to the third generation of French racecourse architecture, which emerged in the 1920s in Paris. Exemplified by the redevelopment of Longchamp in 1921 by architect Charles Adda and of Auteuil in 1924 by Albert-Emmanuel d'Hondt, it combined conventional hierarchical layouts and traditional historicist styles with the innovatory properties of reinforced concrete. Auteuil's new stands, for instance, featured two storeys of seating, the upper of which was a cantilevered platform. This was heralded as an audacious structural achievement, yet it

remained fused with a neo-classicist architectonic. D'Hondt even adorned the buildings with concrete bas-relief medallions.[27] Its gracious, snow-white buildings reflected the elegance that the sport in the French capital was famed for. 'Racing in Paris is racing-de-luxe,' acclaimed one New Zealand paper.[28]

Stylistically, this third generation continued to hark back to the influential model of Longchamp's 1904 stands. The stands seemed to epitomise the essence of the golden age of racing in Europe and beyond. As the sport gained in popularity the world across, time and again we encounter echoes of Longchamp within grandstand construction. The new buildings of Milan's racecourse were one such example.

Opposite above **1.52** Grandstand of the Hippodrome du Tremblay in the Parisian suburbs, which opened to warm welcome in 1906

Opposite middle **1.53** Tremblay was noted for its steel-frame construction

Opposite below **1.54** Rear elevation of the grandstand at the Hippodrome de Deauville, completed in 1919

Above **1.55** The side elevation of Deauville's grandstand illustrates its cantilevered, column-free canopy

Italy

Reinforced concrete, combined with French historicist styles, was a prominent design trend for the Belle Époque grandstand across Europe and beyond. In Italy, the most exuberant exponent of this was the Ippodromo di San Siro, in the outskirts of Milan. The first San Siro had been built in 1888, but in 1911 the Lombard Jockey Club determined that its stands were no longer sufficient to house the Milanese crowds which flocked to its races. A competition was announced for its rebuilding. Delays marred the project's progress. Construction did not commence until 1914 and, hampered by World War I, it took a further six years until the new San Siro was completed. Contemporary commentators agreed, however, that it was worth the wait (Figure 1.56).

Paolo Vietti-Violi (1882-1965), along with prominent Milanese architect Arrigo Cantoni, designed the new complex. For Vietti-Violi, it was the beginning of a distinguished career as an architect of sports facilities, whose output went on to include racecourses in Rome and Merano. Amidst an ensemble of weighing room, stables, entrance buildings and others, the centrepiece of the new racecourse was its two large grandstands. Their reinforced concrete fabric permitted an extensive provision of balconies, stairs and overhanging canopies, which, although not column-free, were supported by few obstructive pillars. This modern framework was, though, cloaked within a distinctly historicist casing. Notwithstanding Italy's venerable architectural heritage, Vietti-Violo turned not to native sources of inspiration for his design but looked instead abroad, in particular to the celebrated precedent of Longchamp's 1904 tribunes. The rear façades of San Siro's two stands were strikingly

redolent of Longchamp in their cadence of projecting belvedere stair towers and double-height arches, coupled with neo-classical vocabulary. The secondary stand was restrained in its classicism, but the principal stand gave vent to a repertoire of Ionic pilasters and columns, swags, urns, rustication, balustrades and central sculpted pediment. Its grandiosity spoke of the heights to which thoroughbred racing reached in the Belle Époque. Moreover, it demonstrated the international character of grandstand architecture, amidst which especial importance was allotted to French architectural precedent. The latter's influence was stretched across the globe, even to the Bay of Benghal.

1.56 The Ippodromo di San Siro, Milan (1920), was reminiscent of the stands of Longchamp

India

Let but a few Englishmen assemble in any quarter of the globe and it may safely be predicated that a horse race would be organised.

(Earl of Wilton, 1869)

Nowhere was this statement more applicable than in the British Empire outpost of India. In the age of high Victoriana, the grandstand was one of the most characteristic structures of India. Under the rule of the Turf-loving British, there was hardly a station in India without a racecourse. The stands were on occasions nothing more than flimsy tents, but at other times they were extremely lavish. Throughout the nineteenth century, their grandeur grew, and by the Edwardian age the clubhouses, stands, stable blocks and restaurants could rival government buildings in opulence. The racecourse of the Royal Calcutta Turf Club was one such example. The racecourse's buildings had been remodelled several times since it had been established on the large, flat expanse of the Maidan in 1819, when, in 1905-6, three new stands were built (Figure 1.57).

At the opening of the twentieth century, Calcutta was enjoying a high point. Unlike most viceroys, the current incumbent Lord Curzon favoured Calcutta and under his administration, the city was boosted by several large building projects. A 'glance at the building of the town, at the river and the roar and the smoke, is sufficient to show that Calcutta is in reality a European city set down upon Asiatic soil,' Curzon said in a 1903 speech to the Bengal Chamber of Commerce.[29] By the opening of the twentieth century, Calcutta ranked as the second biggest city in the whole of the British Empire and it had a markedly classical silhouette. From the dome of its Government House (1803) to the Greek temple-like façade of its Mint (1837), neo-classicism was the language of Calcuttan power and

the Calcuttan elite.[30] It is this tradition to which the Royal Calcutta Turf Club's new grandstands belonged. By 1904 club attendances by far exceeded the capacity of the Maidan's two 1880s stands, and in May the following year Government approval had been granted to build a range of new masonry stands.[31] Their architect was Vincent Esch (1876-1950), a 'Calcuttan architectural institution'.[32]

Esch played a notable role in the forging of a European architectural enclave in the Bengali capital. He had arrived in India in 1898 as a young, newly-qualified English architect. He immediately took up a post as architect to the Bengal Nagpur Railway Company and went on to design a body of work in Calcutta including the Allahabad Bank, Bengal Club, Temple Chambers and the Victoria Memorial. All adopted the restrained classicism which characterised so much of the city.[33] His designs for the Royal Calcutta Turf Club followed suit.

As in his other commissions, Esch relied heavily on concrete for the stand's superstructure. However, he was no modernist. Esch's approach 'was to use modern technology discreetly in support of an historical cultural pattern,' and in the case of the Turf Club, this meant employing the established tradition of European High Victorian stands with a pronounced French classicist flavour.[34] The three stands had a tiered cross section. Two levels of open raked seating and a stepped terrace, which extended to the track apron, provided viewing accommodation for the racecourse's wealthy patrons. At the rear, circulation and refreshment spaces were housed behind stately brick and stone-dressed façades. The most impressive of the three stands was the central one. With its stone quoins, balustrades, pediments, keystones, and three mansard-topped towers, this was a classically garbed building of Francophile inspiration. Its stair towers in particular evoked the grandstands of France.

Early twentieth-century racing architecture was international in character. France, with its cultural prestige and racing pedigree, proved an especial model. Yet it was not the sole exemplar. When in 1921, the Royal Western India Turf Club commissioned three new stands for its Mahalaxmi Racecourse in the heart of Mumbai, it was not France but Australia that they turned to for a model.

> The Indian Turf Club sent a couple of its members as a commission to enquire into and report on the best-appointed racecourses of the world. After visiting England and the principal continental centres, the commissioners came to Australia, and in New South Wales they found what they had made a world tour to find – the best appointed racecourse in the world. Randwick was the place decided upon by the commissioners as the best they had found in their travels.[35]

With their model decided upon, the Turf Club employed Randwick's architects Robertson and Marks to recreate a little spot of Sydney on Indian terrain. The grandstands sheathed their concrete and steel structure in a pared classicist exterior. The Members' Stand was the most attractive and exclusive of the racecourse ensemble. Measuring 80 metres (260 feet) long and housing 6,000 people, it provided open tiered seating over three floors. Borrowing a motif seen time and again within nineteenth and early twentieth-century grandstand design, each end of the building was terminated by a tower; in this case it was capped with a red tile, hipped roof and a deep block cornice. Like Esch's designs at Calcutta, any reference to Mughal architectural

traditions were eschewed; Robertson and Marks were working fully in the tradition in which they were familiar. Simple in form, the design of the stands was, though, less sophisticated than Robertson and Marks's work at Flemington or Randwick. Mahalaxmi's stands were not directly patterned upon any in Australia, yet in embarking upon a world racecourse tour and selecting Robertson and Marks as its architects, the Royal Western India Turf Club was illustrating the international temperament of racecourse architecture of this era. From Milan to Mumbai, racing architecture followed established international currents, and nowhere was this international dialogue stronger than in Latin America.

1.57 The Royal Calcutta Turf Club commissioned three new stands in 1905 from British architect Vincent Esch

South America

The early twentieth century was a time of relative political stability and economic prosperity for the ruling elite throughout much of Latin America, and these halcyon days came lavishly to bear upon the continent's racing panorama. The century's opening decades were a golden age for racecourse architecture as palatial complexes were built for the recreation and relaxation of wealthy society. Horses had been imported centuries earlier by Iberian conquistadors and match races soon became a popular colonial pastime amongst all sectors of society. By the eighteenth century, horse racing was a daily happening in Chilean, Argentinian, Colombian and Uruguayan towns. However, the traditional Iberian races did not outlast the introduction of British-style turf racing in the mid-nineteenth century and quickly the ad hoc, inclusive sport became an aristocratic and institutional one, incarnated in grand new courses such as those of Buenos Aires, Rio de Janeiro and Santiago.

The emergence of British-style racing was not an isolated phenomenon; it was symptomatic of a widespread emulation of European cultures amongst the upper echelons of South American society from the late nineteenth century onwards. By the 1870s, the continent's newly-independent countries were largely enjoying unprecedented social, political and economic health. Their accelerated leap into the world economy had engendered a rising class of socially and materially ambitious bourgeoisie, who were goaded by an ardour to distance themselves from their colonial history and what was perceived as a backward and barbaric past. The antidote to this was perceived as 'civilised Europe', and it was here that the era's elite looked to as a social, cultural and artistic model.

The continent's burgeoning affluence brought an influx of European immigrants to its shores and reciprocally a cross stream of South Americans traversing the Atlantic. This was to have two far-reaching consequences for the urban landscape of the New World cities. Firstly, it supplied skilled labour and, secondly, contact with aesthetic trends and sensibilities unlike those which had preponderated hitherto.[36] As the Belle Époque progressed, architecture across the new republics took a similar path. Great government buildings, stately theatres, palatial residences, vast parks adorned with public monuments, and wide new boulevards arose which bore witness to South America's Europeanisation. Between the 1870s and 1920s, architecture was a vital ideological tool in formulating new republican national identities. Governments and the rising bourgeoisie used architecture as one of the most visible agencies of constructing an image of culture and modernity. From neo-Gothic to Tuscan Renaissance to French Beaux-Arts, a medley of new architectural fashions were embraced. There was, however, an almost ubiquitous recoil from the styles of Spain or Portugal, as reminders of colonial rule, and instead artistic inspiration was sought from the 'enlightened' models of Italy, England, and, most prominently, France.

A host of imported styles and historical motifs transformed city centres. The late nineteenth-century urban panoramas of Argentina in particular came to reflect the growing wealth and social ambitions of society's upper echelons. With the riches of the country concentrated upon Buenos Aires, the city was soon refashioned.[37] The ornamented Beaux-Arts architecture and urban planning of Baron Haussmann's Paris captured the imaginations of Argentina's government and rising bourgeoisie as a physical manifestation of progress and beauty. Buenos Aires's new Recoleta neighbourhood especially reflected the Francophile mentality of its inhabitants. From the late nineteenth century, the city's aristocratic families flocked

to this fashionable suburb and lined its streets with tall Parisian-esque mansions. For these Francophile Argentinians, though, it was not enough that their buildings merely looked French; the marble staircases, bronze and ironwork, crystal chandeliers and even the roof tiles of the Recoleta palaces were imported from Europe.

By the close of the nineteenth century, Buenos Aires boasted all the amenities of the great European cities. And this included a racecourse. Endowed in 1876, the founding of the racecourse went hand in hand with the local desire to ape European customs. The Hipódromo de Palermo, as the course was christened,[38] was sited adjacent to Recoleta in the Parque Tres de Febrero which had been created two years earlier and was modelled upon Paris's Bois de Boulogne and Vienna's Prater. When the hipódromo's wooden Victorian stands were rebuilt from 1908 to 1911 it was again the omnipresent European spirit which stimulated the project.

The hipódromo became home to one of the grandest ensembles of buildings in racing history. Intent on echoing the fashionable Parisian grandeur of neighbouring Recoleta, its owners engaged Frenchman Louis Faure-Dujarric (1875-1943) as their architect. Faure-Dujarric went on to design numerous Parisian buildings and sporting venues, including the 1924 Olympic stadium and centre court at Stade Roland-Garros (1928), but from 1905 to 1914 he was living in Argentina where his marriage to the daughter of a local industrialist introduced him to the elite of Buenos Aires. The racecourse was Faure-Dujarric's most notable commission there.

Faure-Dujarric designed a palatial series of Louis XVI-inspired neo-classical stands at the racecourse, the centrepiece of which was the Official Stand. Serving as the course's principal entrance, the Official

Stand's rigid symmetry and lavish ornament gave the racecourse a stately public façade worthy of its privileged patrons (Figure 1.58). Indeed, its architecture was so majestic that it might easily have been mistaken for a state palace, national library or government offices. The entrance elevation was a two-storey design built in banded, rusticated ashlar masonry. In style, it typified the Beaux-Arts movement in its symmetrical neo-classical architecture embellished with historicised ornamental decoration. The focus of the façade was a richly decorated central curved block. Sculpted garlands, festooned volutes, mascaron keystones and florid cast iron railings bedecked its curving façade, but its most opulent feature was a crowning sculpture of central cartouche intertwined with a profusion of swags and horses inspired by the celebrated Marly Horses (1739) in Paris's Place de la Concorde. The sculpture's rococo bravura imparted a level of grandeur far beyond the average sporting venue and asserted a claim to rank amongst the city's most important buildings.

Opposite **1.58** The impressive entrance façade of the Hipódromo de Palermo in Buenos Aires, built 1908-11

Above **1.59** The trackside elevation of the Hipódromo de Palermo, designed by Frenchman Louis Faure-Dujarric

Whilst less imposing, the Official Stand's trackside elevation was no less elegant (Figure 1.59). The gently curving outline of the canopy that projected from the main body of the building and sheltered its tiered viewing platform injected an Art Nouveau grace which softened the neo-classical rigidity of the public façade. This was complemented by the sinuous staircases which enclosed either end of the raked platform and curled upwards towards a reception room beyond. The Francophile nature of the complex was completed by the formal parterre gardens which surrounded the building.

The Hipódromo de Palermo was not the only racecourse of the age to embody the French spirit in South America. The Francomania was fully entrenched in Brazilian society by the time that Rio de Janeiro's Jockey Club set about to find a plot of land on which to build the city a new racecourse. A large tract of marshland opposite the city's Botanical Gardens in the suburb of Gavea was acquired in 1919 and the Hipódromo da Gavea opened seven years later (Figure 1.60).

One of Brazil's most prestigious architects, Archimedes Memória (1893-1960), in conjunction with his partner Francisque Cuchet, was responsible for its design. In the 1920s Memória and Cuchet established themselves as probably Rio de Janeiro's largest architectural practice based on a reputation of reinterpreting French and Italian styles. Their neo-classical monuments such as the Palácio Tiradentes (1926), the seat of the Brazilian Government, epitomised the grand Europeanisation that transformed Rio's streetscape in the years of the Old Republic (1889-1930).

In their search for a new visual identity for the city detached from any Portuguese legacy, the statesmen and designers of the Old Republic turned to nineteenth-century France. The wide boulevards and neo-classical buildings of the French capital were perceived as pertinent symbols of revolution and a triumphant republic. The government was positive that by moulding Rio de Janeiro into a more 'civilised' city through a new urban landscape populated by sophisticated and showpiece architecture, they would by extension 'civilise' the nation as a whole. [39] In the opening decade of the twentieth century, Rio de Janeiro's chief engineer, Pereira Passos, strove to mimic Haussmann's nineteenth-century remodelling of Paris. Entire working-class districts were demolished and wide new boulevards were created, framed by Beaux-Arts architecture. Public buildings such as the Municipal Theatre, National Library and School of Fine Art espoused the stylistic rubric of Parisian architecture and inaugurated Rio with a fresh, modern outward persona. It was within this context that Memória and Cuchet's racecourse designs were conceived.

The city's new racecourse had five stands. That so many stands were built was indicative not only of the anticipated popularity of the enterprise but also of the strict social hierarchy that the design of Latin American racecourses enforced. Each stand sported a rich design repertoire that Haussmann would have approved of. The ornateness of their neo-classical vocabulary corresponded with the hierarchy of the stands and culminated in the Tribuna Social, overlooking the finishing post. Here Memória and Cuchet gave full vent to their Francophile imagination. The Tribuna Social was a chef d'oeuvre of classical orders, cartouches, and Grecian urns. A play of advancing and recessing surfaces enlivened its façades, detailed with a neo-classical profusion of stuccoed geometric panels, swags and festoons.

Akin to the other four stands that stretched the length of the track, the Tribuna Social employed rigid architectural symmetry and a regular coursed ashlar skin. The stand was divided into two conjoined but distinct sections: a trackside façade with unenclosed tiered benches sheltered by a cantilevered canopy and curving side elevations; and a rear wing fronted by a grandiose entrance façade. The latter was a spacious rectangular block housing the reception rooms which hosted Rio's elite. The two lowest of its three storeys projected outwards to form encircling verandas, along which the prestigious inhabitants of the stand could promenade to overlook the adjacent paddock. On the upper storey above, a central procession of seven tall, arched windows with curving cast-iron balconies was flanked by two towered end blocks.

The tour de force of the elevation was its exuberant entrance (Figure 1.61). From the centrepoint of the façade extended a long colonnaded walkway terminated by a triumphal-arched gateway at the head of the Jockey Club's ceremonial driveway. A more imperial threshold to a racecourse would be hard to find. A whole repertoire of neo-classical ornament decorated its surfaces: engaged pilasters, stylised bands of laurel leaves, swags and margents of bellflowers, and a crowning cartouche edged with laurel. A half-dome glass canopy and geometric panelled metal gates both trimmed with cast-iron festoons completed the ensemble.

The track façade was a simpler affair, sleeker and more contemporary in its silhouette. The projecting canopy, which shielded its raked seating and was curved to echo the arched outline of the stand's side elevations, was a token of modernity amidst the complex's fervent historicism. Like many other classicist architects of their period, Memória and Cuchet embraced modern construction techniques though typically cloaked these afterwards with a historicist patina. At the Jockey Club, the architects made full use of reinforced concrete and the Tribuna Social's canopy was at the time Latin America's largest cantilevered roof in reinforced concrete.

Memória moved with ease between different styles, blending elements of various periods and places at the Jockey Club. However, of Latin America's racecourses, this quality is probably best in evidence at Chile's oldest course, the Club Hipico de Santiago. The club had been founded in 1870, but from 1918 to the mid 1920s, its buildings were completely remodelled under the aegis of local architect Josué Smith Solar (Figure 1.62).

The racecourse's rebuilding took place at the apex of Chile's Euro-mania. Like Rio de Janeiro and Buenos Aires, in the late nineteenth century Santiago had entered into a phase of major economic, demographic, cultural and urban change. Its capital, Santiago, was deluged by European, notably French, influences, from clothing to cookery, for this was the moment in which contact abroad first truly flourished. This oftentimes took the shape of native Chileans embarking to study in foreign climes, nurturing exposure to and understanding of the styles and customs of the western world.

Smith was one such example of this case. Born to an American father and Chilean mother, in 1885 he left his homeland to study architecture at the Polytechnic College of Philadelphia. Four years later, he embarked on a lengthy study trip around Europe before returning to the United States in 1891 where he opened an architect office in Wilmington, Delaware. The experience gave him a fashionable cachet when in 1894 he resolved to settle in Chile and establish an office in Santiago. It was a prosperous office and its output included the Federico Santa Maria Technical University in Valparaiso, the Ministry of Finance and the Metropolitan University of Educational Science in Santiago. His buildings were part of the urban revolution then reshaping Chile's capital in which the colonial city of low-rise, adobe buildings gave way to a new image of Santiago.[40]

The Club Hipico was built on the edge of the city, bounding a wealthy new neighbourhood populated by a clutch of large, new mansions assuming a spectrum of historicising architectural styles. In his design for the racecourse, Smith took his cue from these. In 1918, Smith began work on the course, commencing with a general plan. He created an extensive complex comprising a vast Members' Stand, two smaller public stands, an administrator's house, paddock and club house surrounded by wide tree-lined avenues which connected the elements of Smith's plan. It was a wildly eclectic ensemble. From the English Arts and Crafts style of the administrator's house, to the Mission Revival of the paddock buildings and the Tuscan renaissance flavour of the public stands, Smith embraced the historicist vogue which had swept the city. As at the racecourses of Palermo and Gavea, its focal point was the Members' Stand and it was designed to impress.

With its inspiration taken from the Francophile zeitgeist, the basic formula of the Members' Stand was modelled on that of Longchamp's stands in Paris. Its long rear façade was a tripartite elevation punctuated by four stair towers. Its surface made for a rhythmical panorama of arched and square windows, of colonnade balconies, indented and projecting planes, and surface ornament; the whole regulated by classical symmetry. However, Smith's stand was not a mere copy of Longchamp's stands. To begin with, the former was much larger. And whilst it echoed the Beaux-Arts symmetry, balustraded towers and bold consoles of Longchamp, Smith enriched his building with a stylistic freedom that fused touches of Florentine palace, Renaissance chateau and medieval Italy. Each storey was differentiated by window type and surface ornamentation. The fourth floor was given *all'antica* bas relief panels; the third floor was lit by triplets of arched windows with solomonic columns;

1.61 The neo-classical entrance and façade of the Tribuna Social at the Gavea racecourse

1.62 The Club Hipico de Santiago was rebuilt from 1918 to circa 1924, including two public stands (left and middle) and a vast Members' Stand (right)

on the second floor ran a parade of staid Doric columns. All four towers were embellished with Renaissance-inspired heraldry, winged horses, and barbed quatrefoil windows (Figure 2.38).

Smith's jamboree of historical styles could easily have proved an inchoate pastiche, but instead his bold imagination and adroit sense of harmony resulted in a unique composition that, like the racecourses of Buenos Aires and Rio, perfectly expressed the mores of the society which it served. The three complexes physically embodied the microcosm of South America's highest echelons in their application to the traditional tiered grandstand format of an architectural exuberance perhaps unprecedented in racing. They are reflective, though, of an end of an era.

The early years of the twentieth century had undoubtedly been a golden era for racing. The sport flourished in all corners of the world more than ever before, and its evolution was given palpable form in its architecture. Grandstands continued to use the compositional formula conditioned in the second half of the nineteenth century, but, as racing became more popular and prosperous, its buildings grew larger in size and grander in architectural ambition. Across the world, the genre of racecourse architecture was growing more complex, more variegated and different nationalities demonstrated different approaches to this growth. Australian, New Zealand and British racecourses, for example, expanded upon a piecemeal basis, whilst their French and Latin American compeers favoured holistic, clean-sweep developments. Yet amidst these varying methodologies, continents, and ever-increasing complexity, certain trends are identifiable which profoundly conditioned the evolution of the racecourse building typology in the first decades of the twentieth century. Firstly, subsidiary buildings grew common. Built to house ancillary facilities displaced from grandstands by increased crowds and the clamour

for fixed seating, they were epitomised by the Antipodean tea houses and totalisators. Secondly, amidst new construction, modern materials, specifically reinforced concrete, became increasingly widespread. Thirdly, as the examples of Calcutta, Milan or Rio de Janeiro demonstrate, these materials were habitually clad in historicist or traditionalist idioms. Belle Époque racecourses sported a medley of historic and traditional architectural styles, from the Edwardian red-brick Ascot, to the Anglo-Normand of Saint-Cloud, the stripped classicism of Flemington, or the full-blown neo-classical excess of Francophile Palermo. If there was no absolute consensus on stylistic prototype amongst this generation of racecourse buildings, it did nevertheless seem distinguished by a palpable international outlook. The trends of the age were played out on a global scale. Stylistic and sociological currents flowed between nations. When it came to commissioning new additions to their racecourses, turf clubs and administrators looked for inspiration at celebrated precedents at home or abroad, on occasions embarking upon world tours or employing foreign architects. Often – although by no means always – attention focussed upon France, as most exuberantly demonstrated by the Latin American examples.

The courses of Rio de Janeiro and Santiago embodied the end of the gilded age. The sport of racing was soon to change and so too was the architecture that housed it. These South American examples brought a new degree of opulence and architectural bravura to racecourse design. Moreover, though, they were amongst the last expirations of the set-piece classicist aesthetic of racecourse architecture that had been transported to all corners of the globe. As the twentieth century progressed, modernity encroached. Festooned columns and fluted Orders yielded to a new way of thinking about architecture that emphasised function, purity and, ultimately, a rejection of tradition.

Chapter V

Modernity

Europe

Following the close of the First World War, racecourse buildings entered a new phase in their evolution. Modernism – the buzzword of the age – came to bear. Armistice Day did not mark the sudden rejection of the traditional forms and classicising vocabulary of conventional racecourse architecture – we have seen these used to exuberant effect at the Club Hipico de Santiago. Nevertheless, just as in all other branches of architecture, efforts to reconcile the underlying principles of architectural design with rapid technological progress and the modernisation of society led to a simplification of form and ornament in the structure and theme of racecourse buildings. This came particularly to bear upon the racecourses of the US and Europe.

The Hippodrome de la Canche represents, in many ways, the crossroads between the modern face of horse racing and its traditional guise in the post-war years. Built in 1925 in the northern French coastal resort of Le Touquet, the course consisted of two grandstands, one large and the other a smaller copy, designed by Parisian architect Paul Furiet.[1] The trackside façades of these grandstands embodied the attributes that characterised the new tenor of racecourse buildings (Figure 1.64). The largest grandstand had a deep, reinforced concrete canopy that was cantilevered over open tiered steppings. A simple and rational design, it was without any superfluous details. However, the reverse façade – the entrance façade – was entirely different; no one would guess they belonged to the same structure. Here, the architect fused half-timbering, steep hipped roofs and oculi in the Anglo-Normand style which dominated Le Touquet (Figure 1.65). The ground floor was given over to an arcade of five emphatically pointed brick arched openings,

while at the top level, a row of dormer windows projected from the steeply pitched red tile roof. Each end of the building was flanked by projecting half-hip pavilions, decorated with panels of half-timbering. It was a highly picturesque and highly traditional vernacular language, identical in tone to the hotels and villas which populated the fashionable seaside resort in the 1920s.

The dichotomy in style between the modern rationality of the trackside elevation and the romanticism of the rear façade may seem anachronistic, but La Canche was not alone in sporting this aesthetic and it stemmed from a specific mindset. A cantilevered, reinforced concrete grandstand attached to a rear façade in a neo-classical or vernacular architectural idiom was common in France in the 1920s, motivated by a desire to fuse bold, modern creations with traditional values. The grandstands of the regional courses at Clairefontaine (Deauville), Croisé-Laroche and Enghien are also symptomatic of this phenomenon.

The aberration in approach to grandstand architecture was a continent-wide phenomenon. From the 1920s, strong, modern shapes and modern construction techniques, notably reinforced concrete, came to the fore at courses across Europe. 'One of the outstanding features of recent architectural achievement,' observed a 1927 *Architects' Journal* article,

> is the unprecedented improvement evident in the planning and design of buildings devoted to sport and recreation.... Instead of the fussy prettiness of the pre-war period, we have a bold and simple handling of well-considered masses, carefully disposed and relying for effect on functional fitness, adequately expressed, rather than upon the application of gratuitous embellishments irrelevant to its structural purpose. The controlling influence of material upon

Page 98 **1.63** Epsom Racecourse Derby Day, 1979. The huge, tripartite grandstand was built in 1927

Opposite above **1.64** & below **1.65** Hippodrome de la Canche (1925) exhibited a stylistic dichotomy between the traditionalism of its grandstand's rear façade and modern rationality of its trackside elevation design is nowhere emphasised more strongly than in this type of building in which reinforced concrete has practically revolutionised its architectural character. The practical problem of spanning wide distances without any intermediate vertical support has resulted in the eminently satisfying trabeated effect of light and shadow to which the Epsom stands owe all their beauty.[2]

The Epsom stand which the *Architects' Journal* thought so successfully flaunted the new constructional innovations, was an enormous grandstand completed in 1927 (demolished 2007/8) (Figure 1.63). Built to the direction of two architectural practices, Elcock and Sutcliffe of London and Reeve and Reeve of Margate, it vaulted Epsom Downs into the twentieth century. Its blueprint was enormously ambitious. Projected to be the largest in the world, it was capable of holding 20,000 people. It extended 215 metres (700 feet) in length and rose 20 metres (70 feet) tall in parts. It was, moreover, a curious hybrid of a building. Although built strictly speaking as a single building, the stand was ostensibly three conjoined parts: Club (or West) Stand, Centre Stand and East Stand. Each part differed widely in size and style. The Club Stand, the smallest section, featured three cantilevered balconies, while the East Stand at the opposite end was built to an incredibly basic model of a single tier of covered raked seating. In between, the Centre Stand stood taller and longer than its neighbours. It adopted the large single tier of open raked seating which formed the East Stand, but added atop this three further storeys of viewing and refreshment accommodation. This fusion of three contrasting components into a single entity made for an unorthodox appearance, but its rationale was a pragmatic one. Epsom was attempting to cater for the needs and purses of all strata of its racegoing audience, from the Jockey Club members and Royal retinue in the comparative luxury of the Club Stand, to the rank and file attendees in the basic East Stand.

It was not only much larger than anything that Epsom had ever seen before, but its appearance was markedly different to its predecessors. Gone was the ornamented wooden trusswork, the delicate cast iron balconies and the flat-roof viewing platforms; here was an angular, utilitarian, elongated structure conceived purely for the purpose of giving as many people as possible a view over the track. This was racing for the modern age. In an engineering feat, massive cantilevers enabled tier to be stacked over tier, maximising seating and standing accommodation with a good view over the course. 'Special attention has been paid in the design and planning,' wrote *The Builder*, 'to ensure unobstructed angle of vision for everyone, and the elimination of the usual large number of supporting stanchions.'[3] Securing an uninterrupted view of the course from all parts of the stand through the means of reinforced concrete and cantilevered structures was an increasing priority from the 1920s within racecourse design. The *Architects' Journal*, for instance, advised that 'the construction of the superimposed terraces should be designed with the idea of eliminating vertical supports as far as possible'.[4] The cantilevered concrete Art Deco Members' Stand at Brighton Racecourse on Britain's south coast (built in 1936 by architects Yates, Cook and Derbyshire, demolished 1965) was a stand that illustrated this tenet.[5]

Concrete reinforced with steel came into common usage at the end of the nineteenth century, and by the 1930s was a widespread building material in Europe. One of the most pioneering structural experiments using the material took place upon Madrid's racecourse, La Zarzuela. As part of Madrid's Expansion Plan of 1929, the city's old Hipódromo Real was demolished, and in 1934 a competition was organised to design a replacement. The competition was won by the

architects Carlos Arniches and Martín Domínguez in collaboration with the internationally-celebrated civil engineer, Eduardo Torroja. La Zarzuela's grandstands are the most renowned and important of Torroja's architectural commissions to the extent that their design is often assigned to him alone.[6]

Three stands lined the track. Fundamentally, each grandstand was a simple structure comprising a raked tier open to the elements, below which was housed a betting hall. However, its striking roof transformed the basic building into one of superlative architectonic expression. The roof was a canopy of repeating double curvature cantilevering shells that made for a graceful and audacious visual statement. The bare concrete canopy was formed from a double curved hyperboloid shell, a mere 10 centimetres (four inches) thick, that projected 13 metres (over 42 feet) beyond the vertical supports at the rear of the stand (Figures 1.66, 1.67). The cantilever principle was applied in

1.66 Hipódromo la Zarzuela, Madrid, designed 1934. The grandstands' cantilevered concrete canopies were a superlative example of the application of modern engineering to racecourse design

Hipódromo la Zarzuela. Its grandstands became an emblem of Madrid

partnership with intersecting curvatures to achieve the required rigidity without recourse to beams, resulting in the impressive span which so awed contemporaries. The *Architectural Forum* wrote of it,

> It is difficult to look at the reinforced concrete canopies of the Madrid Hippodrome and still remember that they are static structures. Their shells, their repeated barrel forms rippling the length of each shelter and their great cantilevers... are more like birds which have lighted on the top of the grandstand in that instant before they fold their wings.[7]

The stand's radical simplification of form, honest expression of structure, rejection of ornament and use of concrete were hallmarks of the International Style. Emerging in the 1920s and 30s, this new mode was the single most influential form of architecture in the twentieth century. Amongst its essential characteristics was a reliance upon the intrinsic elegance of modern materials, and in this La Zarzuela's gliding canopies excelled.

Concrete shell structures were not new, but the construction of a cantilevering canopy of the scale of La Zarzuela was a technological coup. In 1930s Madrid, Torroja was responsible for several commissions demonstrating his proficiency in manipulating the most advanced technologies and materials to accomplish bold structural feats. The elegant and daring concrete shells that he produced in these years were of immediate influence to the post-International Style generation, while La Zarzuela in particular influenced many similar structures erected the world across. The soaring concrete canopies fulfilled the functional requirement of sheltering racegoers without impeding their view of the course with visual obstructions; but they also gave to the racecourse a distinct institutional identity and furnished Madrid with an emblem of modernity.[8] In the history of racecourse building, rarely have grandstands been at the architectural avant-garde; La Zarzuela is the exception.

USA

Europe's racecourses saw few architectural innovations of the calibre of La Zarzuela. Across the world, the privations of the Depression and the devastation wrought by two world wars were not conducive circumstances for architectural innovation at racecourses. It was arguably across the Atlantic, in North America, that the most decisive changes in the formula of racecourse architecture of the interwar years were being enacted, changes that were sparked in specific response to the straightened financial climate. By the end of the 1930s, a series of new complexes had been built which, in scale, size and ambience, differed radically from the Saratogas, Churchill Downs and Morris Parks of yesteryear. They were a new ilk of racecourses, created in reaction to a singular external circumstance, namely changing American gambling laws.

Horse racing in the United States had grown rapidly in the nineteenth century, so that by 1890, 314 courses were in operation across the country. In the early 1900s, however, a wave of anti-gambling sentiment shattered the sport. All save two states banned bookmaking, bringing horse racing to a standstill; by 1908 the number of courses had sunk to only 25.[9] The bans, however, proved a boon to the Mexican racing industry and it is here, in the border town of Tijuana, that the story of racecourse architecture continues.

With drinking, gambling and horse racing prohibited in neighbouring California, Tijuana became a playground of drinking and gaming for American excursionists to escape the moral strictures of the US and spend their nouveaux riches. And the most celebrated destination for them to do this was the casino resort of Agua Caliente. The 'Monte Carlo of Mexico', it combined a hotel, casino, golf course, an airstrip and, from 1929, one of the most palatial racecourses ever built. Hollywood celebrities and wealthy Californians of the likes of Clark Gable and the Marx brothers flocked to Agua Caliente's racecourse, eager to revel in its heady atmosphere of vice and luxury. And the setting certainly was luxurious. Costing $2.5 million (over $30 million today) to build, the racecourse was a study in architectural opulence. Owners Baron Long, Wirt Bowman and James Croffroth visited every major American course to draw together a compendium of the ideal facilities, and engaged architect Wayne McAllister to harmonise these into an architectural casing. McAllister, a young San Diego architect who was later celebrated as a leader in the Googie style of architecture, was responsible for every aspect of the resort and racecourse. Out of the barren desert, he created an oasis of opulence. Fusing Mexican Colonial, California Mission and Moorish influence, he gave tangible form to Baron Long's dream of a place built 'by a group of old Spanish missionaries', 'of a campanile and of the sunset being mirrored off gleaming white walls and of an air of peace and quiet, of bells ringing vespers and walks bordered by rich flowers of the tropics'. The result was an architectural fantasia.[10]

The racecourse was known as much for its architecture as its horse racing. It was characterised by red tile roofs, whitewashed stucco walls and colonnades adorned with carved marble reliefs (Figure 1.68). Seating 4,500, the tiered grandstand was an open-arched structure, decorated with

Opposite **1.69** Ornately carved doorway of Agua Caliente's clubhouse, built 1929

Above left **1.70** & above right **1.71** Agua Caliente's interiors glittered with Art Deco opulence

ornate carving and a Mediterranean-esque tiled floor. Alongside it was the clubhouse, smaller but more sumptuous (Figure 1.69). Internally, baroque ornamentation, Mudéjar tiles and Art Deco murals created a jewel-like interior. Externally, the clubhouse was a red-tiled, white washed building with a double-storey veranda overlooking the track. In Agua Caliente fashion, this was no mere utilitarian viewing platform. Swirling classical railings divided the seating whilst the marble arches that upheld the upper storey had been imported from Italy. Bearing Renaissance-inspired hand-carved relief decoration, these arches were exceptionally rich. The upper level boasted further Italian masonry – classical columns and carved balustrades. The grandstand and clubhouse opened forth to a lawn, offering further spectator accommodation, made with turf specially imported

from Europe. Much of the expenditure was, in fact, due to landscaping. Mature shrubbery and palm trees were planted so that from opening day, the effect would have been consummate. The betting hall was Art Deco in its style, and pure Hollywood in its glamour. Silver and nickel geometric leaded-glass betting windows lined its walls, reflecting the influence of the 1925 Paris Exposition des Arts Decoratifs et Industriels upon McAllister (Figures 1.70, 1.71).[11]

Agua Caliente's shine, though, was not to last. Across the border in North America, the Great Depression of the 1930s was to prove the American racing industry's unlikely saviour. With the nation plunged into a financial abyss, legalised betting at racecourses was suddenly looked upon as a quick-fire way to bolster the struggling economy.

Grandstand Entrance, Hialeah Park, Miami, Florida

316

Eager to receive its lucrative revenues, one state after another legalised pari-mutuel wagering on horses in the 1930s. Large crowds once again returned to the country's veteran courses, and moreover, a spate of large, glamorous and ultra modern new racing facilities opened, ushering in a new chapter in America's racing architecture. Legalised gambling in the US meant downfall for Agua Caliente. Shorn of its primary inducement, it never recovered.

The first of the new generation of American racecourses was Hialeah Park in Florida. Hialeah had, in fact, opened in 1925, a product of the state's land boom of the 1920s.

Its setting was a lacklustre one. A utilitarian concrete and steel grandstand presided over an infield of partially burned and charred weeds, set off by the slovenly backdrop of the backstretch washing lines beyond. It was not until 1930 that Hialeah's story really began. It was in this year that wealthy Philadelphian Joseph E. Widener bought the Miami Jockey Club and recast Hialeah from a struggling course to an elite winter resort. Widener had been the prime force behind the remodelling of Belmont Park in New York several years earlier, and at Hialeah he set about making his vision of style, splendour and

1.72 Hialeah Park grandstand. The racecourse was redesigned in 1931-2 under French inspiration

serious racing a reality. Widener outlaid nearly $2 million (approximately $27 million in today's money) to effect a complete transformation of the course, employing Lester Geisler as architect.

Geisler was a protégé of the Palm Beach society architect Addison Mizner, whose Spanish Colonial Revival buildings left an indelible mark upon South Florida. Widener had envisaged a Mediterranean Revival flavour for Hialeah, but, following Mizner's advice in 1928 that 'everybody can build Spanish, from now on we must do French', Geisler set out to persuade his client that they should instead turn to France for inspiration (Figure 1.72). Using a 1924 publication of *French Provincial Architecture, As Shown in Various Examples of Town and Country Houses, Shops and Public Places Adaptable to American Conditions*, Geisler showed Widener a small illustration of the outbuildings of a Loire chateau, Azay-le-Rideau, as indicative of his vision for the complex. Widener was convinced and sent Geisler to France to study architecture and landscape, followed by a grand tour of the classic European and American courses. 'I wanted people to take a walk around Hialeah and see the best features from the best racetracks in the world,' Widener later recalled.[12]

Hialeah sought to fuse the best that Europe's and North America's courses had to offer. Its walking ring was modelled on Longchamp; its tree-lined pathways were taken from Saratoga; and Epsom provided the inspiration for a tunnel leading to its track. Its new look was constructed

between the termination of the 1931 June season and the opening of the January 1932 meeting. The jewel of the scheme was the clubhouse, a striking Renaissance-revival design. Using French Provincial Architecture as his sourcebook, Geisler took the chateau of Azay-le-Rideau as his template. The clubhouse's recessed entrance of tall, carved mahogany doors framed by pilasters was modelled upon another of the book's plates, showing the Annex to the Town Hall in Ivry-sur-Seine. It was roofed by dark, slate tiles supplied from the discarded leftovers of a prominent Georgian tile-maker, producing a delicately variegated roof surface. Heightened by its small size, the building exuded an aura of exclusivity and quality.[13]

As important as the architecture was the landscape. Landscape architect H. L. Clark's conversance with the climate and flora of Florida radiated in Hialeah Park's botanical beauty. The majority of Hialeah's landscape – hundreds of pine and palm trees, 20,000 shrubs and 75,000 bedding plants – could be found in the nearby Everglades and Florida Keys. Royal pines flanked the approaches to the clubhouse and grandstand, while Australian pines circumscribed the track itself. Echoing Azlay-le-Rideau, bougainvillea-covered latticework arches scaled the rear of the grandstand through which direct views were afforded over the paddock.[14] The tour de force of the scheme was, though, an island in the infield lake, or, more specifically, the inhabitants of the island – a flock of flamingos (Figure 1.73). Widener imported the birds from Cuba in 1931 and, although many flew away or died in the initial years, soon a breeding colony was established creating what was, and continues to be, Hialeah's lasting image.

After Widener's death in 1943, the *Bloodstock Breeders' Review* remembered, 'he was chiefly responsible for the creation in Florida of the present beautiful Hialeah Park course, in which he proposed to set a new standard in the outward attractiveness of American racing - and succeeded.'[15] Under Widener's charge and Geisler's direction, architecture and landscape were fused into a unified whole, creating one of the most beautiful sports facilities in the country.[16] Amidst the gloom of the Great Depression, Hialeah's colour, éclat and excitement proved a tonic that transformed Florida, once an outpost of America, into a bastion of winter racing. The crown of winter racing was, however, quickly put into contention. In 1933, on the opposite side of the country, the California legislature passed a bill to legalise pari-mutuel wagering that opened the floodgates for a host of new courses in the Golden State. The first was Santa Anita Park, in Los Angeles County. Undoubtedly, its founding transformed the horse-racing experience for Californians, creating a refined, high-quality setting for the sport. Indeed, so intent were the founders in creating the world's most luxurious racing facility that, by opening day, they had poured so much money into its construction that none was left for the ticket sellers to make change.

1.73 Hialeah Park, postcard view of clubhouse (left) and grandstand. On the infield lake island cluster Hialeah's famous flamingos

From the outset, Santa Anita's physical image was perceived by its owners as a determining factor in its future success. Already-established racecourses such as Tanforan in northern California (founded 1889) and Agua Caliente provided instant competition, and furthermore it was essential that Santa Anita should divorce itself from the ignominy that laid California's racing industry to waste in 1909. Architecture was viewed as a means of setting Santa Anita apart from all that had come before, and the course's investors spent lavishly on it. A high profile, highly eclectic Los Angeles architect, Gordon B. Kaufmann (1888-1949), was given the task of designing the entire facility. The Santa Anita known today was largely shaped to Kaufmann's vision during a 19-year timeframe between 1934 and 1953.

Kaufmann was dismayed by the banality and uniformity of both the style and planning of US courses and at Santa Anita he determined to challenge the mould. Drawing on his diverse body of work which mixed Mission Revival, Art Deco, Colonial Georgian and Streamline Moderne, and ranged from mansions to libraries to churches, Kaufmann crafted a dynamic architectural identity for the new course which melded the élan of the thirties with a reassuring conservatism. He did this by investing the racecourse with two distinct visual characters, one embodied in the clubhouse and the other in the grandstand.

Sleek, mechanical, almost austere in its profile, the grandstand was designed as a building of its time, exemplifying one of the quintessential movements of the 1930s, the Streamline Moderne. Emblematic of the age of speed and of machines, the style was functional and efficient, stripped of artifice and ornament, yet with an engineered polish that made it enormously popular in California. The grandstand was a steel-framed concrete structure, four storeys tall, and it opened in 1934. On its entrance façade, Kaufmann designed one of American racing's most recognisable motifs – panels of stylised racing scenes made from punched steel sheets backed with glass. Alternating with panels of louvers, these bold panels extended the length of the grandstand. Evoking the spirit of flight, of movement, they symbolised the action of the track. Providing a striking contrast to the horizontality of the panels, the elevation's focal point was its entrance pavilion (built in 1938) (Figure 2.47). A vertically fluted frontispiece divided into three bays by engaged columns, the pavilion added a soaring upward momentum to the stand which culminated in crowning lettering spelling 'Santa Anita Park'. The effect was one of velocity, vigour and modernity.

The clubhouse, on the other hand, had historicist ambitions. Borrowing from the residential properties that Kaufmann designed, its façade is that of a neo-Georgian mansion. A tall, semi-circular portico supported by pairs of slender, pared-down columns provided its centrepiece; a flight of semi-circular steps led up to its arched doorway. White louvered shutters, Grecian urns and a belt course trim skirting the windows decorated the building. Regency motifs dominated the clubhouse, yet the whole was treated with a crispness, restraint and bold use of colour that harmonised it with the Moderne building alongside.

Kaufmann saw it as his mission to express the 'colourful aspects of the sport' unconstrained by 'hard and fast architectural traditions', and this attitude explains much of the complex's success. Kaufmann's consummate ability to fuse the traditional and contemporary in a single entity made him an ideal choice as architect. It should not be forgotten that, horse racing having been illegal in California for 25 years, it must necessarily have been viewed with at least a degree of mistrust. Kaufmann's historical quotations imparted a reassuring conservatism to Santa Anita which, when combined with the dynamism of the grandstand, fortified the racecourse for success in an uncertain climate.

Santa Anita Park set an important precedent in Californian racing. Not only was it significant for its racing, but also for its architecture and planning. 'When a structure must serve such a utilitarian purpose it is gratifying to find such harmony of proportions,' wrote *California Arts and Architecture*. 'This is indeed an immense engineering and architectural achievement.'

As the thirties progressed and the revenue potential of horse racing bore fruit, so a flurry of new racecourses opened in California. The Del Mar Turf Club was opened in San Diego County as part of a fairground complex in 1937 by a showbusiness consortium, with members including Bing Crosby and Paramount Studios acting as corporate sponsor. The aura of glamour provided by Crosby and pals, combined with the charm of its architecture made Del Mar unique. The architecture of the Del Mar Fairground and Racetrack

marked the culmination of the vogue for the Spanish Colonial Revival. Popularised by the 1915 Panama-California Exposition in San Diego, the Spanish Colonial style was the paradigmatic built expression of Southern California by the end of the 1920s, characterised by broad expanses of uninterrupted stucco-sheathed walls, rounded arch windows, and low-pitched clay tile roofs. At the Del Mar Racetrack and associated Fairground, a city in miniature was created in which architecture was used to create an ambiance of Spanish romance. Its plan was inspired by that of a Spanish town with two public squares acting as the structural apexes of the racecourse and fairgrounds. One square was allotted to the fairground's exhibition buildings, and the other was given over to the Turf Club. Within this square, the rear of the grandstand lined one side, other Turf Club buildings composed two sides, and the fourth was left open.

The buildings were designed as tributes to the West's and South's missionary history by architect Sam W. Hamill. The grandstand evoked one of the best known of California's missions, the Mission San Gabriel in Los Angeles, especially its great buttressed walls. At the eastern end of the grandstand, Hamill drew from the Mission San José y San Miguel de Aguayo. This eighteenth-century mission near San Antonio in Texas is one of America's most authentic extant examples of Spanish Baroque architecture. It served as the direct model for the clubhouse's entrance and its surmounting window, as well as its tower whose silhouette dominated the racecourse (Figures 1.74, 1.75). Neighbouring the clubhouse

was the saddling shed, described by one commentator as 'the most romantic saddling shed found in any of America's racetracks'. Its dirt floors, adobe walls and roof clad in bark-stripped logs upheld by sturdy wooden posts purveyed the myth of old Spanish days. Hamill specified all construction to be of adobe, a natural building material made from sand, clay, manure, straw and water, which is shaped into bricks and dried in the sun. Not only was this the building method of the missionaries, but it could be made on site and was financially pragmatic. The scale of the complex rendered Del Mar the largest single adobe construction in Californian history.[17]

Del Mar's fairytale Mediterranean flavour and Bing Crosby's star appeal ensured huge crowds flocked to its races. Throughout California, the Hollywood elite played a major part in the cultivation of its glamorous racing industry. A year after Del Mar's launch, the Hollywood Park Turf Club was opened to the public in a Los Angeles suburb in June 1938 under the chairmanship of Jack L. Warner of the Warner Brothers film corporation and backed by shareholders including Walt Disney, Sam Goldwyn, Al Jolson and Bing Crosby. With this pedigree of patronage, Hollywood Park was immediately established as a playground for the movie industry's rich and famous. The clientele were matched in glamour only by the flair of its physical fabric.

The racecourse was one of the best set pieces of Streamline Moderne architecture in California (Figure 1.76). Its architect was Stiles O. Clements. No other city in the country was as receptive to the Moderne avant-garde as 1930s Los Angeles, and no other architectural firm could rival the productivity and pre-eminence of that of Clements. Clements monopolised commissions for shopping centres, movie theatres, drive-in supermarkets, and car-orientated suburban department stores and in so doing perfected the commercial Moderne style that characterised downtown Los Angeles and its environs. Hollywood Park was his sole racecourse commission. Accommodating 30,000 people over 130 hectares (315 acres), he distilled his quintessential streamlined style into a functionally efficient, rationally-planned racing facility. The long, rectangular mass of the grandstand dominated his design. In its sleek lines, smooth stucco surface, and dramatic rounded corners, the grandstand epitomised Streamline Moderne glamour. The reinforced concrete structure was sheathed in blue-green painted stucco. Narrow horizontal windows were stretched in continuous bands along the length of its rear façade, creating a sense of movement befitting a racecourse. Its planar façade was stepped back at mid-height, creating a balcony and relieving the rigour of its horizontal mass while at the far end, it burst forth into a semi-circular bay.

At the centre of the grandstand Clements inserted a striking innovation - an interior paddock. It was a dome-covered space beautified with box hedge and well-insulated for soundproofing to ensure a settled environment for the horses.[18]

'Modernity distinguishes the Hollywood Turf Club,' wrote the *Western Architect and Engineer*, 'a true modernity that combines beauty with functional utility.'[19] Agua Caliente, Hollywood Park, Del Mar, Santa Anita and Hialeah revolutionised the physical setting of US horse racing. Celebrated and imaginative architects were engaged by turf clubs to synthesise architecture and landscape into a unified whole. Never before in this genre had physical appearance been so highly valued and cultivated. Particularly striking is their sheer stylistic diversity. Within a single state and within a four-year timeframe, Santa Anita, Del Mar and Hollywood Park were all built in different architecture styles.

The racecourses of 1930s America or their European cousins - La Zarzuela, Epsom, or Brighton for instance – were not related by any single architectural formula; indeed, their stylistic experimentation was all-encompassing. What they shared, however, was a new approach to the physical fabric of racing. Whether cloaked in historicising Mission Revival or embracing streamlined modernism, racing architecture grew in scale and organisation. Undisguised steel and concrete, big cantilevers and even bigger car parks became common ingredients. Multiple tiers of seating became less prevalent in favour of long stretches of single-storey raked seating. Particularly in the case of the new American courses, the facilities were planned with an unprecedented comprehensiveness. New priorities had changed the milieu of racecourse design, and these established the foundations from which the next generation of racing buildings were to stem.

1.76 Hollywood Park's Streamline Moderne grandstand, designed by Stiles O. Clements and opened in 1938

Chapter VI

Post-War

Horse racing the world across inevitably ebbed during the years of World War II. Courses were requisitioned for army bases such as Warwick Farm in Sydney, transformed into prisoner of war camps like Kempton Park in the UK, or internment facilities for 'enemy aliens' such as Santa Anita Park. The decades following the conflict were, though, ones of recovery for the industry, frequently materialising in extensive construction projects. These projects inevitably bore witness to a new language of racecourse architecture and a new generation of racecourse buildings was born.

With its sleek silhouette, pared lines and glass curtain walls, the 1947 grandstand at the Hippodroom Wellington in Ostend was an early example of this new generation (Figure 1.77). From 1939-45, European architecture came to a standstill. When building resumed, shortages of manpower, materials and money restricted construction to the most utilitarian needs and sober styles. The elegance of Wellington's grandstand, then, built so soon after the war's expiration, comes as something of a pleasant surprise.

The Belgian seaside course suffered extensive damage during World War II. Its late nineteenth and early twentieth-century stands were demolished, but only two years after the war ended architect Albert-Victor Fobert began work on a replacement grandstand.[1] Fobert was one of Ostend's most important and prolific architects. The stand he created for the stricken racecourse was a clear manifesto of modern movement architecture. A curved canopy projected over the single tier of raked seating; on the side elevations, elliptical stair towers were enclosed by walls of glass; and the whole was painted a brilliant white. It was joined in 1955 by the Royal Tribune, built alongside. A small rectangular building with a projecting elliptical tower on its rear façade (topped with a crown to signal its regal function), its skeletal construction was encased in glass curtain walls. Strikingly bold, the buildings possessed a spatial bravura unrivalled in racing architecture. Their straightforward functionalism and monumentality was indicative of the priorities of architects across the world in the new post-war age.

In the decades following World War II, the priorities not only of architects but also of racecourse managements were revised. Post-war society's increasing orientation towards commercialism and leisure shaped new demands at racecourses: more comfortable seating, more seats under cover, more food and beverage outlets. All this 'more' necessitated bigger buildings. The new generation of grandstands was cast in a profoundly modernist aesthetic, dominated by the material of choice of the age – concrete. By the mid point of the century, concrete was established as the quintessential twentieth-century building material. In the post-war world, when a shortage of steel and skilled labour was pitted against a need for rapid rebuilding, concrete's popularity boomed. Concrete lent itself to the 'brave new world's' zeal for 'modernisation', offering new possibilities for flexible and uncompromising design while satisfying demands for a visual split from the past.[2] This attitude moulded grandstand architecture of the 1950s and 1960s. Across the world from Melbourne to Malaysia, racecourse panoramas were permanently transformed by large-scale building ensembles that combined the modern engineering with modern amenities.

THE MANHATTAN SPORTS PAVILION
FRANK LLOYD WRIGHT ARCHITECT

Concrete drew the most celebrated and pioneering architects of the post-war era, producing a spirit of experimentation and innovation. And, on a select number of occasions, this spirit was employed in the service of racecourse architecture. It is no better evidenced than in Frank Lloyd Wright's 1956 designs for Belmont Park in New York (Figure 1.78).

By the early 1950s, Belmont Park, like other New York racing venues, was afflicted by a general decline in its facilities. In fact, the entire New York industry was sinking amidst falling profits and increasing competition. In 1953, a Jockey Club-appointed committee set about to consolidate the disjointed industry, with the result that

a brand new non-profit corporation was formed in 1955 to purchase and operate New York's principal courses – Aqueduct, Belmont Park, Jamaica and Saratoga. The corporation came to be known as the New York Racing Association. Whilst Aqueduct Racetrack was given immediate priority (it underwent a wholesale rebuilding by the virtuoso of racecourse design, Arthur Froehlich, completed in 1959), the 50-year old Belmont Park was part of the fledgling association's long-range plans. For one of the committee's original three members, Harry F. Guggenheim, these plans were of an architecturally ambitious mettle.

Following the death of his uncle Solomon R. Guggenheim in 1949, Harry had been responsible for the Guggenheim Museum in Manhattan going into construction. From this sprang a close relationship with the Museum's architect, Frank Lloyd Wright, which awakened him to the enormous possibilities of modern architecture. Almost immediately after the formation of the New York Racing Association, Guggenheim offered Wright another commission: to design a grandstand for Belmont Park.

The renaissance of New York racing, the pair concluded, presented the ideal moment to devise a new identity for grandstand architecture. Wright's scheme was a world away from the traditional aesthetic of a racecourse. Its dominant feature was an enormous stand built upon a 'massive concrete slab', four storeys tall. For Wright, concrete and steel were the tool box for the twentieth-century architect. Their combination was the single greatest liberating element that opened the door for an entirely new architecture and he demonstrated this conviction in creating an entirely new type of grandstand. Each end of the stand was terminated by two enormous angular concrete towers, which rose above the Long Island skyline into tall pointed peaks. From these a 'lacework of slender tensile steel cables' swooped downwards to suspend a vast translucent plastic roof which covered all four levels of seating. It was a composition of organic, sweeping lines which created a building as streamlined as the horses on the track before it. The cobweb of steel cables created an image of gossamer-like lightness fused with immense tensile strength. It was a quality that the architect particularly admired. 'This beautiful material that spins like a spider and produces a tension so perfect that you can balance a monolith on a pinpoint,' he wrote of the

material.[3] In a grandstand, it was particularly becoming for it abrogated the need for supporting pillars, according total visibility for all of the 75-80,000 occupants of the stand. Guggenheim compared the overall scheme to a medieval joust, with seating concentrated in tall stacks over the finish line.[4]

Dr. J. J. Povlika, a structural engineer who worked with Wright on multiple occasions, wrote of the scheme that it was a 'revolutionary but very practical and economical building'.[5] Yet Wright's pavilion never left the drawing boards. His scheme proved simply too structurally daring for the Jockey Club members, and, notwithstanding Wright's riposte that racing's leaders were unable to grasp the finer points of architecture, it was never built, to the great tragedy of the thoroughbred world.[6]

When safety fears finally closed the ageing Belmont Park in 1963, it was rebuilt along far more traditional lines, by the firm of Arthur Froehlich and Associates. Froehlich (1909-85) was the premier designer of racecourses of the day. The Los Angeles-born architect was responsible for a string of courses across North America – from Hollywood Park in the west to Roosevelt Raceway in the east – but he ranked his finest work as the Hipódromo la Rinconada in Caracas, Venezuela. Beginning in the 1940s, Caracas was transformed by a significant body of modern architecture. Every city has its consummate moment of wealth and development, and for Caracas this was the Venezuelan oil boom of the 1950s. Fuelled by unprecedented oil profits, foreign immigration and political optimism, Caracas emerged as a modern metropolis. From an essentially agricultural town with a 1936 population of 163,000, it became the control centre of the world's second biggest oil producer

1.79 Hipódromo la Rinconada.
Caracas's racecourse opened in 1959,
designed by veteran racecourse
architect Arthur Froehlich

with a population of one million by 1957.[7] The city physically grew under one's very eyes. International architects including Richard Neutra, Oscar Niemeyer and Gio Ponti were imported to mould the modern identity of Venezuela and its capital, and by the time that Arthur Froehlich began work on the Hipódromo La Rinconada in the mid-1950s, the city was a breeding ground for modernism.

Froehlich's racecourse immediately ranked amongst the most sophisticated in Latin America. Horses and racing had long occupied a special place in the nation's consciousness. Caracas's first racecourse had been erected in 1851, but this and its successors were quickly outgrown and the phenomenal mid-twentieth-century alteration in the country's economy prompted the commissioning of a lavish new facility in tune with Caracas's amplified fortunes and aspirations. The new racecourse opened in 1959 amidst the desert hills south of the city. Froehlich designed three stands, a veterinary hospital, stables and dormitories, all set within a tropical landscape designed by Brazilian landscape architect, Roberto Burle Marx (gardens no longer extant). The whole ensemble was a blaze of brilliant colour, modernist spaces and ground-breaking technology. From the track side, the three grandstands were dominated by a vivid yellow roof. The three-inch thick concrete roof cantilevering 27 metres (90 feet) over the three tiers of open seating was a technical feat, but, moreover, its concrete-shell construction was used in the service of creating an eye-catching aesthetic motif.[8] From the front, the roof had the appearance of a string of concrete scallops, and at the centre of each sat a space-age-like silver spherical booth housing announcers and the media (Figure 1.79). It made for a bold vista, enlivened further by the striking palette of red, blue and yellow applied to each level of seats.

Vibrant hues were a recurring feature of Froehlich's scheme (Figure 1.80). Inspired perhaps by Le Corbusier, each surface whether inside or out was emblazoned by distinctive patterns of block colour which counteracted the tremendous bulk of its concrete construction. From the rear, the three stands looked as though they may have been built of Lego. They were long, rectangular slabs whose windowless rear façades were divided into blocks of primary colours. It was not unusual for subtropical architecture of this period to be windowless. Instead, the entire façades were given over to painted adjustable louvers which diminished the intensity of the sunlight and allowed for natural ventilation, thus resulting in a building responsive to climate and site.[9]

The kaleidoscopic colours of the walls, pillars, staircases and seats were of great significance to Froehlich, who considered the psychology of race-going a vital element in the design of successful racecourses. Not only did they relieve the mass of the concrete that formed the hipódromo's vast spaces, but were vital ingredients in creating the 'happy bettor':

> Wagering money is an activity which can very easily bring on moods of depression or annoyance. Froehlich counteracts this by splashing his tracks liberally with color whether in the flowers and shrubbery or the mosaics of building materials. Warns Froehlich: "Somber colors are no incentive." ...A track has to be pleasant and airy and as bright and gay as a state fair.[10]

The modernist sensibility was, arguably, even more in evidence at another South American course, this time in Brazil. The Hipódromo do Cristal in Porto Alegre opened to a euphoric reception on 12 December 1959 to designs by Uruguayan architect Roman Fresnedo Siri (1903-75). Siri was a significant and prolific architect, earning major acclaim for the design of civic buildings

throughout Latin America, as well as the headquarters of the Pan American Health Organisation in Washington, DC (1965). Siri had already designed two grandstands at the Hipódromo de Maroñas in Montevideo (1938 and 1945) when in 1951 he was selected by the Jockey Club of Rio Grande do Sul to build Porto Alegre a new racecourse on a 30-hectare (75-acre) site in the south of the city. While only a section of Siri's design was ever realised, the grandstands that were completed were strikingly ambitious.

The scheme as built comprised three stands all built to the same model, two public stands and a smaller paddock stand (Siri had planned for five). It was a tremendously inventive model. As typified many mid-twentieth-century stands, Siri designed a cantilevered structure of pre-stressed concrete and trussed beams. However, he abandoned the more traditional solution of a roof overhanging the trackside supported upon two rows of pillars and replaced it with a structural system of two overhangs supported upon a single line of pillars with minimal bracing (Figure 1.81). The roof cantilevered 26 metres (85 feet) from the pillars to the front and 17 metres (56 feet) to the rear, where they were balanced by a counterweight of taut steel rods extending from the overhanging roof to the ground. Siri was in pursuit of a lightness and levity never before achieved in grandstand design.

This aesthetic was compounded by Siri's unprecedented use of glass compared to other stands of the time. The side and rear elevations were curtain walls of glass set in steel frames. In this, Siri was responding to one of the most preoccupying and progressive motifs of contemporary modernist design. The 'transparent glass-

Hipódromo do Cristal rear façade (1959). A unique structural system of plate glass and taut steel rods resulted in unparalleled transparency

and-steel box' epitomised the era's most influential architecture, such as Mies van der Rohe's Farnsworth House (1951) and Philip Johnson's Glass House (1949). This modernist aesthetic was adapted to Brazil's tropical climate by shading the rear façade of the grandstand with bold horizontal brise-soleils, which had been frequent elements of Latin American modernism since their innovative use on the Ministry of Education and Culture in Rio de Janeiro (Lúcio Costa et al., 1942). The final product was one of the most dynamic examples of grandstand design of the century, embracing a vanguard vocabulary of modernist architecture. By day, the Hipódromo's concrete, glass and metal stands made for a robust yet transparent ensemble. At night, the structures glowed like luminescent glass lanterns against the dark sky.

Regrettably the progressive spirit of Frank Lloyd Wright's unbuilt Belmont Park, the Hipódromo la Rinconada and the Hipódromo do Cristal did not exemplify the nature of racecourse building in the decades following World War II. The magnitude and multitude of modern sporting events required an ever-increasing number of facilities and the majority of racecourses across the world felt a call towards modernisation. Especially in the UK, USA and Australia, the characterful stands of the Victorian and Edwardian era were deemed too small or functionally inadequate, and were demolished and replaced. Overwhelmingly, these replacements were of a disappointing creed.

Broadly-speaking, the new racecourse buildings embraced the pre-fabricated concrete and stark geometry that characterised so much post-war building, yet they lacked the spirit of innovation and experimentation that defined the best architecture of the period. Functionalism and standardisation were the bywords of the day, and grandstands were created utilitarian in appearance and monolithic in scale. A uniting factor in their design was efficiency, economy and, most importantly, speed of construction. For the most part, redevelopment schemes were allotted the narrowest of timeframes between annual meetings or racing seasons. The redevelopment of the Hippodrome de Longchamp (1966) was one such example. Its picturesque 1904 grandstands, no longer spacious enough to accommodate the course's crowds, were demolished and supplanted by three new stands, within the October to April interval between racing seasons. Designed by architect J. Regnault, the main skeleton of the structure was constructed on rails some 250 metres (820 feet) away from its ultimate destination then winched into its final position.[11] Whilst an ingenious solution, the new stands pursued a rational utility which sacrificed much of the elegance and intimacy of the turn-of-the-century Longchamp. The modular buildings were large and functional, but ultimately lifeless and commonplace. The delicate presidential stand was replaced by 'a sort of air traffic control tower', bemoaned one commentator.[12] It was a worldwide phenomenon. Woodbine in Toronto (1956) and Aqueduct in New York (1959) were set-piece exponents of the trend. Australia's two premier courses built individual grandstands of this type – the Hill Stand at Flemington (1955) and the Queen Elizabeth II Stand at Royal Randwick (1969); as did a succession of UK courses, notably Ascot in 1961, Doncaster in 1969, and Sandown in 1973.

By the 1960s, UK racecourses were suffering from falling attendances and legal off-course betting. Racing's leaders became increasingly receptive to the need to make the sport more attractive to consumers who had more options than ever before as to how to spend their leisure time, and there was a perceptible shift in commercial orientation amongst the country's racecourses. Largely speaking, this meant an upgrading of facilities for spectators. Even the Jockey Club, a bastion of orthodoxy, concluded the exigency of 'making the spectator once more the focus of the sport'.[13]

This mood was palpable in the large-scale redevelopment of venerable Ascot. When the new Queen Elizabeth II Stand was unveiled in June 1961, the face of the racecourse was radically transformed. It endowed Ascot with state-of-the-art facilities. *Sporting Life* hailed it 'the most impressive structure on any English racecourse'; the *Windsor, Slough and Eton Express* wrote:

> For the first time in more than 30 years racing at Royal Ascot, I saw the start and finish of all the races in complete comfort.... For each race I chose a different vantage point in the mammoth building and no matter if I was seated on one of the luxury tip-up stalls, halfway up the terrace, or in a private box I had an uninterrupted view of the horses.[14]

The new stand stood upon ground that had, since 1839, been occupied by the grandstand, a structure which had long been a cause of concern to the Ascot Authority. Belonging to a different era, the grandstand was no longer deemed to offer the convenience and comfort demanded by modern audiences while, moreover, misgivings had been expressed over its safety. By the late 1950s, redevelopment was seen as inevitable and the construction firm, George Wimpey & Co., was engaged as contractor and designer, with Eric Collins acting as their in-house architect. The main requirement of Wimpey was that the building had to be completed within a very rigid timescale; a timeframe of only 10 months was open for demolition, rebuilding and landscaping, in order that the annual summer Royal Ascot meeting would not be disrupted. Such a brief could not be accomplished without prefabricated building technology, and equally without plain, repetitive design (Figure 1.82). In this, the Queen Elizabeth II Stand typified racecourse construction of these years.

Nearly 200 yards in length, the Queen Elizabeth II Stand was a steel-framed and precast concrete structure. It comprised private boxes, tip-up stall seats, and a terrace of steps, and accommodated a

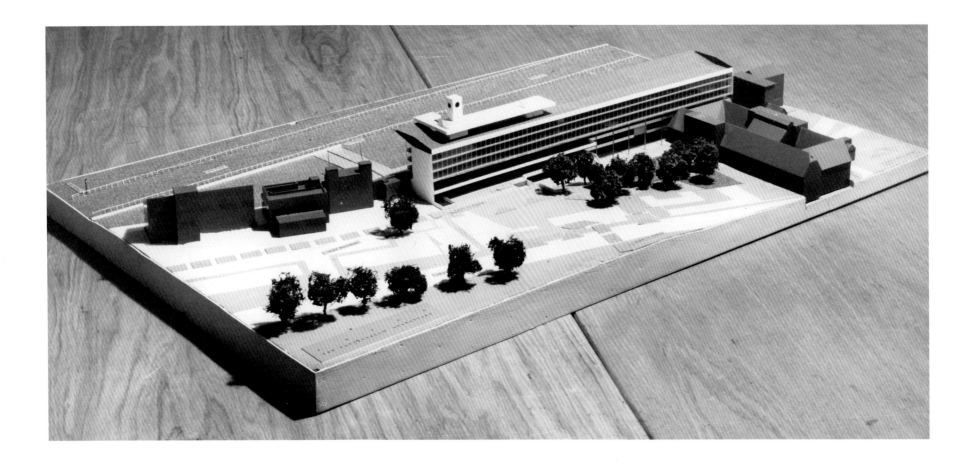

total of 13,000 racegoers. Its design was shaped not only by the desire to provide better viewing facilities, but also by the advent of corporate hospitality to the racing world. Two-hundred-and-eighty private boxes, each with private dining room, were layered in three upper storeys along the longitudinal façade of the stand. The cantilevered design of the giant roof sheltering the stepped terrace removed the need for obstruent supports, while a bank of escalators – the first on a British racecourse – conveyed racegoers from the main entrance at the rear to the first-floor bars and stall seats. These were such an innovation that one reviewer counselled visitors that 'even if you do not need to do so, you should have a ceremonial ride'. [15]

Naturally enough, however, the arrival of this concrete behemoth upon Ascot's hallowed ground did not escape criticism. Racing comm.entator and correspondent Peter O'Sullevan lamented that the stand was 'set at an absurdly inadequate angle for viewing the straight, and incorporated no top-level area for the general public', a stricture echoed by the actor Robert Morley:

> At the cost of a million pounds all that the public is provided with are a few concrete steps rather narrower than before. Profits from Ascot are not used to improve facilities, which are now worse for the Silver Ring and the Iron Stand, but to make bigger profits in the years to come.[16]

1.82 Model for Ascot's Queen Elizabeth II Stand, completed 1961. The building replaced the racecourse's Victorian and Edwardian grandstands

Undoubtedly, the grandstand drastically altered the architectural aspect of the experience of the UK's most celebrated racecourse. Gone was the charmingly varied skyline between the Royal Enclosure and Silver Ring, and instead was a concrete monolith, stark in its outline and resolutely of its time. Even some contemporaries bemoaned that it 'strongly resembles a new skyscraper block of offices'. The new grandstand was utilitarian to the utmost, making little concession to the design heritage of the historic course and instead placing a focus on what was to become an increasing priority in forthcoming years –corporate hospitality.

When a modernisation plan was prepared for Doncaster Racecourse in 1966, the architects' brief envisaged maximum use of the buildings for corporate and non-raceday functions. The result of the plan was a new grandstand, opened in 1969. Improved facilities for racing spectators was the chief priority, but the client, Doncaster Corporation, stipulated a multi-purpose building. The architects, Howard V. Lobb & Partners, delivered a building that could be put to use as an indoor sports centre with restaurants that could double as ballrooms or banqueting suites. Accommodating a total of 13,000, the building was divided into two parts: a five-storey front seating section and a rear three-storey section, holding the betting hall below two levels of stepped terraces. The internal betting hall was the main component of the structure. With the celebrated St Leger meeting drawing around 75 bookmakers, this necessitated a space of 3,700 square metres (40,000 square feet). Not only did the provision of this hall allow the bookmakers' customers the same degree of comfort as those of the Tote, but it afforded an expanse large enough to be used for squash, badminton, boxing, indoor archery and so forth.[17]

The Doncaster grandstand, like many of its generation, was notable for the speed with which such a substantial building was erected. Like Ascot's Queen Elizabeth II Stand, within a mere 10 months all the stands previously situated in the grandstand and paddock enclosures were demolished (including John Carr's 1778 grandstand) and the new one rose in its stead. Once again, these conditions rendered precast concrete the inevitable choice of material. The material was widely favoured at this time for needing negligible maintenance and no external surface treatments, whilst in this case precast construction gave room for structural components to be ordered before a main contractor was engaged. The soaring canopy roof, cantilevering 15 metres (50 feet) with plate glass at each end, was formed of precast lightweight-concrete segmental shells.[18] Unexpectedly, the judges' and commentators' fibreglass box was perched centrally at the outside edge of this cantilever, creating a curious loadpoint. Stylistically, the grandstand again typified its generation. Its design was economical, industrial fare with nothing to interest the eye.

Time and money were also the two driving strictures at work when Sandown Park in Surrey came to be redeveloped early in the 1970s. Since its opening in 1875, the park's natural amphitheatre shape had made it a favourite with racegoers. Yet after World War II, it suffered a continual decline in attendance figures and a corresponding decline in profits. Particularly in the cheaper enclosures, facilities left much to be desired. In a bid to reverse its fortunes, Sandown embarked upon redevelopment on a monumental scale. Seldom in the history of racecourse architecture do we encounter the razing and rebuilding of an entire racecourse, but this is what happened at Sandown in 1973. All its stands were demolished and replaced by one long, continuous structure, containing the members' enclosure and the grandstand (Figure 1.83). The fundamental element of the commission was that construction was limited to a time span of under 12 months. This, together with a tight budget and desire to reduce long-term maintenance work to a minimum, directed the form that the grandstand took.

These specifications made the use of precast concrete virtually unavoidable. Designed by the Fitzroy Robinson Partnership, the basic structure of the precast concrete grandstand took the form of H-frames in parallel rows stretching along its length spanned by pre-tensioned double T-units; this enabled very quick erection. All components were standardised, resulting in a repetitive and cost-effective design.[19] The challenge of roofing the elongated structure without pillar supports obstructing views to the course was solved by anchor-shaped beams that cantilevered nearly 20 metres (65 feet) over the track and sides suspended from stainless steel cables from a row of central towers. The lightweight Perspex roof was applauded by contemporary commentators for the shelter from the weather that its breadth afforded, while the cantilever beams also supported intermediate glazed panels that enabled uninterrupted views alongside protection from the elements. Taken together, it constituted an innovative design.

Like Doncaster, the stand also marked something of an innovation in its mixed-use functionality. With racing restricted to 25 days per year, the grandstand had to entertain other uses and it borrowed from American models to become one of the UK's first to cater for conference, exhibition and dining facilities. On the first floor, large bars were enclosed with glazing giving sweeping views over the course; on the level above, a multitude of lounges, bars, and restaurants with glazed walls, balconies and boxes, were installed. Largely, the new addition was well-received by contemporaries. 'The architect has coordinated the complex structural and planning requirements into a simple coherent statement,' praised *Concrete Quarterly* upon its opening. 'The engineer has made the most of the structural technique and materials at his disposal. And the contractor has put the whole thing into practice with exemplary efficiency.'

Grandstands of the ilk of Sandown are not held in such positive regard today, however. Whilst it seems symptomatic of human nature that each generation looks askance at the architecture of that preceding it, the developments of Doncaster, Ascot, Flemington and others of the same creed from the 1950s to 80s have met with especial criticism. Notable examples do stand out for their imagination and innovation – La Rinconada and Cristal for instance – but these are exceptions and not the rule. Ultimately this was an unsuccessful generation of racecourse buildings. Built quickly during straightened economic times, they were soon arraigned as architectural eyesores and difficult to maintain. At least in terms of Ascot and Doncaster, their efficacy is best assessed by the fact that both have been demolished.

1.83 Sandown Park grandstand. The Victorian racecourse was completely razed and rebuilt in 1973 to designs by the Fitzroy Robinson Partnership

Chapter VII

To the Present

In the past half-century, prodigious changes have transformed the racing industry. From effectively a national sport, racing was restyled on an international scale. In 1952 at Laurel Park in Maryland, the United States' first international race was launched – the Washington, D. C. International. The inaugural running drew entrants from England, Canada, Germany and America. Today, accustomed as the world is to transporting horses across oceans and continents, the event may seem unremarkable, but then it was unheard of. 'International' racing at the time was almost completely confined to French, English and Irish horses competing against one another in their respective countries' most prestigious races. The DC International set a precedent that slowly but surely changed this. The race itself ebbed, flowed and eventually perished, but it gave international racing a footing to build upon.[1]

In the late twentieth century, the emergence of the Japan Cup (1981), the Breeders' Cup (1984), Hong Kong Cup (1988) and the Dubai World Cup (1996) amongst others were symptom and cause of the dramatic globalisation of the sport enabled by improvements in transport and communication. Multi-day festivals, such as the Melbourne Cup Carnival and Royal Ascot, became able to market themselves as major points of global competition. Meanwhile, a select band of individuals were also piloting racing's new direction.

During the 1980s, Dubai's oil-rich rulers, the Maktoum family, and an Irish breeding operation, Coolmore, began a multimillion-dollar buying spree at the American yearling markets. The effect was galvanising. The large-scale import of North American bloodstock changed the course of thoroughbred breeding in the British Isles and a successful international thoroughbred programme was established in the new setting of the UAE, culminating in the richest race in the world – the Dubai World Cup.

These changes have left a distinct mark upon the development of racecourse architecture. As the thoroughbred industry has grown worldwide, so have racing's buildings increased in size, technology and comfort; but, moreover from the end of the twentieth century, several discernable trends emerged which have shaped the panorama of racecourse architecture to the present day: behemoth-scale construction that sacrificed design to functionality; diversification of functions; and a resurgence of innovative design buoyed by leading architects.

Function Over Form

In the last decades of the twentieth century, the age of international racing dawned. Yet, its architecture saw little in the way of international standardisation. Overwhelmingly, the predominant trends that have shaped the design of racing's buildings since these years have been conditioned by the aims and aspirations of individual nations or continents. The international dialogue that engendered the shape of the Club Hipico de Santiago, Mahalaxmi Racecourse or Hialeah Park seem a thing of the past. In other words, in the past four decades, the scope of racecourse architecture has narrowed into a comparatively localised phenomenon.

This has been especially applicable to the industry in Asia. Towards the end of the century, Asian racing mushroomed. Naturally, this was accompanied by a steady period of grandstand construction and, fundamentally, this conformed to a single building typology. Their design took their lead from the post-war designs of Ascot, Flemington, Doncaster and elsewhere, in which architectural merit was forfeited in pursuit of rational functionality. The buildings that resulted were characterised by utility, enormity and banality. At the risk of generalising, little heed was paid to aesthetics. These were not buildings intended to be beautiful objects in themselves, nor were they projected to have long lifespans; instead, they were planned as rational structures built to high technological specifications that reflected the prevailing attitude towards the sport.

One such example of this typology was the new grandstand of Perak Turf Club in Malaysia (1971) (Figure 1.85). In 1964, the Perak Turf Club reached the decision to raze and rebuild their existing grandstand at Ipoh, 225 kilometres (140 miles) northwest of Kuala

Lumpa. This decision was largely based upon a lack of space. The old grandstand had served for 60 years but as attendances at the races increased, and more buildings and facilities were added accordingly, the racecourse became increasingly inefficient. The rebuilding was thus one of rationalisation. A Melbourne firm, Joyce Nankivell, won an international competition to redesign the facility in 1968 and three years later the grandstand was complete.[2]

Seating 10,000 and providing around 46,500 square metres (500,000 square feet) of covered floor space, the new grandstand almost doubled the size of its predecessor. The reinforced concrete structure was built around a structural frame of overhanging cantilever beams spanning 60 metres (190 feet). Utility and efficiency were the specifications underpinning its form. An

Page 130 **1.84** Happy Valley Racecourse from the air

Above **1.85** Perak Turf Club in Malaysia, completed in 1971, was a utilitarian and rational construction

1.86 Sha Tin Racecourse grandstand, seen from the rear, built in 1978

Opposite above **1.87** The Fuji View Stand (2007) at Tokyo Racecourse is the second largest in the world

Opposite below **1.88** Garden State Park, New Jersey. After a destructive fire, the racecourse was rebuilt in 1985 but permanently closed in 2001. The site is now a mixed-use development of shops, restaurants and housing

important component of its design was that it was capable of future extension and it was heralded for including two escalators – the first to be installed anywhere in Perak. While it was no doubt functionally efficient, the grandstand offered little concession to the eye. The most prominent feature of the building were two twin towers, rising 55 metres (180 feet) high on the finishing line to house stewards, judges, committee members and the media.[3] These incongruous high-rises formed the sole interruption to the dominant, repetitive horizontality of the stand, but they made for an awkward, unbalanced addition, seemingly likely to topple over at any moment.

Perak's new facility was built at the turning point of a new age for Asian racing. In the final three decades of the twentieth century, the gambling and horse racing industry there swelled. And grandstands got bigger and bigger. This was especially true of Hong Kong. The city-state's first racecourse opened in 1842 at the heart of the Hong Kong

Island, under the aegis of British rule. The course was christened Happy Valley. It was only in 1971 that racing became professional in Hong Kong, but in the space of a few short years its racing, prize-money and local fervour for the sport skyrocketed, transforming it into one of the world's most important gambling centres (Figure 1.84).[4] Happy Valley quickly outgrew its own success. Situated at the centre of the island and crowded by high-rise buildings, space was in sharp demand. The commodity is in such scarce supply today that horses are stabled in neighbouring tower blocks where they are exercised on the rooftops.[5] In 1975, the Royal Hong Kong Jockey Club proposed that a new racecourse be built to supplement Happy Valley. One hundred hectares (250 acres) of tidal wetlands at the Sha Tin Bay were allocated to build a state-of-the-art complex, which opened as Sha Tin Racecourse in 1978. The grandstand built was simply enormous. It occupied nearly 7 hectares (16 ½ acres) and was the largest single building in the colony.[6] Scale was its defining characteristic. In design terms, it can only be described as 'Asian Functional' (Figure 1.86).

Function and size were the defining characteristics of the succession of ambitious grandstand construction projects that ensued at Asian racecourses. There was no greater exponent of this trend than Japan. European-style horse racing was introduced to Japan in the nineteenth century, when racecourses became popular venues for socialising and power broking amongst the Meiji elite. However, by the turn of the next century, horse racing had been tainted by the introduction of legalised betting, and its associations with the seedy underside of city life. Racing became marginalised to compulsive gamblers and the darker spheres of Japanese society. Bank employees and high-ranking civil servants could even lose their jobs if they were discovered to be racing fans.[7] It was not until the last two decades of the twentieth century that racing in Japan recovered its reputation with the help of two popular heroes: Oguricap - a horse known as the grey monster - and a handsome young jockey called Take Yutaka. The media frenzy which engulfed the pair transformed racing from an insalubrious underworld activity to primetime news. Since then, the sport has thrived.[8] In fact, it grew so phenomenally that Japan today offers the highest total prize money for flat racing.[9] Its grandstand construction – at Nakayama (1990), Kyoto (1999), Tokyo (2007) – was the tangible demonstration of this growth. The scale of Tokyo's Fuji View Stand, for instance, was enormous (Figure 1.87). Stacked 10 storeys in height, the building stretched over 375 metres (1,230 feet). Its sheer size was a matter of awe, but this size was dictated by demand and it was this demand that shaped its form – another example of the 'Asian Functional' typology.

The colourless aesthetic and titanic scale of these grandstands has much to do with the nature of Japanese racing. Whilst the sport has broken loose from its blighted past, it continues to be driven overwhelmingly by gambling. Going to the races does not carry the same social connotations as it does in much of the West or, indeed, did in the Meiji empire, and thus its architecture is not conditioned by the desire for spectacle. It is a house for betting in.

This brand of grandstand construction was not, though, limited to Asia alone; resounding examples exist too in the US. The grandstand of Garden State Park in New Jersey was a large, stacked configuration completed in

1985 to designs by Robert Krause of Ewing Cherry Cole (now demolished) (Figure 1.88). Covering over 46,500 square metres (500,000 square feet), the building placed clubhouse on top of grandstand, inspired partly by financial motivations and partly to give a better view of the racing to more spectators. While the architect aimed to create an exciting atmosphere to lure a younger audience, the buildings' exterior conveyed little of that spirit of innovation. It was a lifeless, bulky structure, enclosed at all levels by large expanses of glass and with an overhanging upper deck. Garden State Park's stacked, behemoth approach, common to Asia and the USA, is brought into contrast by comparison with the grandstand at Arlington Park in Chicago, built four years later by architects Skidmore Owings Merrill (Figure 1.89). Arlington's stand looked diminutive in comparison – spanning approximately 20,500 square metres

(220,000 square feet). It rejected the stacked, glass-encased model seen at Kyoto or Garden State Park in favour of a single tier of seating open to the elements. The result was a far greater intimacy between spectators and horses, more akin to the nineteenth-century grandstands of Saratoga and Churchill Downs than contemporary design practices. Above the open tier of seating, two levels of restaurants and corporate facilities enclosed by glazing conceded the demands of a modern stand. The rear of the narrow building was lined with balconies to bring onlookers closer to the activities of the paddock behind, and conjuring an ocean-liner like appearance (Figure 1.90). The new grandstand countered the mould of American grandstand design in the late twentieth century. Amongst its contemporaries, it stood out like a shining light for its return to a more immediate, intimate spectator experience.

Above left **1.89** Arlington Park (1989) bucked the trend for enormous, glass-enclosed grandstands in favour of a more human-scaled, immediate visitor experience

Above right **1.90** Arlington Park. Balconies overlooking the paddock bring racegoers into greater immediacy with the spectacle, activity and emotions of a raceday

Diversification

In the last fifty years, the world has seen opportunities for leisure multiply beyond expectation. Expanding air travel has enabled foreign holidays; computers, games consoles and the internet have been born from technological advancement; and leisure centres, theme parks and art centres have become common sights. Unequivocally, horse racing has met with increasing competition for consumers' time and income; indeed, it has faced intense pressure. Since the midpoint of the twentieth century, the UK has seen the closure of 16 racecourses, 20 per cent of the total number. According to one study, 'racecourse managements have been faced with a stark choice – modernise and diversify or die'.[10] 'Diversify' has frequently been the motto which has shaped architectural endeavours of recent decades. Racecourses woke up to the idea that they are in the entertainment industry, and that the jaded facilities of the 1950s and 1960s held little appeal for a modern-day public. It was no longer sufficient to cater only for the hardened racegoer; it was necessary to draw both a new clientele and commercial activities to subsidise race meetings. This modernisation in mindset has resulted in a modernisation of building approach.

Amongst the most palpable manifestation of this has been the drive to market race meetings as destinations for corporate hospitality. Corporate hospitality at racecourses was not exactly a new idea, yet in the past decades it has held increasing sway upon racecourse design as courses have sought ever more varied ways to remain viable. Goodwood Racecourse was putatively the first in the UK to build hospitality boxes which face away from its track in 1980.[11] In 2002, Churchill Downs opened 64 luxury suites and meeting areas built atop an existing grandstand, which its management anticipated would generate up to $4 million per year.[12]

Racecourses across the US have suffered from declining attendances over recent decades, precipitating numerous courses to introduce additional leisure elements. The most prevalent of these has been the 'racino'. The racino concept was born in 1994 when West Virginia, Delaware, Iowa and Louisiana passed legislation allowing slot machines at racecourses. This encapsulates the premiss behind the concept. Live racing was combined with casino-style gambling, with racecourses receiving a share of the revenue. Currently, over 50 courses in North America operate as racinos. Development to house the new facilities necessarily followed, such as a new wing added to the grandstand of Oaklawn Jockey Club in Arkansas in 2010 by Hnedak Bobo Group architects. The new structures have, without exception, been of an undistinguished creed.

In a bid to revive the suffering industry, racing in North America has increasingly been coupled with commercial, leisure and corporate projects. 'The racing venue must become part of a larger complex,' Don Dissenger, principal architect at Ewing Cole, has said. 'This includes interactive attractions, game arcades, 'eater'tainment', speciality retail, museum attractions, sports bars, hotel and conference facilities, and luxury spas.'[13]

Many of these so-called 'Destination Entertainment Venue' projects have never left the drawing board, the victims of insufficient finances; one that did, though, was Gulfstream Park in Florida. In 2002 its owners unveiled plans to become a premier regional entertainment venue by creating a three-tier 'sports palace' for live sporting events such as boxing, a concert amphitheatre, an hotel, casino and retail complex, thus pitting the course against other local entertainment options.[14] Its elegant 1950s grandstand was torn down in 2004 and replaced by a multimillion-dollar makeover projected to renew Gulfstream to be all things to all men. Racing veterans mourned the change from 'an old-fashioned racetrack with thousands of outdoor seats to one that emphasises indoor dining rooms', while its aggressively promoted concert series 'significantly alienated its core constituency'. Neither did casino fans delight in the slot machines, to judge by the machines 'anaemic revenue' in 2007, a year after their unveiling.[15]

Gulfstream Park is an extreme example of the diversification trend. Nevertheless, from the late twentieth century glazed restaurants, urbane conference suites and large function rooms came to characterise refurbishment projects and new construction as racecourse managements tried to diversify their appeal. It has been an international current, but one primarily led by the UK and Dubai. The Tattersalls grandstand (2000) at Newbury Racecourse in the UK has been one such instance. The new stand was planned foremost for racing but its design was clearly informed by the vital supplementary income generated by non-raceday use. It housed a 600-person restaurant and bar, plus a large, flexible open-plan hall designated as a betting hall during the racing season and a conference, exhibition or corporate entertainment space at other times. The building provided the commodious amenities expected by a twenty-first century audience and, furthermore, these were housed within a signature Foster and Partners casing (Figure 1.91).

In metropolises around the world, a Foster building equates to a mark of modernity. This, no doubt, was a decided attraction to a racecourse trying to diversify. Moreover, the trademark Foster look – lean, sleek, logical and crystalline – holds distinct advantages for a racecourse stand – lithe, unfettered buildings of the type that the practice is famed for indisputably allow superior views of the Turf.[16] At Newbury, the Foster and Partners practice created a glass-enclosed, tautly-engineered stand. Designed to keep to its functional essence, it was also an economical architecture. Its premise was simple – a structural system based on six oversized X-shaped steel frames. Not unlike an ironing board, the top 'legs' supported the roof while the lowered 'legs' enclosed the ground-floor betting hall and provided the outline of the open stepped terrace. The straightforward logic of the frame system provided a refreshing alternative to the cantilever roof, and was also remarkably efficient in fiscal terms. With the clients stipulating a tight time span, the design allowed extensive pre-fabrication and the frame was delivered on-site in kit form.[17] It is proof that grandstand architecture can be functional and economic but also visually successful. Glazed on three sides, the X-frame makes for a bold, expressive statement while offering flexible internal spaces and sweeping views of the course that satisfy demands for race-day and non-race-day entertainment.

For British racecourses, the value of being able to brand themselves as entertainment venues is particularly pressing. Although Britain is second only to Japan in the total spent on horserace gambling, the returns to the racing industry are substantially lower than any of the other world-leading betting markets.[18] British racecourses draw a mere third of their revenue from betting, necessitating a complex and diverse funding structure based upon admissions, catering, media and non-raceday activities. The premium prices that high-quality raceday hospitality packages command during iconic fixtures such as Royal Ascot are especially indispensable, but in order to justify high-end prices racecourses need to offer high-end environments.

This situation is even more pronounced in Dubai. Thoroughbred racing came late to Dubai, beginning in an unstructured, embryonic form in the 1970s. But, as with all things in Dubai, once the emirate turned its hand to the Sport of Kings it did so with gusto. In 1992 the Dubai Racing Club was established and its first track,

Nad Al Sheba, was completed. Nine years later, it was enlarged with the opening of the Millennium Grandstand. With spaceship-like looks, it housed luxury suites, a nightclub, media seating and a restaurant as well as public seating. 'The new Millennium Grandstand has been designed to create an all-purpose new corporate/leisure entertainment centre...offering sophisticated viewing spaces along with multi-facility corporate entertainment,' boasted Les Benton, the Dubai World Cup Committee Chairman.[19] This new stand was, however, allowed only the briefest of lifespans, for, in 2010 races transferred from Nad Al Sheba to Meydan, Dubai's glittering new racecourse (Figure 1.92).

1.91 Newbury's Tattersalls Grandstand (2000). The sleek steel and glass aesthetic was designed by Foster + Partners

1.92 Meydan Racecourse in Dubai (2010), the largest, most expensive racecourse ever built, houses a hotel, museum, marina, IMAX theatre, and a host of restaurants

The biggest and most expensive course ever built, Meydan was a 'racing city'.[20] Featuring a five-star hotel, a host of food and drink outlets, a museum, marina, IMAX theatre, and a host of business facilities, Meydan's grandstand is an exaggerated banner for the diversification trend that has affected grandstand design. It is apt that Meydan in Arabic means 'meeting place'. At the top of the building was sited a corporate area known as the Sky Bubble lounge which gives up to 5,000 people unparalleled views of the course and Dubai skyline. Below, 78 corporate suites featured restaurants, bars and grandstand seating. The hotel, at the far end of the stand, is the first in the world to be purpose-built within a thoroughbred racecourse grandstand.[21] Ninety-five per cent of its 290 rooms had direct views overlooking the course. 'Meydan is designed as an attraction…an all-year round attraction,' proclaimed its chairman, Saeed al Tayer.[22]

Meydan is, undoubtedly, the most poignant demonstration of the functional diversification of racecourse architecture. With gambling in the UAE illegal, all its profits necessarily derive from creating a leisure experience. Part of its appeal was designed to lie in its futuristic architecture. Its Malaysian architect Teo A. Khing designed a highly polished glass and stainless steel landmark grandstand. Its most dramatic feature was a sweeping crescent roof, inspired by the wing of a falcon, which seems to soar majestically above the stands. Undoubtedly the most awe-inspiring aspect of the building

is, though, its sheer size. This is staggering. The structure extends 1,600 metres (5,250) in length; even the crescent runs 426 metres with a 56-metres span (1,400 by 180 feet). With a capacity of 60,000 (or 120,000 inclusive of full facilities), it accommodates twice as many people as the Nad Al Sheba racecourse.

The guise that Meydan assumed and its focus upon the 'leisure business' went hand in hand with the aspirations of Dubai racing. When he embarked upon his multimillion-dollar spree in the 1980s at America's yearling sales, Sheikh Maktoum was not merely indulging a love of thoroughbreds; it was part of a grander vision. In the face of dwindling oil reserves, the sheikh planned to cast Dubai as a prestigious tourist and business destination. The successful international racing programme that he rapidly set about forging was to act as an advertisement for this. Meydan is a manifestation of these machinations.

The racecourse is a string of superlatives: world's only trackside hotel, world's longest LED screen, world's largest suspended roof. It epitomises much of Dubai itself. The grandstand embodies the era of credit-fuelled building frenzy that engulfed the entire region. Given Dubai's well-publicised economic difficulties, whether this model is responsible or sustainable is equivocal. Whilst it is an exception in terms of global grandstand design, unfeasible at other racecourses and racing clubs, it is nonetheless heightened evidence of the trend of luxury, commercialism and leisure that a select band of racecourses has pursued.

Resurgence of Design

The Meydan grandstand was very deliberately designed as a landmark structure, and as such, it indexes a second phenomenon that has affected the physical fabric of horse racing since the late twentieth century: a reawakening to innovative, high-calibre design within the sporting sector. 'The greatest buildings, the "icons", have always reflected the zeitgeist. And right now, the zeitgeist is sport,' wrote architect Ron Sheard.[23] In an increasingly commercial and secular age, sport has assumed a place as a global culture and, correspondingly, venues of sport have acquired a status of architectural icons perhaps not known since the Coliseum or Circus Maximus. As the last century came to a close and the next began, a revolution commenced, small in scale but significant nonetheless, against the perception of sports buildings as crude, concrete monoliths. As buildings such as the Media Centre at Lords Cricket Ground in London (Future Systems, 1999) and the Beijing Olympics National Stadium in Beijing (Herzog & De Meuron, 2008) demonstrate, sporting grounds again became the subject of leading architects. Although by no means a universal trend, racecourses have too been affected by this change in attitude. In the 1990s a select number of construction projects began to raise the architectural bar, interrupting the pattern of inertia towards design within the racing industry that had prevailed for decades. Imaginative, sensitive and creatively ambitious design was recognised as a desirable commodity by prominent courses trying to cement their prestige amidst growing global competition, and prominent architects once again began designing for racecourses. The trend is most discernable in the UK.

The Queen's Stand (1993) at Epsom was one such example (Figure 1.93). Following a competition in 1984, Richard Horden was selected to design a new building combining clubhouse and viewing stand. Fundamentally, Horden saw the stand as an opportunity to invent a completely new approach to grandstand construction. The Queen's Stand was conceived as a direct challenge to what Horden referred to as the 'autobahn' aesthetic of racecourse buildings, those long monotonous concrete slabs encasing 'red carpeted and curtained dark "betting pub[s]"'.[24] It was to be light, bright and airy. The stand was a comparatively simple building, built in brilliant white precast concrete up to a height of seven storeys with continuous aluminium balconies at every level enveloping all four sides. Horden's buildings are characterised by a structural weightlessness, openness and light, and the Queen's Stand was no exception. In this, it formed a marked contrast with the architectural panorama of late twentieth-century UK racing.

Its form, dramatically different to the grandstand norm, was inspired by an assessment of the psychology of attending the races and designed to respond to the reactions and behaviours of racegoers. From the outset, Horden shaped his design around the truism that racegoing is as much about the social aspects of the event as it is about the sporting ones; it is about seeing and being seen. He drew on a parallel which on first thoughts seems rather curious, that between horse racing and yachting, but one that becomes all the more convincing as the similar natures of the two activities are considered. The purpose of a viewing stand necessitates an outward-looking architecture giving vistas over the course, just as a yacht or ocean liner gives views over the ocean or harbour. The stand's balconies evoke the decks of a liner, and create a spectator experience in which the boundary between inside and out is blurred. Patrons of the Queen's Stand are encouraged to continually move outside and in, alternating between eating and drinking inside, and surveying the events of the course and waving

to friends from the balconies, akin to passengers aboard a yacht or ship. The interior and exterior colour palette of pure white and silver both enhances the jaunty nautical atmosphere, and provides a brilliantly blank canvas to set off the peacock finery of the racegoers. The architect's deliberate omission of escalators in favour of elegant elliptical staircases was motivated, he has remarked, by the natural elegance of the female form in movement which cannot be appreciated on an escalator, as well as the increased potential for social interaction on stairs.[25]

Its design was equally reflective of the financial strain faced by racecourse managements in the upkeep of their facilities. Its white, aluminium-clad surface was a practical as well as aesthetic decision, for it could be hosed down easily after events (akin to swabbing the decks of a yacht), creating a hardy building that was readily renewed to pristine condition. Moreover, it was designed as a flexible space in consciousness of the fact that the stand must generate a living for the greater part of the year as a commercial venue, whether this be for banquets, weddings, or conferences. Its neutral aesthetic made it appropriate for a range of functions, and became a trend within subsequent sporting projects, notably Michael Hopkins's Mound Stand at Lords or Goodwood Racecourse pavilions.

Goodwood Racecourse was profoundly affected by a changing attitude towards design at the turn of the century. Since its founding in 1802, the Sussex course had long been designated the UK's most beautiful racecourse, but this accolade was thanks to its natural setting in the picturesque South Downs rather than any manmade architectural intervention. Beginning in the 1990s, though, Goodwood underwent nothing short of a reformation, leaving it with one of the most innovative and interesting physical sporting set pieces in the country.

The earliest of the transformational projects was the Sussex Stand (1990) by Philip Dowson of Arup Associates. The stand was the manifestation of a three-year master plan which aimed to transform Goodwood's facilities from amongst the most lambasted to the most gratifying in the UK through the application of thoughtful and visually-appealing design. Goodwood suffered from numerous problems. The course had come under fire from its members and the racing press for prioritising corporate racegoers, thus a driving force behind Arup's plan was providing for the non-corporate racegoers - the paddock and Tattersall patrons. The master plan re-orientated the western entrance, moved the winning post to a more central position, and accommodated the Tattersalls and hospitality suites within one new stand, the Sussex Stand. The result was a visual unification of the course's three enclosures, overturning racing's deep-rooted distinctions. Likewise, its organisation marked a departure from the traditional prioritisation of spectator groups. In planning the grandstand, Arup drew from the basic structure of its 1830 forerunner. The stand took the form of standing steppings ascending from ground level up to boxes at the rear, with the principal seating area on an upper level covered by a canopy. From this elevated platform, the paying public were given prime views over the course, outstripping those of the entertainment suites below – a reversal of the arrangement in the 1980 March Stand. The stepped standings rose from a concrete base, sheathed in brick to match surrounding buildings and housing a betting hall, restaurant and meeting areas. Above this, a steel framework encased the hospitality boxes and upheld the distinctive fabric canopy.

The canopy of the seating area is what gave the stand its visual character. Inspired by Edward VII's observation in 1905 that 'Goodwood is really a garden party with racing tacked on', the architects designed a structure that heightened this ambience. The grandstand is, in effect, a permanent translucent tent with a comparable flavour of lightness and festivity to that of the Queen's Stand at Epsom. At the height of summer

during 'Glorious Goodwood', it becomes the largest of the canopies in a sea of marquees recalling the archetypal British partnership of white tents and summer sporting events. With its sweeping silhouette, translucent roof, and brilliant-white painted steelwork, the Sussex Stand made for a light and airy contrast with the neighbouring bulky, concrete March Stand built only a decade earlier. Clear glass windshields protected the high-level seating from the chilling breezes of the Downs, while the steppings led directly to the lawns, paddock and bookmakers' forecourt, creating a sense of openness, fluidity and accessibility that perfectly complemented the festive atmosphere of the occasion.[26]

The Sussex Stand's festal lightweight roof became a local landmark that so successfully personified the race meeting, that when Goodwood selected Hopkins Architects to upgrade the course in 1997, it proved the starting point of the scheme. The project was in essence driven by an awareness that the racecourse had fallen behind its competitors in catering for the corporate entertainment market, and it focussed on improving the quality of the winner's enclosure, parade ring and weighing-in room behind the March Stand. Completed in 2001, the Hopkins practice reorganised the layout, utilising the natural slope of the terrain to create a terraced mound with spectator seating overlooking the parade ring and enclosure (Figure 1.94).[27]

The promenade from parade ring to grandstand was remodelled as a tree-lined boulevard and issues of hospitality and catering were addressed. Here Michael Hopkins turned to the precedent set by Arup Associates, and designed three pavilions to house these facilities between the promenade and parade ring. Formed of PVC canopies upheld by white steel masts, these pavilions chimed with the 'garden party' atmosphere of Goodwood. The Hopkins practice in fact pioneered the use of permanent

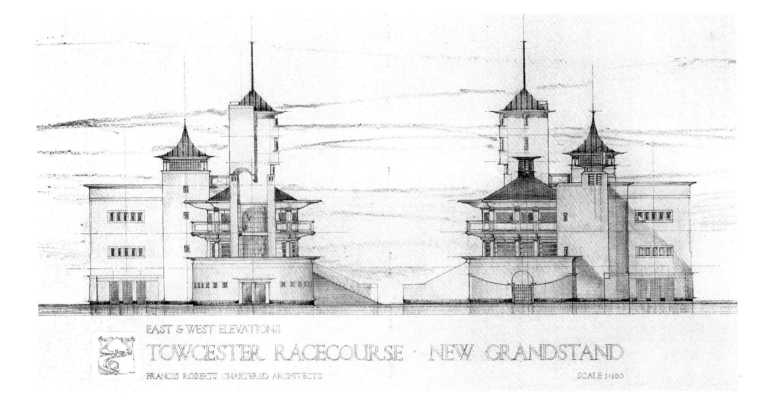

EAST & WEST ELEVATIONS
TOWCESTER RACECOURSE · NEW GRANDSTAND
FRANCIS ROBERTS CHARTERED ARCHITECTS   SCALE 1:100

lightweight fabric structures in Britain, as illustrated by the 1987 Mound Stand at Lords and at the Hampshire County Cricket Club (2001). The style resulted in pragmatic, high-tech buildings, ideal for sporting contexts. At Goodwood, the Hopkins pavilions made for a light, open architecture. Each pavilion was structured around a central bar or server, surrounded by tables but not enclosed by perimeter walls. As few structural elements as possible were used so as to dissolve the boundaries between the spectators, horses and the legendary beauty of the Downs landscape. Only two, free-standing glass screens, purposed to shield against the strong southerly winds, created any division between the pavilions and the surrounding course.

The project facilitated the racegoers' experience but also complemented Arup's earlier work in creating for Goodwood a physical identity that encapsulated the light-hearted festivity of the meeting. The two schemes demonstrated the expediency of simple, yet high-quality design.

High quality design was also the driving force behind a new grandstand in 1997 at Towcester Racecourse in Northamptonshire, UK. Towcester was a modest local steeplechase course with inferior facilities. Having opened in 1928, by the early 1990s it possessed two decaying stands and a lacklustre image. This image its owner Lord Hesketh set about to rejuvenate and the result was one of the most unexpected grandstand designs on these shores. One critic enthused:

> Built in the true tradition of the architecture of entertainment, the new stand at Towcester is a triumphant breath of fresh air. A beautifully executed flight of fancy, it flaunts itself in the face of the myriad of dreadfully dreary, ungainly and inappropriate new stands which abound on our racecourses.[28]

1.95 Grace Stand at Towcester (1997) was an eclectic, traditionalist building commissioned to revitalise the image of the course

The Grace grandstand, as it was christened, was more akin to a park folly or hunting lodge, in the spirit of the seventeenth-century Lodge Park, than a modern-day stand. It was a small building, built in a traditionalist vein that combined vernacular details with meticulous craftsmanship. Sporting a warm, buff-coloured render, it was an asymmetrical structure with irregular towers at either end, a red tile gable roof, capricious buttresses, windows of all shapes and sizes, and white painted woodwork (Figure 1.95). On the rear façade, a triple-height projecting bay with balustraded balcony overlooked the paddock. On the opposite elevation, fluted wooden Doric pilasters framed a wall of windows opening from restaurant onto steppings outside; above, a white-painted Chinese Chippendale balustrade railed a balcony running the length of the stand. Its inspirations were eccentric and eclectic. The Chippendale balconies were inspired by Thomas Jefferson's early nineteenth-century architecture at the University of Virginia; the Doric pilasters referenced the Greek temples of Paestum; whilst the long, locally-crafted iron strap hinges on its main entrance evoked the style and craftsmanship of the Arts and Crafts Movement. Its historicist heterogeneity was characteristic of its architect, Frank Roberts.

Roberts's portfolio is made up of unique buildings inspired by traditional architecture, which place a premium on craftsmanship, an approach directly influenced by the Arts and Crafts Movement. At Towcester, he avoided turning to past grandstand precedents for stimulus and looked loosely instead to the tradition of pavilion architecture. He sought to capture a celebratory, theatrical ambiance, befitting for a day out at the races, and in this he succeeded. Roberts's building was a blithesome addition to the corpus of grandstand design. His task was, admittedly, made much easier by the modest size of both the racecourse and the

building itself. It is, as a generalisation, a far easier matter to design for small-scale projects than larger ones.

Whilst its design is whimsical, its basis was pragmatic. The design of the Grace Stand has much to do with the nature of jump racing in Britain. Held in winter, racegoers are unlikely to want to spend much time on the outside steppings, thus this area was kept basic in design. Similarly, the attendees are as likely to be wearing waterproof boots as dainty heels, so the interior too was kept relatively plain. Racing was only scheduled for 14 days a year, however, and for the structure to be commercially viable it also had to be adaptable to host conferences, parties, weddings and corporate hospitality year-round. Its restaurant, bar and six top-floor private boxes with balcony were planned for maximum flexibility and panoramic views over the course.[29]

In today's climate, it is rare for a sports venue to embrace historicism as Towcester has done. Respect for the past was, however, a driving facet of Ascot Racecourse's most recent redevelopment (Figure 2.1).

At the world's most famous racecourse, modern ambitions sat side by side with a reverence for its 300-year history. With ageing facilities and increasing international competition, from 2003-2006 Ascot embarked on its first major remodelling for 40 years. The racecourse was transformed: circulation patterns were overhauled, the track was realigned, the parade ring was moved to a more central location, and the nineteenth- and twentieth-century perimeter buildings were substantially renewed. Most notably, its red-brick turnstile building (1876) was stripped of its later additions and returned to its stately Victorian glory to create a new majestic, colonnaded entrance façade for the racecourse.

When it came to rebuilding the grandstand, however, a historicist approach was held ill-suited for twenty-first-century racing at the scale of

Ascot. At the heart of the scheme was built a vast, curving grandstand to replace its dated 1960s stand. With a palette of aluminium, steel, terracotta and glass, this unquestionably marked the racecourse as a twenty-first-century venue. The man responsible for the grandstand's design was Rod Sheard of HOK (now Populous), whose projects included rebuilding Wembley Stadium in London and designing the 2000 Olympic stadium in Sydney. Whereas so many modern-day stands have a generic appearance, Sheard set about to create a site-specific building. Fundamental to its design was the creation of a dialogue between the building and its landscape setting. Hugging the brow of the hill on which it sits, the grandstand curved with the contours of the land from its highest point at the centre downwards. Its roof was upheld by 'structural trees' – stylised with tubular aluminium columns with fanning branches – intended to respond to the wooded landscape of Windsor Great Park, onto which the grandstand looked out (Figure 1.96). The stand's sleek lines and sailing roof made for an architectural spectacle as unique as the racing spectacle of Ascot's Royal Meeting itself.

The spectacle, theatre and drama of racing were the buzzwords behind another innovative UK project: the building of two twin grandstands at Aintree Racecourse in Liverpool (2007). Aintree is home to the Grand National, the world's most watched steeplechase. Every April, 600 million viewers worldwide tune in to watch this National Hunt race. 'As a result,' wrote architectural critic Martin Spring,

> Aintree's buildings are on show nearly as much as the horses themselves. Until very recently, though, the potential of the architecture to promote the event was lost on the racecourse owners. The four existing grandstands were about as inspiring as a 1970s business park. But no longer. At last, the excitement of a top horse race is properly expressed in Aintree's two latest grandstands.[30]

In a bid to capture the energy, thrill and ritual of the event, international architectural practice BDP defied the usual structural expression of contemporary grandstands to create instead what they referred to as 'theatres' of sport.

Part of a wider scheme to reorganise Aintree's entrance, pre-parade ring and stables, the new stands replaced a host of temporary stands and marquees with permanent spectator and hospitality facilities housed within two bold, flamboyant structures sited at a sharp corner of the track (Figure 1.97). Accommodating 6,500 people, the two new stands are far smaller than Ascot's 2006 grandstand. Instead of a single, larger grandstand, the decision was made to harmonise with the scale of Aintree's existing buildings by creating two smaller ones. The paired buildings each assumed a fairly conventional arrangement of three tiers of viewing accommodation plus an upper storey of suites; but to BDP, the pair were not mere stands but 'theatres'. Capturing, utilising and enhancing the atmosphere of the Grand National day was the driving force behind BDP's master plan and grandstand design. The culminating expression of this design philosophy was the glazed drum which linked the two structures and which crossed the wide, open-air gateway between them. Serving as a triumphal arch

Opposite **1.96** Ascot Horse Walk from pre-parade ring to parade ring. The historic racecourse was redeveloped from 2003-6

Above **1.97** The Earl of Derby and Lord Sefton Grandstands (2007) sit at the corner turn at Aintree, the home of the Grand National

through which the horses and riders processed from the parade ring to the starting line and back again, this gateway elevated a racing ritual into a ceremonial pageant. The central drum housed bars glazed to all sides, giving unparalleled views of this ritual as well as of the saddling paddock to the rear and the finishing and starting posts at the front. Racegoers were, therefore, always at the heart of the drama of the turf. The white fabric canopy roof of the drum enhanced – as at Goodwood – the festal spirit of the day.[31]

The cantilevering roof of the main stands, on the other hand, was modelled on the peak of a jockey's cap. Constructed in shiny zinc, it was a striking statement. At the back of each grandstand, the curve of the roof was extended in one fluid movement down the rear façade (Figure 1.98). This motif had pragmatic as well as aesthetic foundations. South-westerly winds glided smoothly over the top of the stands rather than reverberating into the paddock. Either side of the sloping zinc banks rose a pair of service towers. Their warm larch cladding provided a welcome textural and chromatic contrast to the coolness of the zinc.[32]

The arresting materials and theatrical forms of the exterior of the two stands have transformed Aintree's physical image. They demonstrate the employment of an unusual, bold design in capitalising on the potential of architecture to promote a course and an individual sporting event. UK racecourse administrators have become progressively more attuned to this potential. It is no coincidence that the UK has been the focus of the resurgence of design within racing. Its racecourses face a situation, arguably more acute here than elsewhere, in which they are compelled to jockey on a national level against other sporting and entertainment venues. The number of racing enthusiasts is not high enough for racecourses to feasibly operate for them alone;

the racecourses need to present themselves in terms of destinations for entertaining days out. This is no new concept. Harking back to Longchamp or Palermo at the turn of the century, these venues attracted swarms of patrons drawn largely not by the sport but their position as a hub of society life set within handsome surroundings. Racecourse managements are awakening to this outlook. Courses such as Ascot, Goodwood and Aintree are in competition not only amongst themselves, but with major sporting destinations such as Wimbledon or Lord's Cricket Ground.[33] A distinguished physical setting can be a proficient way towards gaining the edge. Impressive architectural schemes such as Ascot have been driven by the need to provide a superlative holistic experience to entice patrons, and leading architects, such as Michael Hopkins or Philip Dowson, have been engaged to direct them.[34] This is a prodigious leap from the days when Ascot entrusted its redesign to Wimpey's in-house architect in the 1960s.

The trends of diversification and resurgence of design that have shaped racecourse architecture from the late twentieth century onwards spring, ultimately, from the same motive: financial survival. The third principal trend, that of large-scale construction sacrificing design to functionality, sits somewhat apart. While the first two trends have been led by the UK, the latter is embodied in Asia, at the racecourses of Sha-Tin, Kyoto or Tokyo for example. A dichotomy is striking: as racing is becoming ever more globalised through ease of international travel and growth of rich, international races, the nature of racecourse architecture has grown more localised.

There is at least one common point, applicable to all racecourses, from Tokyo to Toronto. Racecourse design is growing more complex. These are sophisticated, capital intensive venues. As the twenty-first century progresses, and tomorrow's technologies overtake those of today, this is only likely to become truer.

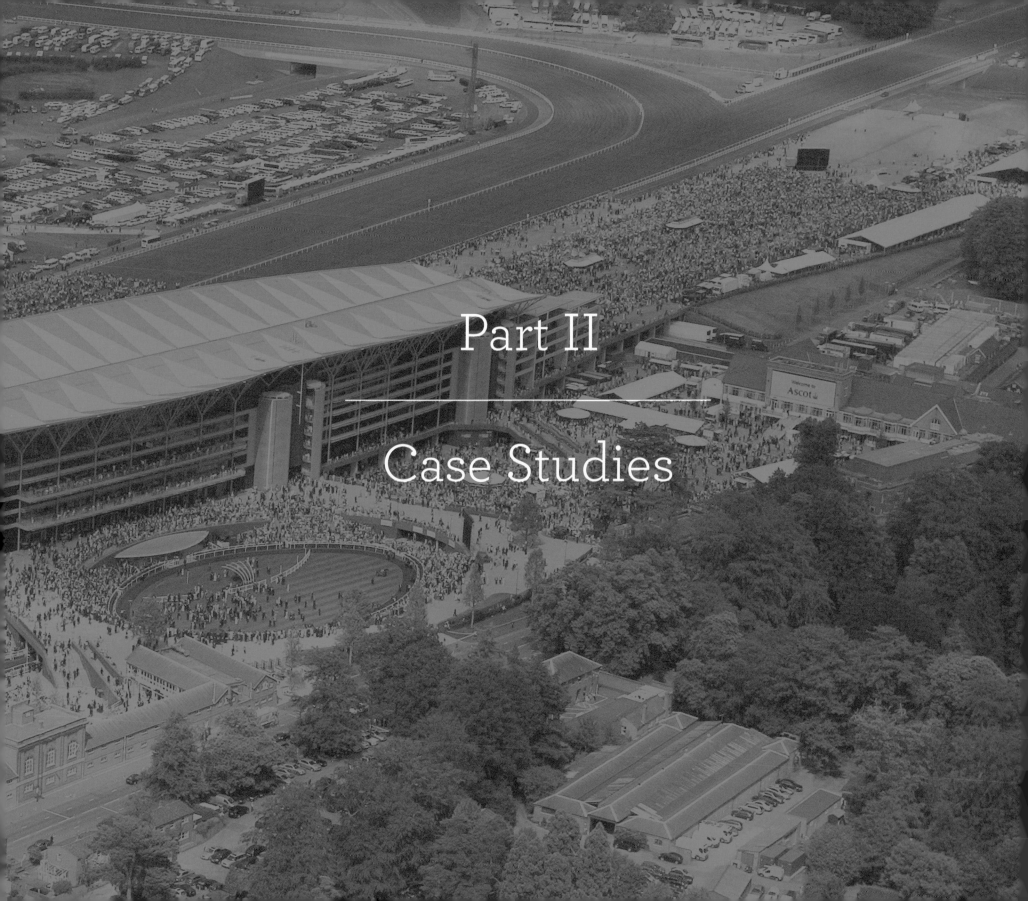

Part II

Case Studies

Ascot Racecourse
Berkshire, UK

Since the day of its founding in 1711, Ascot has been a royal racecourse. Over three centuries, its connection with the crown has shaped its prestigious reputation and its architectural environment. Its 2006 redevelopment is evidence of the importance given to physical setting in upholding its renown.

Ascot derives its renown as a fashionable gathering chiefly from the circumstance of the sports on the Heath having for a lengthened period been one of the especial objects of Royal patronage.

(*Sporting Life*, 15 June 1859)

Legend has it that in the summer of 1711, Queen Anne was riding in her carriage on the open heathland near Windsor Castle, when she was struck by the potential of the heath for 'horses to gallop at full stretch'. This was the genesis of Ascot Racecourse. Described as 'exceeding gross and corpulent', Queen Anne (1707-1714) perhaps cut an unlikely figure to found a racecourse. Yet she had a tireless enthusiasm for hunting and horses and her impulse to establish a racing circuit on crown land at Ascot was quickly set in motion. Its first fixture was held on 11 August 1711.

Anne would, no doubt, be proud. The course that was her brainchild is now renowned the world across, ranking amongst the most hallowed of sporting grounds. After three centuries, Ascot stands firm as one of the most prestigious racecourses, consistently hosting the best thoroughbreds in the sport. Its physical environment, furthermore, is one of the best in racing. Today, its grandstand stands at the forefront of this architectural genre.

The course was, however, slow to begin its architectural endeavours. Notwithstanding its royal pedigree, there were no lavish appointments at the Queen's course. Anne never erected a stand, electing to the watch the races from her own carriage. This was not unusual. Stands were not necessary accoutrements of an eighteenth-century racecourse, and those that did exist were often

Page 154 **2.1** Queen Elizabeth officially opens the new grandstand in 2006. Royal patronage has been key to Ascot's evolution since its inaugural meeting in 1711

Above **2.2** For its first 82 years, Ascot had no permanent buildings. Crowds on foot and horseback jostled amidst tents and wooden viewing platforms. (Paul and Thomas Sandby, *Ascot Heath Races*, circa 1765)

rustic, temporary viewing platforms. Contemporary depictions show that several of these makeshift, portable timber stands lined Ascot's track, beyond which crowded 'an absolute town' of refreshment and entertainment tents (Figure 2.2).[1] For the most part, racegoers clamoured to glimpse the action of the track from horseback, on foot, or, for the well-heeled, within the comfort of a carriage. Even the royal stand was wooden and moved around the course to obtain the best views of the racing. It was not until 1793, 37 years after the opening of John Carr's grandstand at York Racecourse, that Ascot acquired its first permanent stand, the Slingsby Stand (demolished 1859). Named after its builder, master bricklayer George Slingsby, the stand was commissioned by George III and accommodated 650 attendees. Gradually Ascot's architectural tally grew as it entered its second century.

The nineteenth century was one of progress at the racecourse. An important step came in 1807 with the inaugural running of the Gold Cup, today one of Britain's most eminent and popular races; in 1813, Parliament passed an Act of Enclosure which ensured the site's future as a public racecourse; and, in 1822, the new king, George IV (1820-1830), commissioned a Royal Stand from celebrity architect John Nash (1752-1835). The first permanent royal stand had, in fact, been built 15 years earlier for Queen Charlotte but little is known of this building for it was all swept away for George's bigger and better version.

George had a taste for high living and decadent excess, and in his unrepent pursuit of pleasure he was especially fond of horses. 'Amongst the prominent racing men of this time there was none more ambitious nor more risky than the young Prince of Wales', wrote one Ascot chronicler.[2] At the age of 21, he purchased his first racehorse, three years later came his first Ascot victory, and by 1791 his Newmarket Stud had won a total of 185 races.[3] His passion for the turf, though, could not compete with his appetite for architecture. Licentious and libertine he may have been, but he was also a discerning patron of the arts, one that was obsessed with building. Spending lavishly on a portfolio of glittering royal palaces, he employed the greatest architects of the age. The most notable of these was John Nash. It is to Nash, upon George's commission, that we owe the most ambitious planning project London has ever seen – the creation of the modern-day Regents Park and the extensive network of elegant terraces and canal which surround it. The architect is probably best remembered for the oriental-fantasy Royal Pavilion that he created at Brighton for the profligate prince.

George's zeal for racing and building was united when he commissioned Nash to design Ascot's new Royal Stand. Erected in only five weeks, it was a white, stucco structure, indebted to the Grecian aesthetic which dominated Georgian architecture (Figure 2.3). Akin to the typical grandstand formula at that time, the stand had two storeys plus rooftop viewing platform (added 1824). In other respects, however, its design reflected its singular royal raison d'être. Intended only to house the royal party, it was small in size with each floor measuring only eight by five metres (27 by 17 feet). No balconies extended from its reception rooms overlooking the course nor was its ground floor open to the trackside as was the norm. On the upper storey, this façade was given over to the Doric order with column-framed sash windows

2.3 First running of the Gold Cup (then the Emperor's Plate) in 1845 in front of the Royal Stand, built in 1822 for George IV

and entablature with prominent triglyphs. To the sides of the stand was a small lawn, entrance to which was strictly reserved for the king's guests, rendering it the precursor of the modern Royal Enclosure.[4]

The Royal Enclosure provided an important platform for the spectacle of kingship, in other words a chance for the public to see the monarch long before the advent of newspaper photos. The *Windsor and Eton Express* chronicled in 1829 that the 'popularity of these races arises more from the sanction afforded to them by His Majesty, than from the mere running. Horses may be seen every day, but King's [sic] are scarce.'[5] George, quite intentionally, lived his life on a public stage and relished putting the monarchy on show.[6] He made the crown less remote, more overt, and at Ascot left a legacy of 'king-seeing' that has continued to the present. Its most poignant manifestation was the Royal Procession. Stately

arrivals were not uncommon, but in 1825 the sovereign instituted a formal carriage procession up the Straight Mile surrounded by a resplendent royal retinue. Ever since, the procession has stood as an inveterate image of the connection between Ascot and the monarchy.[7]

By the end of his life, George's patronage rendered the Ascot races one of the most fashionable social events of the year. Adjurations for reform, however, began in the mid-1830s. Stakes had reduced in number and entries were appreciably less; complaints were levelled against the condition of the turf; even the quantity of beggars prompted criticism. So too did Ascot's paucity of stands. 'It has long been a subject of surprise and regret, that while Epsom, and almost every other provincial racecourse in the kingdom, was provided with a grand stand, Ascot should have been...without one.'[8] Accordingly, in 1838 foundations were laid for a new grandstand.[9]

It was by far the largest building on the course. With a capacity of 3,000, it measured 30 metres in length and 17 metres in height (97 feet by 55 feet). Crowds filled its ground-floor benches, its first-floor drawing room, and its tiered flat-roof seating. Its architect was a little-known man, William Higgins. Classically proportioned and sheathed in stucco, the stand made for an elegant addition to Ascot's ensemble (Figure 1.16). Engaged Doric pilasters divided its side and rear facades, while on the trackside elevation the Corinthian order was employed on ground and first floors. Importantly, it brought Ascot's facilities for the public in line with Britain's other courses. In addition to tiered benches on all floors, the building offered a wealth of retiring

2.4 Plan of the course, circa 1932. Ascot's physical fabric expanded during the opening decades of the twentieth century with a new Royal Enclosure, public stand, restaurants and bars

Opposite **2.5** Ascot from the air, photographed 1946. The Royal Enclosure buildings (1902) are shown at the centre: (from left to right) Royal Enclosure Stand, Royal Stand and Jockey Club Stand

Above **2.6** Edwardian Ascot from the infield

and refreshment rooms, a spacious saloon and betting room, plus a paved colonnade affording 'shade and shelter from sun and rain for visitors occupying seats on the lawn in front'.[10] 'In fact,' wrote one enthusiastic commentator, 'the conveniences are more numerous than at any other building of the kind in England'.[11] The grandstand was an instant success.

The Grand, Royal and Slingsby Stands now made up Ascot's physical ensemble, together with a host of wooden platforms. It was a motley assortment of buildings of different styles, sizes and ages, creating a piecemeal panorama. This epitomises the approach to growth that has shaped the course ever since. Ascot's architectural story is no smooth evolution; it has none of the wholesale razing and set-piece rebuilding of Chantilly or Longchamp but rather follows a methodology ingrained within British racing of fractional, progressive development. Beginning

with the 1839 grandstand, Ascot's physical environment has steadily evolved, in tune with the latest fashions in stand design or the changing nature of the Turf's popularity and demographics. The 1839 grandstand, for instance, reflected the surge in racing audiences in the Victorian age.

Queen Victoria had come to the throne in 1837 and the following year the railway arrived within 16 kilometres (ten miles) of Ascot. The expansion of the railway network in the 1830s and 40s had a dramatic impact upon racecourses across Britain. Uncomfortable and unsafe they may have been, but excursion trains introduced swarms of passengers to the thrills of travel – and to the thrills of organised spectator sports. Horse racing had long drawn a large following, but the railways vaulted it to commercial success on a national scale. As getting to fixtures became quicker, cheaper and easier, the number of racegoers

2.7 The three stands of the Royal Enclosure (1902). At the centre projects the Royal Balcony, remodelled in the 1930s

swelled, particularly the number of middle-class patrons, and Ascot slowly but surely became a destination for the burgeoning middle classes. Growing attendances squeezed the grandstand and, bit by bit, new buildings were erected to ease the pressure. Circa 1859, the so-called Iron Stand (or Subscribers' Private Stand) was erected a few yards west of the grandstand solely for the use of gentlemen members. The public grandstand was extended circa 1863 with an eastern extension known as the Alexandra Stand. In 1876, a majestic colonnaded entrance building was erected, creating a long, red-brick public façade to the racecourse property. This was followed twenty years later by a small, adjacent hospital building.

Gold Cup Day of 1902 – coronation year of King Edward VII – saw the biggest attendance of Ascot's history. It signalled the dawn of a new epoch for the course under the new sovereign. Racing had held little interest for Queen Victoria; for the new king, however, the very opposite was true. 'I fear, dear Mama,' Edward once wrote to his mother, 'that no year goes round without your giving me a jobation on the subject of racing.'[12] The older he grew, the more he felt racing's lure. 'Restless and craving amusement, he delighted in what he described as its "glorious uncertainties",' one of his biographers wrote of him.[13] A contemporary writer chronicled that, 'it is impossible to over-estimate the good service that our monarch has rendered to the King of Sports during the thirty-five years that his colours hath [sic] adorned both flat and steeplechase courses'.[14] Like George IV before him, Edward's passion for horses and special attachment to Ascot yielded an enormous impact upon the royal racecourse, not least upon its physical evolution.

The opening decade of the twentieth century saw physical changes at Ascot unprecedented in their extent. Immediately after the 1901 meeting the king ordered the razing and rebuilding of the entire royal enclosure – effectively all stands to the west of the Iron Stand, including the 1822 Royal Stand. Work progressed quickly. Around 500 men worked day and night to designs by architect A. W. Stephens, and by May the following year three new stands – Jockey Club Stand, Royal Stand and Royal Enclosure Stand - were complete (Figure 2.5).

The impact on Ascot's architectural setting was substantial. Propelling its tired accommodation into the twentieth century, the buildings belonged unmistakably to the Edwardian era.[15] Each differed in shape and size, but they shared a palette of red brick, ornamental cast iron and sash windows. The Royal Stand was the most ornate of the three, although far from being ostentatious. Indeed, its rear façade had a strikingly domestic appearance. Here was a two-storey elevation with bipartite sash windows, red brick lintels and quoins, and moulded cornice. Its principal feature was a white cast-iron porte-cochere and balcony, whose lacework spandrels epitomised Edwardian elegance. Decorative cast iron continued on the trackside façade. Three tiers overlooked the course, from the lowest of which projected a curving royal balcony and a curving double staircase railed by decorative cast iron (Figure 2.7).[16]

The new buildings were, seemingly, unanimously applauded. 'Everywhere are to be seen signs of a desire to move with the times,' admired the *Times*.[17] They were, though, only for the privileged few. Providing the best view of the races, they were a socially exclusive domain. Admittance could only be gained by personal royal invitation. However, change was also afoot for Ascot's rank and file. Again, Edward VII seems to have played a guiding role:

> His Majesty always thought that not quite enough was done for the comfort of the ordinary public at Ascot, and it was through his active interest that arrangements were made whereby it was possible to clear the ground for the erection of the new stand.[18]

The said stand was the Five Shilling Stand (later rechristened the Silver Ring Stand) and it was erected in 1908.

As transport to the course grew easier and Ascot's popularity increased, the necessity to provide facilities for the less well-heeled became evident. The Five Shilling Stand offered lower priced admission for those unable to afford grandstand rates. Built at the eastern end of the trackside buildings, it was simple in shape and modest in cost but, stretching 90 metres (300 feet) in length, it could accommodate up to 12,000.

> In design, the new stand is a red-brick building covered with tiles, and presenting an un-shuttered front to the running course. It has 22 tiers... At the back are the luncheon rooms, refreshment bars, and necessary offices, these leading out to a courtyard, where a bandstand betokens the fact that musicians will find employment there during the races.[19]

Its front elevation overlooking the course had no architectural pretensions, but its long rear elevation shared the same red brick Edwardian aesthetic as the 1902 structures. This was a two-storey façade with stone dressing, and wide relieving arches which gave a robustness to its architecture. 'Progressive Ascot' was the label applied by *The Sporting Life* upon the stand's completion.[20]

The paddock area to the west of the Royal Enclosure was radically expanded with facilities for the public. Lining its perimeter was built a luncheon room and bars in 1911, further luncheon room accommodation in 1926 and an enormous totalisator building in 1930. Totalisator betting had been legalised in Britain only the year before, so this was a completely novel building type. Ascot converted its red-brick Victorian loose boxes for the purpose, building upwards to create a vast blank façade on its north elevation for the display board.[21] It was 'the largest totalisator board in the world' according to a headline in the *London Illustrated News*.[22]

After this flurry of excitement, the racecourse's pace of development slowed to a standstill. By the late 1950s, its facilities were jaded. Racegoers' expectations of comfort and visibility were no longer those of the nineteenth century, and the Victorian stands made for uncomfortable and unprotected viewing, especially in inclement weather. To the Ascot Authority, the 1839 grandstand was a relic of a bygone age and in 1960 ground was broken on a towering new grandstand. The sweep of redevelopment that followed in the next four years was prodigious. It was the most profound at Ascot since the day in 1711 when Queen Anne had directed its creation.

After only ten months of construction, in June 1961 the new Queen Elizabeth II Stand was officially opened (Figure 2.8). Replacing the Victorian Grand, Alexandra and Iron Stands, the building was vast. Nearly 200 yards long and seven storeys tall, it accommodated 13,000 spectators. The construction firm, George Wimpey & Co., served as both contractor and designer, with Eric Collins acting as in-house architect. The stand was state-of-the-art: 280 private boxes

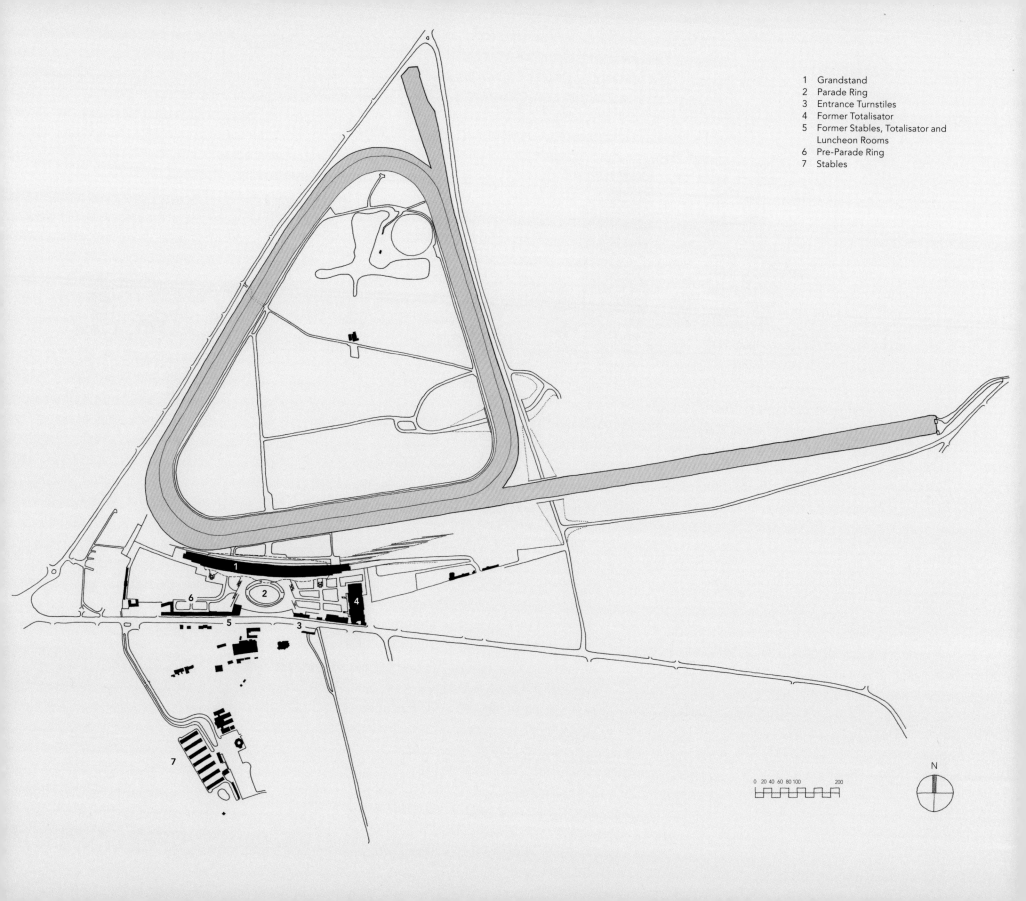

1 Grandstand
2 Parade Ring
3 Entrance Turnstiles
4 Former Totalisator
5 Former Stables, Totalisator and
   Luncheon Rooms
6 Pre-Parade Ring
7 Stables

0 20 40 60 80 100   200

N

each with their own dining room; the first escalators on a British racecourse; and a deep cantilevered roof which eliminated the need for obstructive supporting columns. British racing had not seen anything like it.

The grandstand had some onerous conditions to meet. This was an era of falling attendances at race meetings nationwide, and the building was tasked with both drawing audiences and introducing corporate hospitality. Ultimately, though, the most decisive proviso, and the one which really shaped its design, was timescale. To ensure that the annual summer Royal Meeting was not disrupted, a rigid timeframe of only ten months was allotted for the whole project, from demolition to construction. Such a brief could not be fulfilled without prefabricated building technology and a rigidly repetitive

design. In this, Ascot's new stand epitomised the predominant ethos of racecourse construction of the period. Constructed from repeating pre-cast units, the stand made for a long, faceless building. Three years later, Ascot's new look was complete with the erection of an adjoining Royal Enclosure Stand, which replaced the three Edwardian Enclosure stands with a single, large structure. It doubled the size and capacity of the previous Royal Enclosure and continued the scale and aesthetic of the Queen Elizabeth II Stand.

The redevelopment was almost unanimously welcomed upon its opening. 'For the first time in more than 30 years racing at Royal Ascot, I saw the start and finish of all the races in complete comfort,' wrote the *Windsor and Eton Express*.[23] 'It is the most impressive structure on any English racecourse,' lauded *The Sporting Life* in

2.9 Grandstand cross-section, designed by HOK (now Populous). The building was vertically divided, with viewing accommodation on its north façade, dining and refreshment facilities to the south and a light-filled atrium in the middle

Opposite **2.10** Racegoers overlook the parade ring from a fourth-floor balcony

1961.[24] Yet only two years later the same paper was calling it 'that calamitous main stand'.[25] Criticisms stemmed chiefly from the angle of the stand: 'When will racecourse planners realise that grandstands must be set at an angle to the course if everyone is to have a fair view?'[26] Some reservations were also expressed about its design. 'The structure strongly resembles a new skyscraper block of offices,' wrote one newspaper.[27] The two new buildings wielded an unparalleled impact upon the architectural nature of the course. Instead of the charmingly idiosyncratic silhouette of Victorian and Edwardian Ascot, an elongated concrete monolith loomed over the 250-year old course, utilitarian in outline and decidedly of its time.

Fast forward 40 years later to the opening of the twentieth-first century, and its 1960s aesthetic had fallen drastically out of favour. Besides, the facilities were deteriorating, costly to maintain and unable to cope with the crowds of the Royal Meeting. The pedigree of Ascot's racing was simply not reflected in the utilitarian appearance of its buildings. Redevelopment was desperately needed, and in 2004 Ascot embarked upon its most adventurous modernisation project yet, presided over by Queen Elizabeth II.

'The brief for the project was simple', said its lead architect, Rod Sheard of firm HOK (now Populous). 'They told us to build the best racecourse in the world.'[28] The scheme was hugely ambitious: the nineteenth-century entrance buildings were restored, the Edwardian and interwar structures were renovated, circulation patterns were revised, the track was re-aligned 42 metres (140 feet) to the north, and the parade ring was moved from its location west of the stand to a central, easily accessible position behind a vast new grandstand. This new building lay at the heart of the plan. Ascot's 1960s Queen Elizabeth and Royal

Enclosure Stands fell victim to the wreckers' ball and in their stead rose a 480-metre (1,575-feet) long grandstand capable of holding 80,000 spectators (30,000 seated). It opened in 2006 (Figure 2.9).

The building took the form of a shallow arc, crowned by a dramatic, sailing roof. Its palette of materials – steel, glass, aluminium, tensile fabric – marked it out as a product of its age, but its external appearance was in fact shaped almost wholly by a response to its location. Hugging the brow of the hill on which it sits, the building curved subtly downwards from a high point at its centre where the greatest concentration of activity was converged. With views across Great Windsor Park, the grandstand was imagined as 'a building between trees'. Its roof was designed to replicate the wooded landscape through what its architect termed 'structural trees' – stylised tubular aluminium columns whose fanning 'branches' supported the parasol canopy (Figure 2.10).[29] A world away from the conventional grandstand appearance, its sleek lines and responsiveness to setting made for a unique building.

Internally, its design was no less intent upon dispensing with the traditional grandstand mould. 'The quality of the architecture and the improvements to the layout of the racecourse are hugely impressive, but most impressive of all is the improvement in the experience of the average racegoer,' commended the *Daily Telegraph*:

> Viewing facilities at racecourses are traditionally arranged horizontally; the less you pay the further away you are likely to be from the winning post. Ascot's vast new curving grandstand introduces vertical segregation: those in the cheap seats can be as close to the finishing line as those paying top prices. They will just be on a different level.[30]

In a unique move, Sheard vertically divided the whole building in two by inserting a huge central atrium, known as the galleria. Viewing accommodation was structured to the north of the galleria overlooking the track, while its southern elevation was given over to dining and catering facilities. This rational division of use was driven as much by the social character of the racecourse as by pragmatism. Ascot had long been more than a place to watch horseracing. 'This is a place for promenading, to see and be seen', Sheard recognised. Running the length of the building, the galleria was conceived as the ideal space for this promenading. Bathed in natural light (10,000 square metres or 110,000 square feet of glass was used in the stand), the galleria connected all aspects of the stand via 40 internal bridges and a network of escalators from which attendees could survey their fellow racegoers and be surveyed in turn. The building demonstrates that however important it is to address the logistical demands of a racecourse grandstand, the psychology of racegoing should play a fundamental role in their design. Ascot has always been about far more than horse racing alone and Sheard's design recognised this.

The scheme was a brave move on the part of Ascot Authority. Placing a wholly modern structure upon a site as venerated as Ascot is always going to court controversy. There were undoubtedly teething problems – notably the sightlines from the grandstand[31] - but the project was adroitly conceived. Ascot's history, in the form of the restored perimeter buildings, was not only recognised but also enhanced. It sits side by side with the modern. As such, Ascot has carried off a dexterous two-step; it has one foot in the future, whilst always treasuring its past.

Goodwood Racecourse

Sussex, UK

Since its founding at the beginning of the nineteenth century, Goodwood's architectural evolution has reflected many of the most significant chapters in the history of British racecourse design: the formation of a new grandstand typology in the 1830s, new grandstand buildings by the turf-loving Edwardians, and a resurgence of innovative design in the late twentieth and early twenty-first centuries.

A stranger would indeed be fastidious who did not consider the Goodwood Racecourse the perfection and paradise of racegrounds.

(A visitor, 1845[1])

Perched on a spur of the Sussex Downs 150 metres (500 feet) above sea level, the natural amphitheatre of Goodwood has proved to be a supreme location for a racecourse. Panoramic views sweep across rolling cornfields, undulating hills, ancient woodland and beyond, to the English Channel (Figure 2.12). 'Much has been written, and many have eulogised, about those views, but it rarely palls,' one recent commentator has extolled.[2] The consistently striking topography that envelopes Goodwood has drawn racegoers for over 200 years. The vista towards the medieval spire of Chichester Cathedral or the unfurling avenues of copper beaches is the stuff of panegyric. It is no stretch to imagine that views such as these would lure racegoers even if the racing at Goodwood faltered far below average. Amidst such emotive scenery, therefore, how can man-made buildings compete? Perhaps architecture is fated to play second fiddle at Goodwood, yet the story of its built environment is far from commonplace. Since its genesis at the start of the nineteenth century, Goodwood's evolution has fallen into three distinct chapters which parallel the most dynamic episodes in the trajectory of British racecourse design as a whole. And within these chapters, Goodwood's position has consistently been at the vanguard.

Legend has it that Goodwood's history began with a chance decision. By the turn of the nineteenth century, the third Earl of Egremont had for some years played host to a race meeting held by the Sussex Militia on his country estate, Petworth Park. In 1801, however, the Earl made a seemingly vagarious resolution to withdraw his patronage. In their disappointment, the officers appealed to their colonel, the third Duke of Richmond (1735-1806), for assistance. Richmond did not fail them. A major-general by the age of 26 and founder of the Royal Horse Artillery, the third duke was a military man. With Britain in the throes of the Napoleonic conflict, he was well aware that the militia required their fun. And so, in 1801, he invited the regiment to hold their race meeting at his Goodwood estate, marking the first staging of what was to become a venerable tradition.[3]

The Times wrote of the meeting that it was 'very well attended and afforded good sport', whilst the Sporting Magazine commended it was 'much admired by the acknowledged amateurs of the turf'. The races were run upon a triangular course and large pitched tents provided the sole accommodation. The event won such plaudits that a second meeting was planned for the following year, this time to be open to the public.

The 1802 meeting was the beginning of a permanent racecourse infrastructure at Goodwood. A small stand had been erected for the private use of Richmond and his most especial guests. Its architectural prowess left much to be desired, though. No records survive but it was built in the most rustic tradition of early viewing stands, a timber-framed structure with thatched roof providing elementary shelter from which to view the racing. It was not until the 1830s that Goodwood's architectural story truly began, when, under the tenure of the fifth Duke of Richmond (1791-1860), the racecourse was vaulted to national importance. The fifth duke marshalled a series of improvements: the course was relaid, gallops were set out (complete with the Victorian equivalent of all-weather surface) and a large grandstand was erected (Figure 2.13). 'To the exertions of the present Duke of Richmond, the celebrity which these races have now obtained is entirely owing,' chronicled one writer in 1839.[4] Credit did not lie exclusively with the duke, nonetheless. The transformation may never have materialised were it not for one man, Lord George Bentinck (1802-48).

Bentinck was amongst the most influential racing personalities of the century. As senior steward of the Jockey Club, he was a passionate reformer of the turf; his determination to root out skulduggery was relentless. He owned one of the greatest stables of the day, and competed as a 'gentleman rider' himself. Moreover, in the 1820s he forged a racing partnership with the fifth duke which began one of the most enterprising phases in Goodwood's history.

The precise starting date of Bentinck's involvement with Goodwood is lost to time, but by 1829 the course was being re-laid and the finishing straight was extended by two and a half furlongs. Bentinck is credited with several major innovations, not least the introduction of a pre-race parade, public saddling and varying-priced enclosures. The alterations elevated Goodwood from an interesting but essentially local meeting to one of Britain's leading courses, in the league of Ascot, Epsom and Newmarket.[5] Not least of the improvements was the erection of Goodwood's first grandstand in 1830. With this, opened the first chapter in Goodwood's architectural history.

The 1830s were important years for grandstand design in Britain. The eighteenth century had provided an effectual template for the grandstand genre, but as the nineteenth century progressed

growing numbers flocked to the nation's racecourses and this template no longer met the demands placed upon it. The eighteenth century models were simply too small to hold the burgeoning crowds, and moreover, they placed too great a priority upon social spaces in preference to spectator seating. In the 1830s, a revised formula for grandstand design was forged, and a new generation of stands was built. The first was Epsom's Grand Stand in 1829-30, but Goodwood followed close on its heels.

Built to replace the small, private stand which had been erected in 1802, Goodwood's new building was an archetypal illustration of British grandstand design in the second quarter of the nineteenth century. It melded the eighteenth-century model developed at York, Doncaster and other racecourses with, firstly, a significant aggrandisation in scale and, secondly, modifications such as raked benches within the principal rooms and on the roof top. Its

Page 170 **2.12** Goodwood from the air

Above **2.13** *Adine Leads in the Goodwood Stakes*, 1853. The three-tiered grandstand was erected in 1830, and in 1837 was expanded by the addition of the first-floor balcony

architect was a local man, George Draper. Measuring 36 by 21 metres (120 by 70 feet), it housed refreshment rooms on its ground floor, a glazed saloon with adjacent betting rooms on the first floor, and was topped by a large, steeply raked benched terrace, titled the Betting Stand.

> On the ground floor there are two large refreshment rooms, weighing room and other offices. The first floor – approached by two large staircases – is occupied by retiring rooms and a refreshment room ninety-six feet in length; and immediately above this is the Ladies Stand, ninety-six feet in length and forty feet in width, which being formed in a series of raised benches is capable (without crowding, or the least obstruction to a full view of the Course) of containing six hundreds persons... On the third floor is another refreshment room principally for the use of gentlemen who occupy the Betting Stand and through which they have egress thereto. The Stand when filled, is capable of containing nearly three thousand persons.[6]

From 1837, it also featured a balcony extending from the first-floor saloon. This balcony alone was capable of holding three or four hundred people.

The stand was a smaller, simpler building that that of Epsom's almost coeval precedent, reflective of the more modest status of the Goodwood meeting at the time, yet both shared a neo-classical vocabulary inherited from the first generation of grandstands in the eighteenth century. The front elevation of Goodwood's first floor was given over to a parade of tall arched windows, whilst its balcony was railed by a classical balustrade and upheld upon Doric columns.

'At once tasteful and convenient', 'elegant and commodious' – contemporaries enthused about the improvement that the new grandstand made to the course. 'I have read somewhere that perfection is not to be found on this earth; now, with due deference to the uttered judgement, I think I might safely challenge the assertion,' rhapsodised one visitor in 1840.[7] The enhancements of the 1830s pushed Goodwood to the vanguard of modern racecourses.

A weighing room, in classical style, followed in 1841, whilst the sum of refreshment booths, Punch and Judy tents, coconut stalls and others grew into a sea of pitched canopies around the racecourse's edge.[8] With the spread of rail travel, access to the course was expedited and numbers attending its high-summer annual meeting multiplied. Nonetheless, after the spate of activity in the 1830s which culminated in the weighing room, architectural development at the racecourse came to a standstill. Attendances continued to thrive, but for the rest of the century no new buildings were erected on its grounds. It comes as little surprise, then, that by the turn of the twentieth century its former gloss had faded.[9] Fortunately for Goodwood, when in 1903 the seventh Duke of Richmond (1845-1928) acceded to the title, he was determined to reverse this ebb.

The seventh duke was perhaps an unlikely white knight. Dour, punctilious, a stern military figure, he nevertheless had a passion for racing.[10] The trait came to bear in the commissioning of a new grandstand to replace the out-dated 1830 stand. Erected in 1903-4, its architect was Arthur Henderson, who had designed a grandstand (demolished 1972) at Sandown Park Racecourse which the sixth duke had much admired. Goodwood's new building epitomised the Edwardian grandstand in Britain. With a palette of red brick and decorative cast iron, it offered patrons two tiers of unenclosed seating overlooking the course. 'More than four times the length of the old stand, and stretching from the lawn to the boundary of the paddock,' wrote the *Chichester Observer and West Sussex Recorder* in May 1903, 'the new stand will have many advantages in addition to the enormous increase in accommodation which will be afforded.'

The grandstand was born of a spirit of renewal to restore the pride of the Goodwood meeting, and the endeavour was a resounding success. If the partnership of Bentinck and the fifth duke in the 1830s marked the first great chapter of racing at Goodwood, then this was the second. In racing history, no other generation had given themselves up so fully to the fervour of the turf as did the Edwardians. With more leisure time and disposable income than ever before, the British threw themselves into the whirl of race meetings, gambling, buying thoroughbreds and building studs. Racing became the national pastime at all levels of society.[11] Of no little importance in this was the influence of Edward VII, Britain's playboy monarch. Edward patronised the Sport of Kings with relish, and, given his friendship with the seventh duke, this included the Goodwood races. Amidst an exuberant eddy of high-spirited house parties, royal guests and unstinting entertainment, Goodwood arrived at its social apotheosis. Christened 'Glorious Goodwood', its July meeting became the apogee of the summer season for all, from the nobles of the land to labourers and shop hands. 'There is an atmosphere of gaiety and irresponsibility which one does not associate with any other meeting', explained a journalist in 1903.[12] It was 'really a garden party with racing tacked on', summarised Edward VII.

2.14 In the foreground the parade ring and to the rear the Trundle hill, Goodwood's 'glorious free grandstand'

Goodwood's new grandstand incorporated a specially-designed royal pavilion at the west end of the stand, for which no expense was spared. Its luxuriance was such that the king's lavatory was of monogrammed marble and mahogany. Amendments were made at the behest of Queen Alexandra, notably a subway which stretched from the main box at one end to the ladies' box at the other and to the paddock west of the stand. It allowed the queen to avoid 'the crowd which is always to be seen in front of the stand'.[13]

At the same time as the grandstand, a press stand was erected immediately to its west. Deemed by Nikolaus Pevsner, 'a jolly Edwardian building, like an enlarged Oxford college barge,' it echoed the red-brick and cast-iron fabric of the grandstand. The press stand – or Charlton Building as it became known – contained offices on its ground floor and stewards' and press balconies on the first floor.

The king's patronage boosted Goodwood's prestige and popularity, but it was not until a quarter of a century later that further physical expansion took place. The course's first public stand, the Lennox Stand, was a very different affair to its predecessors (built circa 1935-8). It was a red-brick structure built in stripped Art Deco style and it is the sole of Goodwood's buildings discussed hitherto that survives today. A single tier of concrete steppings was built above betting space beneath. Spare and utilitarian to the utmost, it is indicative of the attenuated depression years of the 1930s. Its appearance was, moreover, token of its purpose as lower-priced accommodation for the general public. This was emphasised by its position – far removed to the east of the grandstand and remote from the finishing line. Far more fortunate were those patrons privileged enough to gain admittance to the new Private Stand (later called the Richmond Stand). Opened in 1938 and capable of holding 2,400

(members only), it overlooked the head of the track from its front and the paddock from the rear. Conforming to the Goodwood palette of materials, it too was a red-brick structure.

With the coming of the motorcar, travelling to the racecourse was easier than ever before. Crowds swelled. By the 1950s, its summer festival drew a daily average of 50,000.[14] Over a third of this total, however, found accommodation not within Goodwood's four stands but on the natural grandstand known as the Trundle hill (Figures 2.14, 2.15). 'The most glorious free grandstand in the history of racing,' the Trundle had made for an ideal vantage point over the track and parade ring since the 1830s when, thanks to Lord Bentinck, 400 yards were added to the finishing straight extending it to the foot of the hill. On the Trundle, travelling vendors had jostled against strolling players and even acrobats, amidst refreshment booths, tented pavilions, shooting galleries and skittle alleys since the mid-nineteenth century. Its holiday spirit characterised the course.[15]

The Trundle's vista was checked, however, in 1976 when the parade ring was moved to the rear of the grandstand. Recent years have seen a tendency amongst racecourses to relocate their parade rings to more 'spectator-friendly' locations, Ascot (2006), Chantilly (2007), and Ayr (2008) being such examples; but in 1976, Goodwood was very much at the vanguard of that trend.[16] The relocation of the parade ring marked the beginning of a wholesale redevelopment programme shaped largely by architect Philip Dowson (1924-), which continued intermittently for the rest of the century. Within this programme, no project made greater impact upon the physical panorama of Goodwood than the building of the March Stand in 1980 (Figure 2.16).

1 March Stand
2 Sussex Stand
3 Parade Ring
4 Charlton Stand
5 Lennox Stand
6 Trundle Hill

0 20 40 60 80 100   200

N

Designed by the Howard Lobb Partnership and Dowson, the three-storey March Stand swept away the Edwardian grandstand, Charlton Building and Richmond Stand. Its rear façade was built upon a red-brick base and it incorporated cast-iron balustrades salvaged from the 1904 grandstand in concession to Goodwood's architectural heritage, but in all other respects it was resolutely modern. Dowson – who served as president of the Royal Academy from 1993-9 – had developed a distinctive approach to architecture which placed the science of function, construction technique and character of materials at the heart of his design. The precast concrete March Stand exemplified this philosophy. Precast concrete was employed to its most rational, lucid conclusion to create the stand's most striking feature, its roof. A vast, cantilevered canopy made up of ten lightweight elliptical vaults projected over stepped terraces. An example of cable-stayed design, the roof was supported by stainless steel tensioning cables. The building ranked amongst the era's few instances of large-scale modern design projects commissioned by a traditional landowner upon a country estate. The stand, though, prompted debate about more than just its aesthetic.

The March Stand espoused a theme common to post-war grandstands in that corporate entertainment was given precedence over the bread-and-butter racegoer. Goodwood was now 'in the entertainment industry', the Earl of March had announced in 1970.[17] The bottom level of unenclosed steppings was assigned to the public, while above were 30 glazed private boxes. Eighteen of these overlooked not the course but the paddock. It was the first time in the UK that this had been done and it was a controversial move. Esteemed racing commentator and correspondent Peter O'Sullevan bemoaned,

The paradox is that the only desirable viewing areas are being allocated to those who appreciate them least. Goodwood have proved it with their aesthetically laudable but practically less acceptable grandstand.... Here they have sold as many boxes facing the Solent as those looking onto the racecourse.[18]

The stand's configuration was a pronounced indication of the increasingly heavy reliance that the UK racing industry placed upon revenue earned from corporate hospitality.

Goodwood's bias towards the corporate racegoer did not go unnoticed. The racecourse came under fire from both the racing press and its membership for its neglect of the paying public. The reproaches, however, bore fruit. In 1987, Arup Associates led by Philip Dowson were appointed to prepare a master plan for Goodwood. The master plan began a new era for the racecourse. Over the next 15 years, it underwent an architectural transformation which yielded one of the most distinctive and well-designed environments of any sporting ground.

The reformation commenced with the opening of the Sussex Stand in 1990.[19] Its organisation was a breath of fresh air for the racing world. The Tattersalls public was allotted the best views from the top tier of the three-level stand, whilst the 'privileged' hospitality suites had to be content with the tier below. Flouting racing's traditional hierarchies, it was a comprehensive inverse of the formula of the decade-old March Stand.[20] No less refreshing was its aesthetic.

In many respects, the Sussex Stand adopted a conventional architectural approach. It was built upon a

2.16 The Sussex Stand (1990) with its tented canopy and, to its right, the March Stand with its cable-stayed roof (1980)

concrete base sheathed in red brick to harmonise with the adjacent March Stand. Likewise, its rear façade featured two tiers of balconies overlooking the parade ring, echoing faithfully those of the older grandstand. Less traditional, though, was its roof. The stand was crowned by a brilliant-white, fabric-canopy roof, seemingly floating above the lower tiers (Figure 2.16). It instantly made for a striking architectonic statement. Amidst the body of burly, bland concrete grandstands that had come to dominate racecourse design, the small, translucent Sussex Stand was something novel, rejuvenating. Inspired by the ocean of temporary tents and marquees that covered the racecourse during the summer months, the Sussex Stand was designed to be the largest of this cluster of canopies. It was to be a permanent manifestation of the 'garden party' atmosphere savoured by Edward VII. The lightweight canopy roof created a soft silhouette, whose agility and buoyancy brought into sharp relief the hefty bulk of the cantilevering concrete roof of the March Stand.[21]

The Sussex Stand was essentially a simple building, yet almost instantaneously its tented roof became an emblem of the relaxed, summertime ambiance of the Goodwood meeting. So successful was the structure, in fact, that when Goodwood came to remodel the course at the turn of the twenty-first century, it formed the starting point of the new scheme.

Following the opening of the Sussex Stand in 1990 the course had undergone a period of consolidation. More race days were added, sales totals grew, and its five-day summer meeting was cemented as one of the most important entries on the European flat-racing calendar. Yet, concerns mounted

that Goodwood was beginning to trail behind its competitors, particularly in terms of hospitality. It needed to move forward to contest with the demands of the new century, but this had to be done without diminishing its famous festive atmosphere. In 1997, the Hopkins Architects practice was engaged to determine how this could be achieved.

The heart of the new scheme lay in upgrading three of the racecourse's key spaces - the winners' enclosure, parade ring and weighing-in building, which had been relocated to the rear of the March Stand in 1976. The area was in acute need of rationalisation. It was a 'messy back-of-grandstand in which the flow of people from stand to ring was obstructed by the weighing-in building', wrote *The Architectural Review*.[22] Completed in 2001, Hopkins remodelled the parade ring, introduced three hospitality pavilions around its perimeter, removed the old weighing-in building and repositioned it within the new ring (Figures 1.92, 2.17).

From a hitherto obstructive structure, the weighing-in building became almost invisible. Built into the new retaining wall of the parade ring, it was designed to be effectively underground with a single-aspect glazed elevation overlooking the winners' enclosure and parade ring beyond. Wrapping around the weighing-in building and the parade ring were tiers of spectator steps bounded by neatly-clipped box hedge. The steps were made from flint, a particularly resonant choice of material for it has long been one of the most characteristic building materials of the South Downs landscape. Flint cottages and walls are plentiful sights in the immediate environs of the racecourse and its use within the parade ring instantaneously rooted the new addition within its historic topography. The most distinctive elements of the Hopkins scheme were, though, its three hospitality pavilions.

The pavilions were a light-weight, light-hearted reinterpretation of the canopy of Arup's Sussex Stand. Since Hopkins Architects' pioneering use of white masted tents for the Mound Stand at Lord's Cricket Ground in 1987, Michael Hopkins (1935-) had become perhaps the greatest practitioner of high-tech tent design. His exploitation of the canopy solution at a range of quintessentially British institutions such as Glyndebourne Opera House (1994) and Buckingham Palace (1995) had won him many plaudits by the time the firm came to upgrade Goodwood. The parade ring's three new pavilions followed identical plans: a central bar or servery was sheltered beneath a PVC fabric membrane structure supported upon a steel framework. Two of the pavilions were sheltered from the southerly winds with free-standing glass screens, but the principle of the design was to include as little structure as possible, not only to ensure unimpeded views over the parade ring but also to augment the Goodwood 'garden party' ethos.

The Sussex Stand and Parade Ring were essentially summer structures, in effect updated versions of the village green marquee or the white pitched tents which are indelibly associated with summer sports in Britain. The two schemes, although separated by over a decade, formed a harmonious entity which has cemented the course's identity as racing's 'garden party'. Their festal, open aesthetic represented a turning point for Goodwood, and for racecourse architecture in

the UK as a whole. Grandstand design was no longer confined to burly concrete automatons; leading architects of the likes of Dowson and Hopkins were entering the field and the result was lightweight, high-tech construction which combined pragmatic simplicity and attention to detail.

The open, masted construction of the Sussex Stand-Parade Ring ensemble delineates the culminating phase of Goodwood's physical history to date. This history is, in many respects, a very tidy one; following the first public meeting in 1802, Goodwood's architectural development can be broadly segmented into three key chapters: circa 1830, the 1900s, and the late twentieth century. These chapters mirror the most dynamic phases in the development of British racecourse architecture at large since the date of Goodwood's foundation: the reinterpretation of the established grandstand formula in the 1830s; the passion for racing amongst Edwardian society; and the resurgence of design in the late twentieth century, in which imaginative architecture became a focus for racecourses looking to set themselves ahead of their peers. In terms of architectural evolution, Goodwood can be said to be the archetypal British racecourse. But it is more that this. At each stage of its lifetime, Goodwood has been at the frontline of British racecourse design, consistently setting itself as a pioneer in its sphere. Goodwood's combined sense of continuity – in its repeated use of red brick and white canopies – and locality – capitalising on the quality of its views over the countryside and using vernacular flint, for instance – is unparalleled amongst Britain's courses and has invested it with a character all its own.

2.18 The Sussex Downs landscape, viewed from the Sussex Stand. Goodwood's natural setting is hard to rival

Hippodrome de Chantilly
Picardy, France

The Hippodrome de Chantilly is one of Europe's oldest and most prestigious racecourses. Its physical environment reflects this. Its architectural setting, although small in scale, is sophisticated and at its heart is the oldest surviving grandstand in France, built 1880-1.

One autumn evening in 1833, after a day of hunting Prince Lobanov emerged on horseback from the forest of Chantilly onto the vast grass sward that ran alongside it. Inspirited by the thrill of the day's hunt and the beauty of the setting, he and his companions made a wager: the first to arrive at the doors of the Great Stables (*Grandes Écuries*) on the opposite side of the lawn would win 100 louis. Lobanov lost the bet, but what he and his comrades discovered was perhaps a greater prize: a soft and silky terrain, ideal for racing. A year later, that grassy plain became home to the Hippodrome de Chantilly.

The Hippodrome de Chantilly is the oldest extant racecourse in France and one of the most picturesque in the world. Since the 1830s, *turfistes* have made annual pilgrimage to the hallowed ground some 40 kilometres (25 miles) north of Paris. Encircling the town, a domain of training tracks and stables covering 1,900 hectares (4,700 acres) forms the largest training centre in the country. Chantilly is certainly *la ville du cheval*. Its association with the horse is both long and deep-rooted, born long before the arrival of Prince Lobanov. The unique story of its racecourse and its beautiful setting can be traced back to another prince a century earlier, Louis-Henri de Bourbon, Prince of Condé (1692-1740).

Thanks to Louis-Henri, the hippodrome has one of the most spectacular backdrops in racing. At the far turn, for 185 metres (600 feet) the track is bounded by the *Grandes Écuries*, a magnificent structure commissioned by the prince in 1719 to house his hunting and carriage horses (Figure 2.19). To call it a stable would be a misnomer; the *Grandes Écuries* are nothing short of a palace. According to lore, Louis-Henri had an unshakeable conviction that,

after his death, he would be reincarnated as a horse. So he set about building the most beautiful stables in the world. Completed in 1736 to designs by architect Jean Aubert (circa 1680-1741), it consisted of a central octagon flanked by two long wings pierced by tall arched windows. Giving free rein to rococo bravura, Aubert adorned the facades with a plethora of sculpted keystones, bas-reliefs, pilasters and statues. Rearing horses were sculpted on its entrance portico, a symbolic winged Victory crowned the central octagon, while a sculpted repertoire of stags, wild boars, lions and hunting trophies completed the exuberant decoration. 'These stables are ridiculously beautiful,' commented the Prince de Ligne wryly in 1754. 'The building is more elaborate than the palaces of several kings together.'[1] What more fitting setting than this could be found for the heart-stopping contests run today on the lawn before it, some of the most celebrated in the thoroughbred calendar?

When the *Grandes Écuries* were built, however, the sport of racing was unheard of in France. The first races were held in 1776 on the Plaine des Sablons in Paris, but it was not truly until the 1820s that the sport was established in France upon the British model. A wave of anglomania had swept through France's upper echelons; everything and anything Anglo-Saxon was in vogue, the Turf being no exception. Around 1825, at the Rue Blanche in Paris, Briton Thomas Byron established an English Jockey Club and Pigeon-Shooting Club, an exclusive coterie of 18 members four of whom were British. From this sprang the birth, in 1833, of two associations: the French Jockey Club and the Société d'Encouragement pour l'Amélioration des Races de Chevaux en France (henceforth shortened here to Société). Their aim was twofold, to improve the breed of horses in France and to be an elite, luxurious and fashionable club. Headed by eccentric Englishman Lord Henry Seymour, their members included the royal princes duc d'Orléans and duc de Nemours. The Société organised match races in Paris's Bois de Boulogne, Champ-de-Mars (future site of the Eiffel Tower) and Versailles, but these were largely ad hoc stages without any such luxuries as grandstands. Moreover, their terrain left much to be desired. In 1833, 'save here and there in the provinces perhaps,' wrote one nineteenth-century authority, 'there were in France no racecourses on which a conscientious owner could invite a respectable horse to risk his limbs in a serious race'. The ground at the Champ-de-Mars and Versailles was condemned as 'simply detestable'. At Versailles, for example, 'in wet weather, the course was so deep in mud that the horses could hardly move, and in dry weather so hard as to endanger the strongest legs'.[2] The timely discovery of the quality of the plain at Chantilly must have, therefore, appeared fortuitous indeed.

The rich Chantilly estate had been inherited only a few years before by the young duc d'Aumale (1822-1897), fourth son of King Louis-Philippe. Aumale's tutor conveniently happened to be Société member, the duc d'Orléans, and thus the way was paved for racing to be held at Chantilly in the shadow of the *Grandes Écuries* under the aegis of the newly-formed Société. The first meeting took place on 15 May 1834. The town's residents were thrilled with the trade that the meeting brought and, when a second meeting was organised the following year, the municipality of Chantilly and the Société erected lightweight, temporary stands (Figures 2.20, 2.21).

Racing was still in its infancy in France, though. The industry was limited to approximately fourteen days of racing. 'And if the number of meetings was small,' wrote turf historian Robert Black, 'so

was the number of competing horses, and so was the value of the prix.'[3] The meetings drew a small, elite and dandified band of followers. 'All rich Paris, the Paris of the idle and the young, who know how to make even their leisure and their follies useful, had repaired to the vast *pelouse*,' wrote French critic Jules Gabriel Janin of Chantilly in 1844.[4] Chantilly was a new playground for fashionable haute society. Its audience was narrow and exclusive, but by 1847 its appeal was enough established for permanent stands to be built (Figure 1.20).

Commissioned by the duc d'Aumale, these buildings were the first permanent racecourse stands in France. Architect Grisard designed a grouping of three structures which accommodated a total of only 700 spectators. It made for a distinctive, influential ensemble, one that was very different to the tradition of racecourse architecture that had been pioneered in Britain. Société members and other privileged patrons were housed in two covered stands. Comparison

Page 184 **2.19** The *Grandes Écuries*, completed in 1736, form the majestic backdrop to the Hippodrome de Chantilly

Above **2.20** The running of the Prix Spécial in 1841. Three lightweight, temporary stands were erected in 1834, at the centre of which stood the *Tribune des Princes*

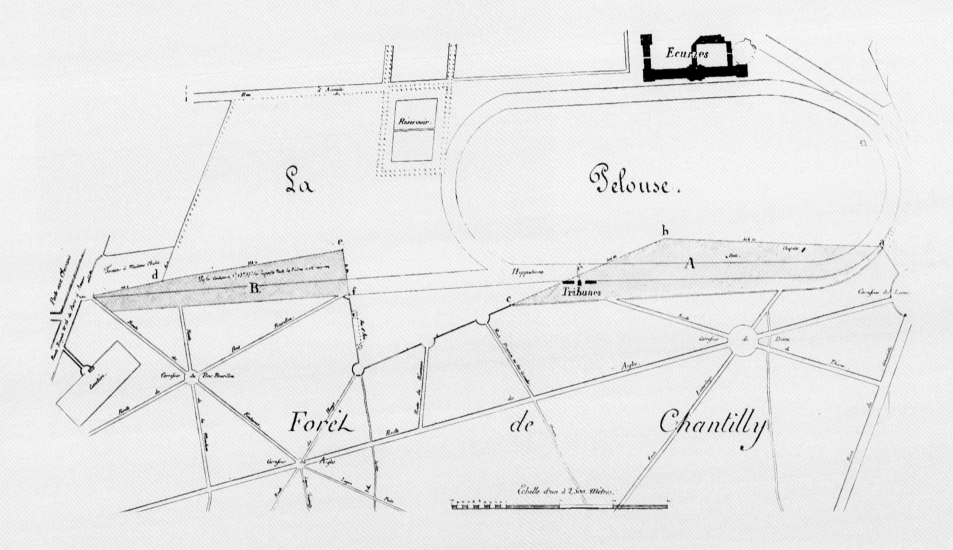

Ecuries

Reservoir

La   Pelouse.

B

d   A

Tribunes

Hippodrome

Forêt   de   Chantilly

Echelle d'un à 2,500. Mètres.

2.21 Plan of Chantilly, 1845. At the southern perimeter of the track stood the three stands, behind them grew the vast Chantilly Forest, and to the north presided the *Grandes Écuries*

with Ascot's grandstand built only eight years earlier shows the very different tenor which the buildings of French racecourses adopted from the outset. Chantilly's stands were not only smaller but also much simpler than the triple-storeyed, classical robustness of the British example. A single tier of raked benches overlooked the track; unlike Ascot's seating, they were open to the front and sides. The roof comprised a flat viewing platform, accessed by a square stair tower at the midpoint of the rear facade. The tower motif was to be a frequent one of French racecourses. They were not only functional circulation towers; they were also belvederes, offering panoramic views over track and paddock.

Chantilly's centrepiece was its so-called *Pavillon du Prince*, a small, two-storey pavilion reserved for the personal use of the duc d'Aumale. This stand-alone structure, reflective of the aristocratic provenance of the racecourse, was not of British inspiration. It is true that Ascot had since the early nineteenth century possessed a royal stand, but it is the sole example of such an edifice in the British Isles. There was no tradition for this building type in earlier racecourse architecture, and yet it was to become an almost ubiquitous motif on the major racecourses founded in nineteenth-century France. Longchamp (1857), for instance, had its Pavillon de l'Empereur, as did Vincennes (1863) and Auteuil (1873). Chantilly's *Pavillon du Prince* had a cruciform plan with a glazed octagonal salon overlooking the track. From its rear rose a tower, taller than those of the other stands. The tower's upper level was glazed and gave forth onto a flat viewing balcony.

All three structures shared a particular stylistic vocabulary, the so-called *pittoresque* style. This was the architectural language of leisure in mid nineteenth-century France. Inspired by the chalets of Switzerland, *pittoresque* houses populated popular holiday towns; Napoléon III commissioned a private *pittoresque* chalet in the Bois de Boulogne. Chantilly's prominent timber construction, its wide eaves, large exposed brackets and balconies railed with carved wooden balustrades were symptomatic of the style. On the rear facades of all three of the buildings, timber balconies overlooking the paddock were a conspicuous feature. The paddock was a planned aspect of the original layout. Situated to the rear of the stands, it was a semi-circular space delineated by stalls, a stewards' room, weighing room and covered gallery.

The layout of the stands and paddock buildings was hierarchical and multipartite, and it was united by a common architectural vocabulary. This was a 'set-piece' design approach. This approach, the antithesis of the incremental development of British racecourses, set a lasting precedent in France. Chantilly's layout and style characterised the first generation of French racecourse construction, also embodied by Longchamp, Vincennes and Enghien (1879), as the sport slowly but steadily gained a hold.

Between 1840 and 1845, the number of horses in training in France increased three-fold. During the Second Empire of 1852-70, economic expansion, moreover, brought to France an era of prosperity which was by no means unfavourable to the racing world. New racing stables were created, old ones grew in size, and the breeding of thoroughbreds in France advanced in strides.[5] The

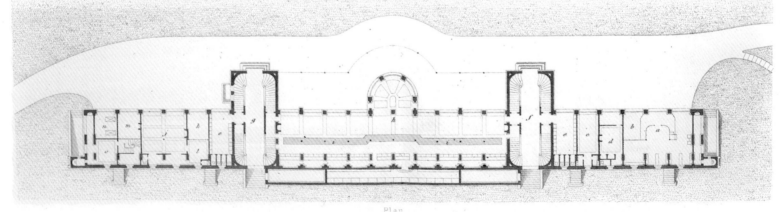

Plan
à 0.m.0025 p.r mètre

Opposite **2.22** *Grande Tribune*
(1880-1), designed by architect Honoré
Daumet and built to hold Chantilly's
growing crowds

Right **2.23** The *Tribune du Prince*
(1880-1) was substantially altered and
enlarged in 1891 and circa 2002

number of meetings grew, as did the number of entrants, the value
of the purses and popular interest. In 1873, the Société held 23 days
of racing; by 1890 this had risen to 35. From 1871 to 1890, no less than
125 publications on the theme of racing and breeding were printed.[6]
Chantilly never drew the mass audiences of Longchamp with its city-
centre location, but its tally of racing days and popularity gradually
grew, helped in some measure by the arrival of the Paris to Chantilly
railway line in 1859. Inevitably, it outgrew its 1847 buildings.

In 1879, it was decided to rebuild. The decision was not solely
a matter of replacing its timeworn stand; the track was enlarged and
its buildings were relocated westwards and southwards to allow this
reconfiguration. The duc d'Aumale contributed 250,000 francs towards
the redevelopment, of a total cost of 560,000 francs. By this time, the duc
had earned himself a reputation as a distinguished patron. A discerning
art collector, he spent a lifetime amassing a celebrated portfolio of
paintings, sculpture and manuscripts. His long-lasting affiliation with
artistic and architectural projects earned him election to the French
Academy and Academy of Beaux-Arts in 1873 and 1880 respectively.
Moreover, from the 1870s to 80s, he reconstructed the Renaissance
Chateau de Chantilly which had suffered extensively during the
Revolution, engaging Honoré Daumet (1826-1911) as his architect. It was
Daumet that the duc selected to design the hippodrome's new buildings.

Daumet's buildings were altogether more substantial than
those they replaced, both in size and fabric. Capable of holding over
3,000, they used a palate of cast iron and ashlar stone. Furthermore,
they diverged from the layout of the 1847 ensemble. Under Daumet's
plan, three structures were reduced to two: a *Grande Tribune* (Figure
2.22) and a *Tribune du Prince* to the west (Figure 2.23) (built 1880-1).

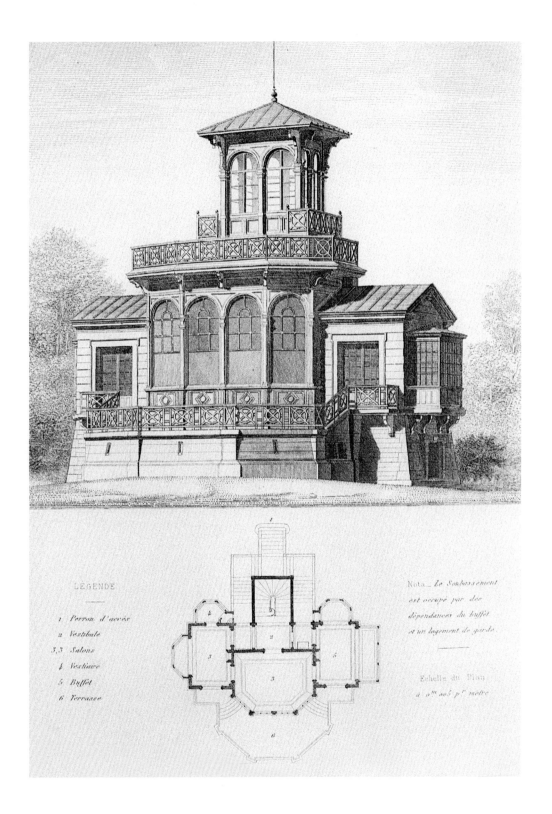

1 Grande Tribune
2 Tribune du Comité
3 Parade Ring
4 Weighing Room
5 Old Weighing Room
6 Grandes Écuries

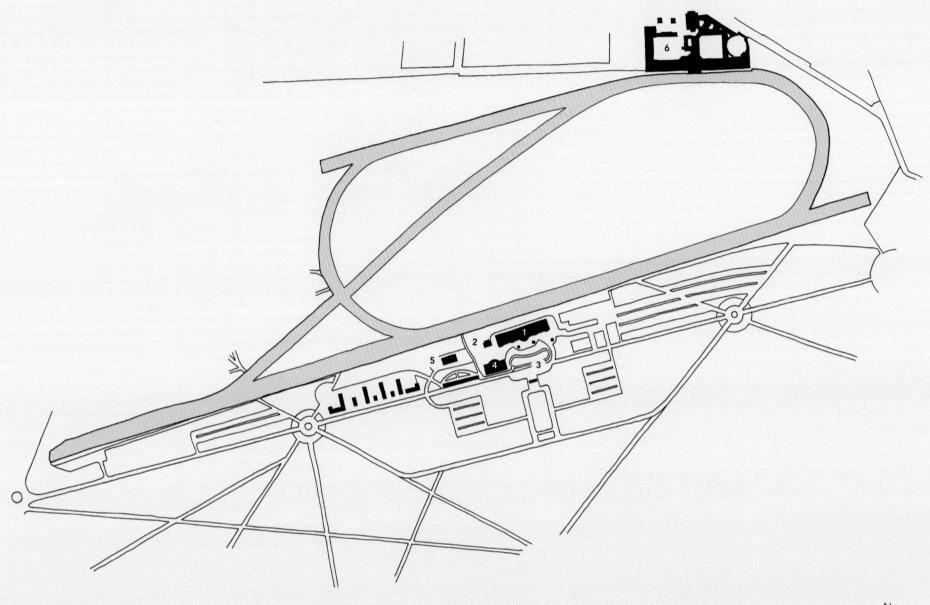

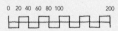
0 20 40 60 80 100   200

N

Stylistically, the *Tribune du Prince* echoed its predecessor; the *Grande Tribune*, though, represented a marked step in architectural evolution. It was classical in its bearing. From the rear façade of the long, rectangular building, a semi-circular rotunda projected. To either side stood a square stair tower, yielding panoramic vistas from the upper storey, which also gave access to the tiered, uncovered rooftop seating. An arcade articulated its rear façade, sculpted horse-head medallions filled the pediments of the towers, and curving consoles embellished entrances and stairways. Its simple, classical mien and repertoire of stone and cast iron were symptomatic of the second generation of racecourse architecture in France, of which Chantilly was a prescient example. The stand survives today as the oldest grandstand of any racecourse in the country.

Additions followed. In 1891, the *Tribune du Prince* – or *Tribune du Comité* as it is now known – was substantially altered by architect Saint-Ange, to create a larger, taller stand in ashlar stone with three tiers of balconies overlooking the track (Figure 2.24). Two decades later, in 1911 a brick and timber weighing pavilion was designed by Daumet's pupil Charles Girault (1851–1932). The paddock and pavilion had been relocated to the west of the *Tribune du Comité*. Girault's building was basic in style, more evocative of the *pittoresque* 1847 stands than Daumet's noble stone grandstand. Its rear façade was lined with horse stalls (removed circa 1948) and in 1962 a simple tiered terrace was built atop its roof.[7]

The 1960s, and the decade either side, were years of modernisation for French racecourses. Venues such as Saint-Cloud (1955), Longchamp (1966) and Maisons-Laffitte (1972) replaced their historic fabric with bigger, modern grandstands. Thankfully

for posterity, Chantilly's nineteenth-century structures escaped the bulldozer. With its elegant stands, sweeping expanses of soft, manicured turf, breath-taking backdrop of the *Grandes Écuries*, and the natural beauty of the neighbouring forest, Chantilly was by this time regularly heralded as the world's most beautiful racecourse.[8]

The last significant new building erected at Chantilly had been the weighing pavilion in 1911. Its physical evolution had stood more or less still. From a preservation or historic standpoint, this was no bad thing; however, by the 1990s, its untouched facilities almost caused its demise.[9] After years without investment, Chantilly's future seemed bleak. 'No amount of elegance can disguise the genteel shabbiness of the environment,' one journalist lamented in 1994.

> The setting cannot be matched, but the grandstand, the stabling, the facilities are now flawed, and it will take more than a coat of paint to put them right. The place needs a lot of money spent on it, for safety and aesthetic purposes.[10]

2.24 *Grande Tribune* and *Tribune du Prince* – now named the *Tribune du Comité* – rank amongst the world's oldest surviving racecourse buildings

The French racing industry was in a parlous condition. Betting revenue was sinking, crowds were down, and a government financial contribution in 1992 was made on condition that at least one Ile-de-France course would be closed. By the opening of 1994, nine out of the 12 members of French racing's ruling body voted to close Chantilly with immediate effect; its celebrated fixtures the Prix du Jockey Club and Prix de Diane were provisionally scheduled at Longchamp. 'Now it is almost certainly defunct,' augured one British newspaper.[11] Chantilly, though, got its eleventh-hour saviour. A consortium of local advocates, the Institut de France and the Aga Khan, owner of an extensive training facility in the town, formulated a last-minute rescue package. With that, Chantilly set out onto the slow road towards modernisation.

In 2005, the first phase of a two-stage physical redevelopment of the racecourse was completed. Architectural firms Claude Penloup and Didier Lefort Architectes extended the *Grande Tribune* with the creation of a panoramic restaurant on the first floor, basement kitchens, press room and private boxes (Figure 2.25). The redevelopment was complicated because the site stood in the shadow of significant historic monuments – namely the Chateau and *Grandes Écuries* – not to mention that the grandstand itself was a protected structure. Building constraints were consequently tight. Nevertheless, for the second stage of the plan, permission was secured to realign the road running behind the grandstand, pushing it back into the protected forest territory. This was no mean feat.[12] The displacement of the road allowed a new paddock to be laid out behind the grandstand, repeating the original 1847 arrangement. Hitherto, the trek to and from the paddock at the west end of the complex had been an inconveniently long one for racegoers. A sunken,

kidney bean-shaped parade ring was completed in 2007, flanked by a new weighing room with roof-top terrace and complemented by new entrances and landscaped parking. The weighing room was somewhat uninspiring in its architecture, with none of the charm of the nineteenth-century structures. Its aridity was, though, partly redeemed by the use of stone cladding to harmonise with these neighbours. The new layout was, nonetheless, an unmitigated success. The displacement of the road and re-siting of the paddock greatly ameliorated circulation; no longer was the public tightly compressed along the finishing straight. Overwhelmingly, reaction to the redevelopment of the hallowed site was positive, not least because with its completion Chantilly's future was secure. 'These days, the track is state-of-the-art, yet it has retained its old world charm', praised the *Daily Telegraph* upon the unveiling of the new facilities.[13]

The graciousness of Chantilly's environment is world-renowned. Its stately nineteenth-century stands have the effect of a time warp, transporting today's racegoers back to that golden age of racing. Its *Grande Tribune* is, indeed, one of the oldest functioning grandstands in the world. Chantilly's architecture is remarkable, though, not only for the heritage that survives today, but also for the vanguard position it has held in piloting French racecourse design. Its 1847 stands codified the nature of the building typology in France, providing a template for the first generation of racecourse structures there, whilst its *Grande Tribune*, built 1880-1, was a precocious example of the second generation. In 1934 one Australian journalist wrote that Chantilly 'has been the birthplace, the nursery, and the academy of the Turf'.[15] Undoubtedly, it has also been the birthplace, nursery and academy of French Turf architecture.

2.25 *Grande Tribune*. In 2005 the building underwent a major remodelling comprising glazed flanking extensions, semi-circular drum on rear façade, and the glazing of the front elevation

Saratoga Race Course
New York, USA

Saratoga Race Course is the oldest sporting venue in the United States.
Unlike many other racecourses, it has largely resisted the temptation
to raze and rebuild its facilities in a race to modernise. Therefore,
today, it stands peerless amongst American courses for the extent and
quality of its historic fabric.

For try as their builders and sponsors may try to duplicate or even approach duplication of the picturesque Saratoga track and its incomparable atmosphere, there is only one Saratoga. New tracks may come, some of them stay and some of them go, but Saratoga goes on forever. And it will continue to exist and prosper as long as there are sportsmen and sportswomen whose pulses quicken to the beat of flying hooves and whose red blood tingles at the sight of a good-looking thoroughbred racing in the beautiful setting his royal lineage deserves.

(Dick Powers, 'Clear and Fast', *Times Union*, July 30, 1939)

To visit Saratoga Race Course is to engage, whether knowingly or not, in a pilgrimage. In an age when sporting traditions are more manufactured than made, Saratoga's spirit of romance and history stands as a beacon. Nestled in leafy Saratoga Springs in up-state New York, it is America's oldest sporting venue; and this is no empty rubric. The racecourse is a multi-layered tapestry of trees and buildings, a visible product of decades worth of growth since the colourful days of the nineteenth century when Saratoga's first racing circuit came into being.

When the nineteenth century opened, barely 1,000 travellers passed through Saratoga Springs in any one year; by 1900, the picturesque, upstate New York town was attracting almost 200,000 visitors annually.[1] With the help of a handful of visionary individuals, the tiny community in the southern foothills of the Adirondack Mountains had transformed itself into the 'Queen of Spas', where pleasure seekers from across the land were drawn to its hotels and boarding houses, to enter into its round of dancing, banquets and gaming. Two of these visionaries were Alfonso Patten and James M. Cole, one a local butcher and the other a livery keeper. Seizing upon the arrival

of the New York State Fair in Saratoga in the summer of 1847, the pair laid out a new trotting track – Saratoga Springs's first racing circuit. Its oval track had a seven-furlong circumference alongside which was built a grandstand. Little else is known of Saratoga's first racecourse. While the *New York Herald* sneered that 'such an establishment is not much of a recommendation for the morals of a neighbourhood', the trotting course was largely enthusiastically received.[2] Its site is well known today as the location of the present-day Horse Haven, Saratoga's bucolic training and stabling ground.

Several buildings still standing at Horse Haven date from this early period, notably an ice house, farmhouse and large barn all bearing Greek Revival detailing typical of pre-1850 domestic construction in the United States. As the racing venture prospered scattered groupings of stables appeared on the infield. Dating probably from the late 1840s to early 1860s, they were timber-framed structures all built to a basic formula of single-loaded stalls below a half-storey loft space roofed with slate. They continue to be as much a part of the Saratoga season today as they were in the days of Patten and Cole.

For 16 years Horse Haven served as the popular staging ground of Saratoga's trotting races, but the town's racing credentials were about to step up a gear. On 3 August 1863 while bitter civil war was consuming the nation, thousands gathered to watch Lizzie W., a three-year old filly, beat the colt Captain Moore to the post in the first race of an experimental meeting of thoroughbred running races at Saratoga's trotting course. The 1863 meeting was the brainchild of one of the biggest, if

Page 196 **2.26** Saratoga Race Course, an aerial view circa 1940s

Above **2.27** The Carpenter Gothic-style grandstand, erected in 1864

not the biggest personalities in American gambling history – John Morrissey. With 'sledgehammer fists', a ruthless ambition and visionary ingenuity, Morrissey propelled himself from an impoverished childhood as an illiterate Irish immigrant, to become the nation's first sporting hero, a New York gambling tycoon, and an influential politician.

The meeting was a resounding success, and on the day after the last race Morrissey drew together a band of society magnates and turf enthusiasts to found a jockey club – the Saratoga Association. A new track was summarily planned on land opposite the trotting course. It opened on 2 August 1864 to a jubilant reception. Its opening was a landmark day in American sporting history – the track was the United States' first modern sports facility and one which continues today as the oldest extant example in the country.

The complex featured an eight-furlong circuit and a simple, timber grandstand, architecturally modest but functionally appropriate (Figure 2.27). Raked tiered seating for spectators was

provided beneath a slate gable roof, below which were 'retiring and refreshment rooms, ladies boudoirs and every needful convenience'.[3] The building's sole decoration were the shamrock-shaped 'gingerbread' cut-outs on its gable ends, evocative of the Carpenter Gothic architectural style, a curious nineteenth-century hybrid unique to America. Judging by the commendations of the contemporary press, the complex was an uncontested hit. 'Neither pains nor expense have been spared to render it perfect in all departments,' rhapsodised one commentator. It was 'a model institution', he continued.[4]

Nevertheless, in the last decade of the nineteenth century, Morrissey's 'model institution' was thoroughly transformed by a comprehensive architectural remodelling under the aegis of the course's new owner, Gottfried 'Dutch Fred' Walbaum. Walbaum was an ignominious figure of the New York underworld who, it was reported, made his money running a brothel and gambling house in Manhattan as well as the Guttenberg track in New Jersey, a track so notorious that it became 'a synonym for all the crookedness…in

SARATOGA RACING ASSOCIATION.

WATER JUMP IN FRONT OF GRAND STAND.

RACING DURING JULY AND AUGUST IN EACH YEAR.

the horse-racing business'.[5] Yet it was during the tenure of this unlikely architectural patron that in 1892 Saratoga entered its golden age of architecture with an inspired state-of-the-art racing complex featuring a new grandstand, clubhouse and betting ring (Figure 2.28).

Its architect, Herbert Langford Warren (1857-1917), injected a sense of style into what had previously been an essentially sober and serviceable building type. Warren was a renowned figure in Boston's Arts and Crafts movement, who had studied under one of the nineteenth century's most celebrated architects, H. H. Richardson, and by the time of his death was dean of Harvard's School of Architecture. Regrettably, of the complex that Warren designed at Saratoga, only the grandstand survives today. It is not only the oldest stand still in use in American thoroughbred racing, but moreover the oldest continuously-used stand of any professional sport in the country.

Extending 60 metres (200 feet) in length, the grandstand was a timber building with raked seating. Its basic construction was spartan and functional, but it was crowned with a strikingly unique feature – a vast slate roof supported by a timber trusswork system (Figure 2.29). The roof's sweeping silhouette, dominated by clusters of sloping turrets at its centre and ends made for an iconic outline. It was reflective of the widespread popularity of the Queen Anne style in United States architecture between circa 1880 and 1910, in which steeply sloping roofs were a key feature. The roof was carried upon a heavy timber frame of exposed Howe trusses. Its most unique

and distinctive feature was the cross-bracing that extended along the grandstand's roof plate, which made for a singularly bold and effective motif. While the frame was undoubtedly a structural device, under Warren's skillful hand it was elevated to a decorative piece of design in its own right.

At the western end of the grandstand, Warren designed a clubhouse (replaced 1928). A two-storey, timber-framed structure, it was built smaller, lower and at an angle to the grandstand. Its steep, slate gable roof with a peak at either end provided a continuation of the horizontality of the grandstand's roof and extended over the clubhouse's elegant, curving, double-height

Opposite **2.28** From left to right, the clubhouse, grandstand and betting ring, designed by Herbert Langford Warren in 1892

Above **2.29** Racing, against the backdrop of the sloping peaks of the grandstand's iconic roof

Opposite **2.30** The Saddling Shed (built 1902) stood at the heart of the paddock, where horses, jockeys and fans co-mingled informally

Above **2.31** The clubhouse, grandstand and betting ring, photographed circa 1940. The clubhouse, built 1928, replaced the 1892 version

veranda which projected outwards onto the trackside. The roof's overhanging eaves and conical peaks again evoked the Queen Anne style, but other design influences were at work too. The long and low profile, overhanging eaves, and exposed timber structure of the structure equally revealed the contemporary vogue for Japonisme – the taste for the arts of Japan. Japan had opened its doors to the West in the 1850s, precipitating a flurry of American interest in its architecture. The fashion was most emphatic in Warren's design for the betting ring.

The betting ring (demolished 1963) stood at the opposite end of the grandstand. It was a single-storey, exposed timber-framed construction which housed the stalls, or cages,

of the bookmakers. The pavilion was open to all sides, but a long, low slate roof sheltered the bookmakers from above. Like the clubhouse and the grandstand, the roof was the building's distinguishing motif. From a hipped peak, the slate roof sloped gently outwards into flaring, overhanging eaves making for a low and swooping silhouette.

The new complex was nothing short of an architectural revolution. For the first time, the racecourse's pleasure-seeking patrons could enjoy the sport in surroundings not only commodious but at the height of architectural fashion. However, beneath the surface all was far from well. Walbaum's infamy caused a media storm and a tidal wave of antigambling sentiment. Many of the most prominent stables deserted Saratoga and racing programmes languished. The track drew an unprofitable and insalubrious crowd and the resort as a whole was tarnished.

Mercifully, though, a savior emerged in the form of politician, speculator and scion of one of the country's most prominent families – William Collins Whitney. The public-spirited lodestar of New York society, Whitney had a distinguished record as the corporate counsel of New York City; had served as secretary of the navy under President Cleveland; and had made his fortune in the heady days of American industrial expansion.

In 1900 he joined forces with financier and Saratoga partisan, Richard T. Wilson Jr., to rescue Saratoga Race Course, and the following year bought out the vilified Walbaum. No sooner than the deal was done, the reborn Saratoga Association led by Whitney embarked upon an immediate and momentous transformation of the course. The buildings, backstretch and landscape were coordinated in an integrated design under the direction of landscape engineer Charles Leavitt (1871-1928). Leavitt produced the earliest-known master plan of the Saratoga Race Course. The circuit was enlarged from eight to nine furlongs, rotated 25 degrees and slid westwards. The grandstand was lengthened, increasing its seating capacity by fifty per cent to 6,000, and rotated to accord with the new track layout. To the rear of the clubhouse, a vast saddling shed (76 x 22 metres, 250 x 72 feet) was erected (extant). Containing 25 stalls, it was here that the horses were saddled and paraded on rainy days until 1963 (Figure 2.30). Akin to the spirit of the grandstand and clubhouse, it was a

simple, timber-framed structure with an exposed, heavy timber truss frame which upheld a slate mansard roof.

The saddling shed stood at the heart of the paddock, a vast lawn behind the clubhouse within the wider expanse of the Back Yard. The paddock was the location of the great Saratoga tradition that took place from the earliest days of the Saratoga Association - the saddling of the horses under the trees surrounded by the racetrack community of jockeys, grooms, trainers, owners, and clientele.[6] The groupings of tall trees that populated the paddock served as informal stalls and exercise rings where the pre-race saddling ritual took place, unless of course rain drove it under the cover of the saddling shed. Anyone and everyone could here get within touching distance of the equine stars; no fences separated the public.

Substantial sums were spent to create a garden idyll in the track environs. Trees were planted throughout and at the main entrance, a new gate created an impressive, well-groomed street frontage. 'The track was always a beautiful spot,' wrote the November 1902 edition of *Munsey's Magazine*, 'under the magic touch of its new owners it became a paradise.'

From the late 1920s, the frontside as Dutch Fred or Whitney would have known it changed considerably. It was a time of growing attendances at Saratoga Race Course, and the demand for boxes outstripped supply. 'Society Throngs Clubhouse at Spa; Stands Prove Inadequate for Crowds', ran a *New York Times* headline on 21 August, 1927. The 1892 Queen

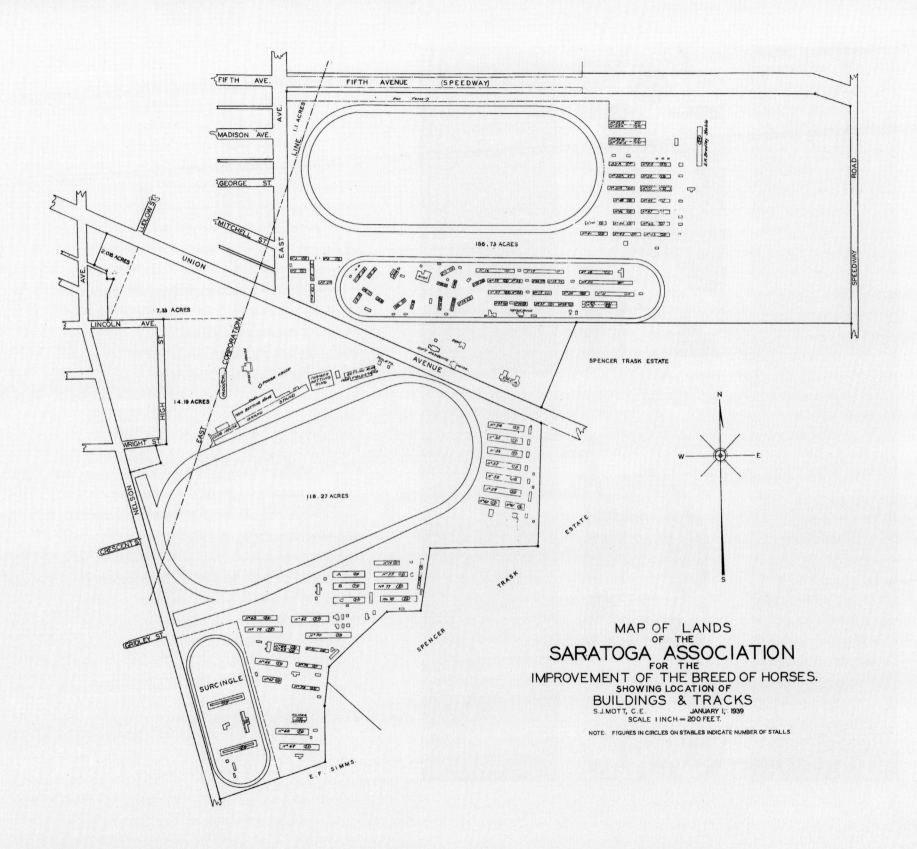

MAP OF LANDS
OF THE
SARATOGA ASSOCIATION
FOR THE
IMPROVEMENT OF THE BREED OF HORSES.
SHOWING LOCATION OF
BUILDINGS & TRACKS
S.J. MOTT, C.E.   JANUARY 1, 1939.
SCALE 1 INCH = 200 FEET.

NOTE: FIGURES IN CIRCLES ON STABLES INDICATE NUMBER OF STALLS

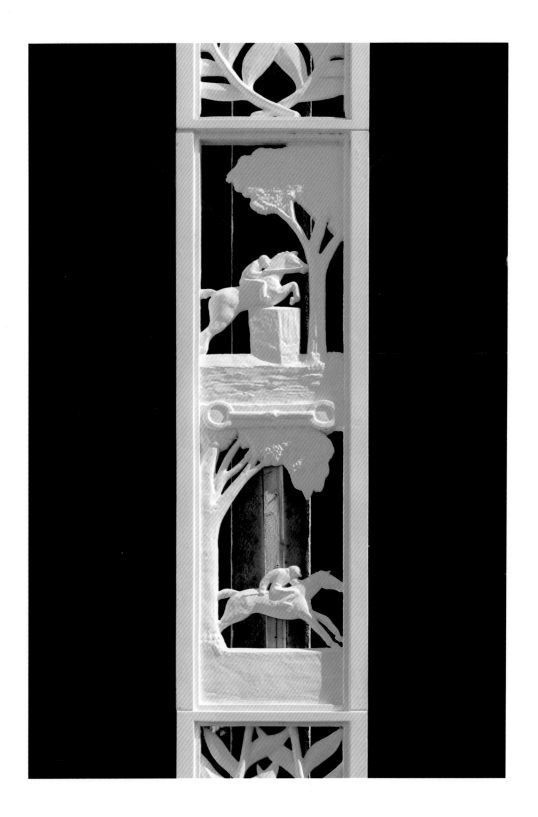

Anne Clubhouse, while picturesque, was simply too small and in 1928 it was supplanted by a substantially larger replacement which directly abutted the grandstand and still stands today (Figure 2.31). At three storeys tall, the steel-framed clubhouse towered over the grandstand. Gone was the curving outline of the old clubhouse, this was a long, rectangular structure roofed by a simple slate mansard roof with a single finial at each end. It had none of the drama or imagination of the sloping planes of the Victorian structures. The building's most distinctive feature was its western end, where architect Samuel Adams Clark had created an august-looking porch, referred to as the 'Landing Stage'. Bringing a touch of Ancient Greece to Saratoga, it consisted of two rows of thickly-set Doric columns, heavily fluted and emphatically tapered which upheld the floor above.

From 1937 to 1945, the architectural character of the whole complex changed with the appointment of architectural firm Marcus T. Reynolds to design two consecutive betting ring extensions to the rear of the grandstand and clubhouse (Figure 2.32). Although largely unsung since his death, Reynolds was a leading Albany architect, creating some of the city's greatest landmarks at a time when it was experiencing a golden age. The two conjoined extensions ran the entire length of the grandstand-clubhouse complex, consisting of ground-floor betting space to accommodate the state-wide legalisation of pari-mutuel machines in 1939 and an open terrace on the upper level:

> Every detailed piece of reconstruction has been worked out to accomplish two purposes – elimination of crowded conditions and convenience to patrons and employees. And, at the same time,

construction has been so modelled that rather than detracting from the natural beauty of the long-famous track it adds to the advantages by modern building in style of simple good taste.[7]

In sharp contrast to the dark wood and slate-roofed Victorian grandstand and 1928 clubhouse, the Reynolds addition made extensive use of metal roofs and ornamental white cast iron. The ground floor featured cast-iron panels imaginatively shaped into racing scenes (Figure 2.33) and horse-head brackets; matching cast-iron grilles railed the terrace. The extensions were painted white, as were the rear and side elevations of the grandstand and clubhouse too. The distinctive design aesthetic of crisp white paint and ornamental iron work has been integral to Saratoga's environment ever since and has been echoed in construction projects of the ensuing decades.

The construction projects of the post-war decades did not, perhaps, treat Saratoga kindly but its historic fabric arguably fared better than that of many of its peers. These were years of profound change for New York racing. Since the Civil War, New York had been the fountainhead of American racing. The charm, glamour and high-quality racing of the metropolitan Jerome and Morris Parks and up-state Saratoga drew wealthy patrons and the best stables to the state. Yet by the mid twentieth century, a handful of other states was challenging its crown and, both in prestige and financial health, the New York industry was floundering. Fortunately, a white knight was ready to spring into action.

The white knight came in the form of a three-man committee of entrepreneurial Jockey Club members who quickly set to work establishing a non-profit corporation to purchase New York's four principal tracks – Saratoga, Belmont Park, Aqueduct and Jamaica. Inaugurated in 1955, this was the New York Racing Association (NYRA). NYRA had big plans. Aqueduct (opened 1894) was rebuilt as a state-of-the-art modern racing facility, completed in 1959; Jamaica (opened 1903) was scheduled for closure as soon as the new Aqueduct was complete; Belmont Park (established 1905) was rebuilt from 1962-8, opening in time for the 100th running of the Belmont Stakes. Attendances at New York courses surged, and the money

Opposite **2.33** 1930s additions introduced cast iron decoration to the racecourse

Above **2.34** The distinctive design vocabulary of the 1930s additions included carved wooden horse-head brackets

rolled in. Amidst this spurt of activity, though, Saratoga was left comparatively unheeded. By 1959, nearly $34 million had been expended on Aqueduct and over $7 million on Belmont Park, compared to $1 million on Saratoga. This may well have resulted from Saratoga's sequestered Hudson Valley location. Had the Adirondack Northway been complete by the 1950s, perhaps Saratoga's buildings too would have been razed in favour of a vast, contemporary, Aqueduct-like complex. Posterity can only be thankful for this accident of history.

Saratoga was not forgotten completely, though. In 1965, work was completed on a 150-metre (500-feet) extension to the Victorian grandstand by Arthur Froehlich and Associates. The firm may have been the doyen of state-of-the-art racecourse architecture, working at Belmont Park and Roosevelt Raceway in New York amongst others, but it was less renowned for sensitive extensions to historic buildings. This experience was pronounced at venerable Saratoga. Whilst the Froehlich stand reproduced the elongated shape and height of the elevation of the Walbaum/ Whitney era grandstand, little attempt was made to achieve more than a superficial continuity between the new and the old. The steel frame of the addition was a marked contrast to the wooden trusses of the original building. Moreover, the beauty of the sweeping outlines of the Victorian grandstand was not replicated. While two turrets capped with golden finials were incorporated into the roof of the new extension, the relationship between the 1965 stand and the 1902 structure was merely perfunctory. The latter had a gently curvilinear profile, but the 1960s roof was rigidly angular and pitched at a milder angle,

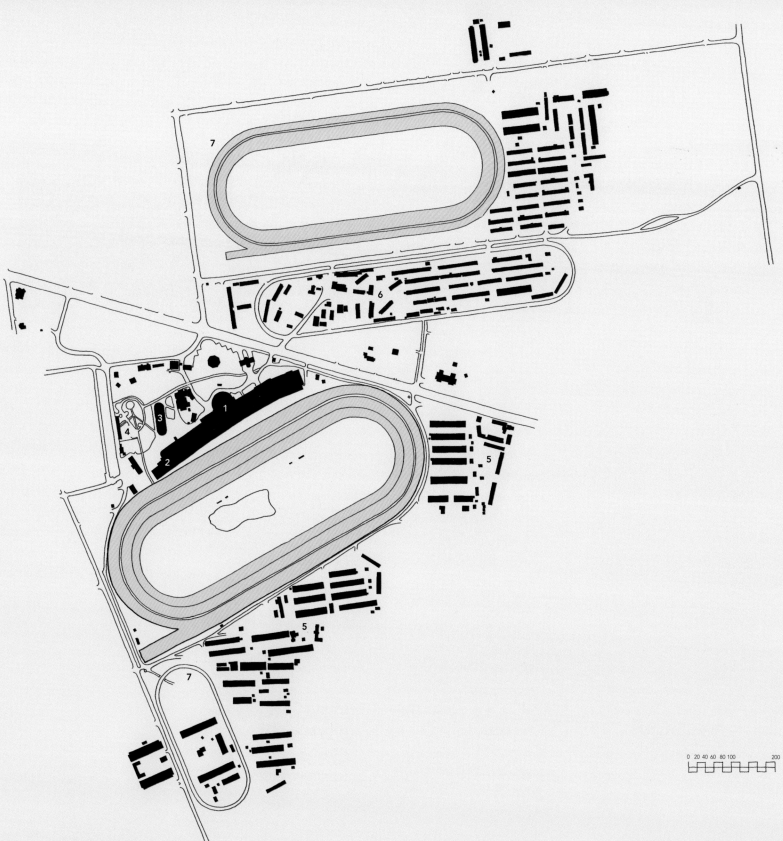

1 Grandstand
2 Clubhouse
3 Saddling Shed
4 Parade Ring
5 Stables
6 Horse Haven
7 Training Track

0 20 40 60 80 100   200

N

resulting in an awkward intersection between the two roofs. The grandstand may now have been fit to shelter modern crowds, but this was arguably at the expense of its quality of design. This insensitive precedent was followed by a major remodelling of the grandstand's rear façade two decades later.

With racing's traditional fan base ageing, enticing new and younger crowds was imperative to NYRA and the means to achive this, the association concluded, was by providing modern amenities. The rear grandstand extension was a manifestation of this (Figure 2.35). From 1985 to 1991, a great semicircular pavilion was erected extending from the building. Christened the Carousel Pavilion, the two-storey building housed food concessions, television monitors, and seating designed by Philadelphia architects, Ewing Cole Cherry Parsky. It mimicked the white horse-head bracket details and sloping, standing-seam metal roof of the Reynolds era, yet it made for a lacklustre addition to the track. Unlike the Reynolds' extensions, the cast iron horse heads had no supportive function and were applied decoratively to the

outer face of the steel columns which upheld the structure. The result was pastiche.

Yet, notwithstanding the unwise and insensitive additions made to Saratoga in the past half century, the underlying historic fabric that remains is unparalleled in North America. Throughout its lifetime, it has resisted the urge to raze and rebuild bigger and better. It has admittedly suffered losses – principally the clubhouse and betting ring, both sophisticated examples of design – but Saratoga Race Course has been for the most part very fortunate that since the late nineteenth century its owners have largely taken an additive approach rather than that of the wrecker's ball. Saratoga is peerless in the integrity of its historical fabric which gives physical expression to over 160 years of continuous evolution. The lofty trees, the festal cast-iron equine decoration, and the soaring planes of the grandstand's roofline are a tangible chronicle of sporting, architectural and national history. At Saratoga, history can be seen, touched and sensed. And this is why, despite uncomfortable seats and no air conditioning, legions of fans return year after year to Saratoga's famous summer meeting.

2.36 The trackside panorama of the twenty-first century

Opposite 2.37 Saratoga Race Course today

Club Hipico de Santiago
Santiago, Chile

The Club Hipico de Santiago is a beautiful, architecturally eccentric example of 'whole-cloth' racecourse design, physically expressing the golden era of horse racing in South America in the early decades of the twentieth century. Its original master plan and architecture have been carefully preserved by succeeding generations.

Chile's oldest racecourse is one of the world's most beautiful. The Club Hipico's palatial complex is a vast green oasis at the south east of Santiago's bustling city centre. Together with the adjoining Parque O'Higgins, it forms the metropolis's largest open space. Yet it acts not only as the lungs of the city, but forms a physical expression of a momentous urban and architectural revolution in Santiago's history.

The design and inception of the racecourse is intimately woven with the development of the city itself. The second half of the nineteenth century was a period of far-reaching, unforeseen transformations in Chile and above all in Santiago, the country's political and economic hub. Domestic revolutions in 1851, 1859 and 1891, foreign wars in 1866 and 1879-84, plus new-found prosperity through the mining of potassium nitrate, silver and coal resulted in profound economic, cultural, architectural and urban changes, not least the emergence of an ambitious bourgeoisie. Changes in thinking brought about by the nineteenth-century Enlightenment and a desire to break away from retrospective Hispanic culture nurtured an era in which Chile looked to Europe, particularly France, as a model for modern civilisation, especially for artistic inspiration. An influx of European immigrants to Santiago brought not only a supply of skilled labour and architects but moreover exposure to new styles and tastes. From the 1870s to the 1920s, the Chilean state and burgeoning bourgeois society made fervent use of European architectural models as a cogent tool to ennoble themselves, transforming the visual and cultural panorama of its cities.

The neo-Romanesque, Gothic Revival, Florentine Renaissance and Beaux-Arts flourished side by side in a Latin-American architectural amalgam. So long as the new buildings lay claim to the ideal of civilised Europe, it was a stylistic free-for-all.[1]

Santiago was bent upon becoming a splendid European city and determined to supplant its 'colonial drowsiness' with the vivacity of modern life. To Chileans, the epitome of this was Paris. The colonial city of adobe houses, rarely exceeding two storeys in height, underwent an urban transformation, as new plazas, parks, and promenades were shaped by town planners and foreign architects. New neighbourhoods were created to the south and west of the city, with a predominantly French flavour. In 1872 alone, at least 340 new buildings were erected in the most conspicuous of the new neighbourhoods, known as the 'enlightened city', all marked by lavish expenditure. It was on the edge of this neighbourhood that the Parque O'Higgins and Club Hipico were sited.[2]

Whilst the park was modelled on Paris's Bois de Boulogne, the Club Hipico was envisioned as Santiago's very own Longchamp. To contemporaries, if Santiago was to fully evolve into a leading modern city, it was imperative that it possessed its own racecourse. The Club Hipico ran its first races in 1870. Horses had been introduced to South America by Iberian conquistadors, and by the eighteenth century straight sprint match races were daily events in towns across the continent. These traditional *carreras a la chilena* were displaced, however, in the mid-nineteenth century by

Page 212 **2.38** The Members' Stand, the chef d'oeuvre of the Club Hipico de Santiago

Right **2.39** Members' Stand trackside elevation

carreras a la inglesa (English-style turf racing). Santiago's first jockey club, the Sociedad Hipica de Chile, was inaugurated in 1866, but it soon gave way to the Club Hipico de Santiago, founded in 1869. The new association laid out a course on land opposite the Parque O'Higgins to designs by French architect Lucien Henault, and it immediately became a leading venue for Santiago's elite.

The expansion of the club's property in 1907 prompted it to engage French landscape designer Guillermo Renner to beautify its setting. Avenues of oriental plane trees were planted around its periphery in evocation of the Bois de Boulogne, and a wholesale remodelling of the course's buildings was planned (although this did not begin until 1918). The design of the new buildings was entrusted to architect Josué Smith Solar (1867-1938), who devised a set-piece ensemble perfectly attuned to Santiago's infatuation with all things European.

Although a native Chilean, Smith was well versed in western architectural fashions. Born to a Chilean mother and American father, he trained in Philadelphia and toured Europe from 1889 to 1891, when he returned to the US to open an office in Wilmington, Delaware. When he relocated to Santiago in 1894 to set up in architectural practice, his experience abroad gave him a distinct professional advantage and, moreover, a taste for the eclectic which came to characterise his work. The Club Hipico was Smith's first major project. He was to control each of its building projects for many years to come, first working alone and then in partnership with his son José Smith Miller.[3]

In 1918 Smith produced a general plan for the facility. Three grandstands – one exclusive Members' Stand and two for the general public - were positioned on the west side of the track with views across the Andes, and formal gardens were laid out at the rear. Their design was a fundamental expression of Santiago culture at the time. The complex was built as a platform for social encounters and worldliness, a place for Santiago's elite to see and be seen and it was situated within the wealthy new 'enlightened city', which was populated by huge historicist mansions. Smith's designs were smoothly attuned to this context. His buildings were impressively splendid and suitably lavish, resonant of the prevailing historicism of the neighbourhood.

The Members' Stand was the chef d'oeuvre of Smith's complex (Figure 2.38). Its rear façade was the representative face of the racecourse, which welcomed the race-going elite upon entering its gates and it was composed of a skilful blend of various styles. Its basic formula was derived from the stands built at Longchamp in 1904. Longchamp was France's premiere racing venue, its popularity greatly enhanced by its location on the outskirts of Paris just as the Club Hipico was sited at the edge of Santiago. Its clientele and its ambiance appeared the height of Parisian chic to Santiago's aspirant society and, moreover, the designs of its 1904 grandstands were internationally recognised. No evidence suggests that Smith made a first-hand visit to the French course, but his designs bore a striking parity (Figure 1.50). Like its Parisian forerunner, the length of the Club Hipico stand was divided into three sections by four projecting square towers. The trackside elevation featured tiered seating beneath a concrete, cantilevered canopy and an uncovered terrace above (Figure 2.39). On the rear elevation, the design was governed by symmetry and a rhythmical procession of arched and rectangular windows. The Club Hipico Members' Stand was, however, larger than any at Longchamp. It rose six storeys tall and stretched 121 metres (400 feet) in length. Furthermore, it demonstrated a unique stylistic fluidity. Whilst echoing the Parisian stand's Beaux-Arts architecture in its symmetry, its balustraded towers (Figure 2.40), arched windows and doors, and bold consoles, Smith enriched his building with touches of Florentine palazzo, Renaissance chateau and medieval Italy. This eclecticism would characterise the whole of the racecourse's physical fabric.

Smith was an architect known for his love of detail. From festooned consoles, to oversized keystones, balustraded balconies and Grecian urns, there are few surfaces of the Members' Stand left unembellished. Each storey is differentiated by window type and decoration. The building's four stair towers were ornamented with a melange of Renaissance-inspired heraldic reliefs, sculpted winged horses, and medieval barbed quatrefoil windows. The two central towers were lit by bands of diagonal windows, which both identified their function as stair towers and interrupted the horizontal rhythm of the building with a vertical accent. The ground floor of the stand was given over to a cathedral-crypt-like space, a vast marble-floored salon beneath a groin-vaulted ceiling.

The emblem of the club - the initials CHS intertwined in a florid, classicist design - was emblazoned across the facade within its wrought iron balconies, stamped in stucco on the consoles, and in miniature form on the window handles. The motto was repeated in wrought iron on the exuberant entrance gates which led to the formal sunken garden and Members' Stand. Each of the three grandstands had its own entrance gate, differentiated in style to accord with the prestige of the stand. That of the Members' Stand was the most ornate (Figure 2.41). Consisting of a curving white stucco wall with black iron gates at its centre, the entrance was bedecked with a plethora of classical detail. Stately orbs, wrought iron lamps and urns crowned each pillar; cornucopias, garlands and antique grotesques filled its stucco surfaces. Its rococo profusion was the prelude to a ceremonial sunken garden. Designed by Guillermo Renner, who was responsible for a number of city parks and gardens in central Chile, it was a French-inspired parterre with a fountain at its centre. Like the grandstand, it was of rigidly axial design with its line of symmetry leading the eye directly from the entrance gate to the centre point of the stand.

The garden's ceremonious classicism was complemented by a grandiose odeon, or musicians' pavilion, at the north end of the Members' Stand (Figure 2.42). This Grecian temple was the utmost symbol of unrestrained splendour. Here, in this half-domed, semi-circular building, musicians would play to entertain the club's members within their palatial stand. With classical pilasters, balustrades, swags, urns, the building gave full vent to Smith's neo-classical imagination.

Smith's historicising architecture made the seamless transition to Quattrocento Italy in his designs for two further tribunes, to the south of the grandstand (Figure 2.43). Built lower and smaller than the members' pavilion, these two public stands were rusticated cement structures with raked seating on two levels overlooking the track. Much simpler than the Members' Stand, they were redolent of the Renaissance architecture of rustic Tuscany. With none of the French Empire swagger of the members' grandstand, they derived their interest from tall stair-towers crowned by peaked roofs upon open timber frames and polychromatic stonework in bands and roundels. On these, as on all his buildings on the property, Smith proudly identified himself as their designer by plaques placed on their exteriors.

Moving from Italy to Iberia, the paddock to the rear of the grandstands was given a Mission Revival flavour (Figure 2.44). Inspired by eighteenth-century Spanish Franciscan mission churches of the south-west United States, from the late nineteenth century to

Above left **2.41** The impressive Members' Stand entrance gate

Above right **2.42** The odeon, where musicians would play to entertain racegoers

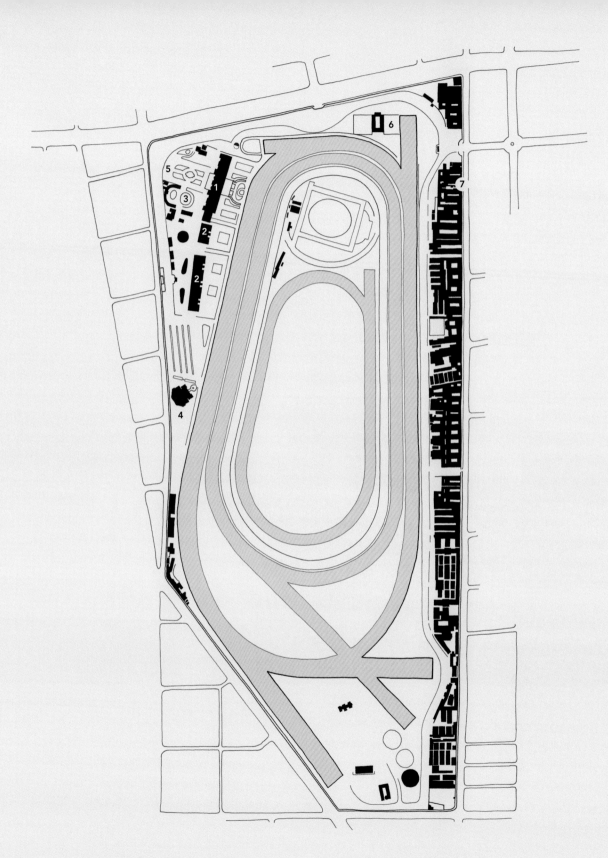

1 Members' Stand
2 Public Stand
3 Paddock
4 Administrator's House
5 Entrance Garden
6 Club House
7 Stables

Opposite **2.43** Trackside panorama. In the foreground is the Members' Stand and beyond are the two public stands

Right **2.44** The paddock. Architect Josué Smith Solar introduced a Mission Revival flavour to its stalls

the 1920s the Mission Revival movement transformed the architectural panorama of California, from whence it spread. The stalls at the western perimeter of the Club Hipico's oval saddling arena bore the round-arched openings, low-pitched roofs sheathed in red tiles, white stucco walls, barbed quatrefoil windows, plus a bell tower-like projection at its centre, which characterised the style. To either side of the paddock were office and jockey buildings which continued the mission theme. Here, the round arched windows, heavy wooden doors, overhanging eaves, and intricately carved wooden trim which typified mission architecture were fused with flourishes of Baroque swags and cornucopias applied to their stucco surfaces.

Mission revival was married with English Arts and Crafts in the architecture of the administrator's house south of the paddock complex (Figure 2.45). With strong resemblance to Smith's typical residential oeuvre, the white-stucco house had a charming asymmetry redolent of the Arts and Crafts movement. The silhouette of its shingle roof was a composite of peaked gables, an eyebrow dormer and polygonal turret; a tower extended from its front façade giving wide-angled aerial views across the racing circuit; and windows came in all shapes and sizes from roundels, to rectangles to lunettes, reflecting the internal arrangements of the property. The entrance porch bore all the hallmarks of the Mission Revival. It featured three round arches and decorative tiles on the façade, shaded by the building's overhanging eaves (Figure 2.46).

Smith's complex was completed in 1927 with a club house at the north east turn of the track. This was not a clubhouse in the convention of American courses. It was not designed as another stand; indeed it had no view over the course at all. A place for Club Hipico members to socialise, dine and relax, it was a chalet with tennis courts and swimming pool at

2.45 The administrators' house introduced domestic-scale design to the Club Hipico

Opposite **2.46** The spacious, arched portico of the administrators' house

the rear. As revealed by the building's signatory plaque, the chalet was the work of Smith in partnership with his son, José Smith Miller. It introduced yet another architectural idiom to the Club Hipico's historicist facility, this time of English neo-Tudor inspiration. Faux half-timbering characterised the building, both internally and on the ends of its projecting gable roofs. At the rear, however, the architects introduced an Italianate motif in the form of a colonnaded arbour surrounding the pool sheltered by vines and upheld by texturised stucco piers. Arbours were a favoured motif of Smith Sr., used frequently in his domestic work and even upon the roof level of the members' grandstand (later replaced by an additional storey).

This jamboree of architectural genres may easily have resulted in an overpowering confusion of styles. Yet Smith's bold combination of historical styles yielded a unique composition that perfectly expressed the mores of the age. Academic classicism, baroque exuberance and rustic Mission Revival worked in parallel, united by symmetry, grandeur, inventiveness and quality. What is more, almost all of Smith's original concept has been preserved by succeeding generations. The Club Hipico is not only the best example of the diversity of Smith's work within a single property, but also arguably the most awe-inspiring, imaginative and picturesque example of racecourse building of its age.

Santa Anita Park
California, USA

Built in 1934, Santa Anita Park was the first in a series of new courses to open in California following the end of a prolonged gambling ban. It is a superlative example of how consummate planning and sleek architecture was used by this generation of racecourses to attract patrons and set themselves apart from competitors.

In December 1934, the dark cloud of the Great Depression loomed low over the United States. In the city of Arcadia, however, a chink of light gleamed through. On Christmas Day, shortly after half past one in the afternoon, cheers rang jubilant through the air in Arcadia, 23 kilometres (14 miles) from Los Angeles. A brown mare named Las Palmas became the first horse to pass the finishing line at California's first new racecourse in over a quarter of a century – Santa Anita Park. Amidst a glittering fanfare comparable only to the biggest movie premieres, a crowd of over 30,000 eagerly poured through its doors on opening day. Many had never attended a race meeting before, many were more concerned with securing a glimpse of the host of movie stars present; but all were enthralled with the spectacle that was presented to them. Santa Anita Park was 'one of the show places of the world,' applauded the *Los Angeles Times*.[1]

Santa Anita's oval circuit, its stabling for 1,000 horses, and its sleek, aquamarine grandstand had been built in a mere nine months on an 80-hectare (200-acre) tract of land once owned by the early California pioneer and legendary horseman Elias 'Lucky' Baldwin. It was Baldwin, in fact, who first dreamt of building a

course there against the rugged backdrop of the San Gabriel Mountains. Baldwin had already established his reputation as a foolhardy speculator and libertine, when in 1875 he purchased the large estate and christened it Rancho Santa Anita. There, he established probably the best stable of the day and in 1907 embarked on the project which would ultimately prove his undoing. That year, on a lot just southeast of the present racecourse, Baldwin opened Rancho Santa Anita's first track (Figure 2.48). The eight-furlong oval was dubbed 'the prettiest track in America', but its success was shortlived. A fatalistic shadow was about to be cast upon North America's racing industry. From east coast to west, moral reform movements had been gaining momentum since the late nineteenth century. Politicians vowed to reclaim the nation's moral fibre by rooting out iniquity in all its guises. As places closely associated with drinking and gambling, racecourses were especial targets for reformist vitriol. Baldwin's circuit operated for a mere two seasons before, in early 1909, the California Legislature passed an anti-gambling bill. The day before the legislation was formally

Page 224 **2.47** The sleek, Streamline Moderne grandstand façade of Santa Anita Park, opened on Christmas Day 1934

Above **2.48** Lucky Baldwin's original Santa Anita racecourse. It operated for a mere two years from 1907-9

approved, Lucky Baldwin collapsed and never recovered.[2] The bill tolled the death knell for racing statewide. The outlawing of bookmakers in California in 1909 ended racing in the state for 25 years, and Baldwin's Santa Anita fell into disuse. It was destroyed by fire in 1912.

In the early 1930s, however, economic privations dampened the influence of the anti-gambling lobby. Impoverished state governments began to look to racecourse wagering less as the root of all corruption, and more as a source of easy and much-needed revenue. With the widespread legalisation of the pari-mutuel machine – a wagering system perceived as far more honest than the old-time bookmakers and one that gave state authorities a share of each bet made – circuits up and down the country began to resume business. Following California's repeal of the ban in 1933, sportsmen across the state clamoured to revive the Sport of Kings.

As early as spring 1932, rumours of a revived Santa Anita racetrack were rife. And the rumours proved to be true when Baldwin's daughter Anita – now owner of the Rancho – joined in partnership with Joseph Smoot, who, only a few years earlier, had built a track at Hialeah in Florida. The pair established the Los Angeles Jockey Club and, by July, excavation work had begun. Smoot had grand plans. The new venue was to be a lavish Colonial Mission creation designed by prominent local firm, Walker and Eisen. In March 1933, however, work on site came to a standstill. Amidst suggestions of infighting and unpaid bills, the Jockey Club offices were shut down, Smoot faded from view and the Arcadia property

was left abandoned.[3] Not for long though. Santa Anita's potential was quickly realised by another duo determined to win the race to bring racing back to the Golden State. They were Hal Roach and Dr. Charles Strub.

Surprisingly, Charles 'Doc' Strub was a dentist by profession. He was, though, an entrepreneurial dentist with a passion for sports whose successful string of offices enabled him to generate the capital to first become an owner of the San Francisco Seals baseball club, and then to join forces with filmmaker Hal Roach to form the Los Angeles Turf Club. To Roach and Strub, the uniquely dramatic setting of Baldwin's ranch framed by a mountainous backdrop was the ideal location to build a racecourse to rival all others.

Raising the necessary funds for the Club was a gruelling process; Strub later recalled literally going 'from door to door', eventually selling the 200 shares at $5,000 each which enabled the fledgling organisation to purchase an 87-hectare (214-acre) tract to the east of the Smoot excavation. Once ground was broken in March 1934, construction on Santa Anita Park progressed rapidly.[4]

From the outset, Santa Anita Park was designed to be different. Billed as the 'million-dollar racetrack with the $100,000 horse race', it immediately grabbed headlines for offering the first six-figure prize money in history.[5] Prodigious purses may have been used to draw the best horses, jockeys and trainers, but it was arguably the quality of the physical experience that made Santa Anita an enduring success. From the project's conception, the design

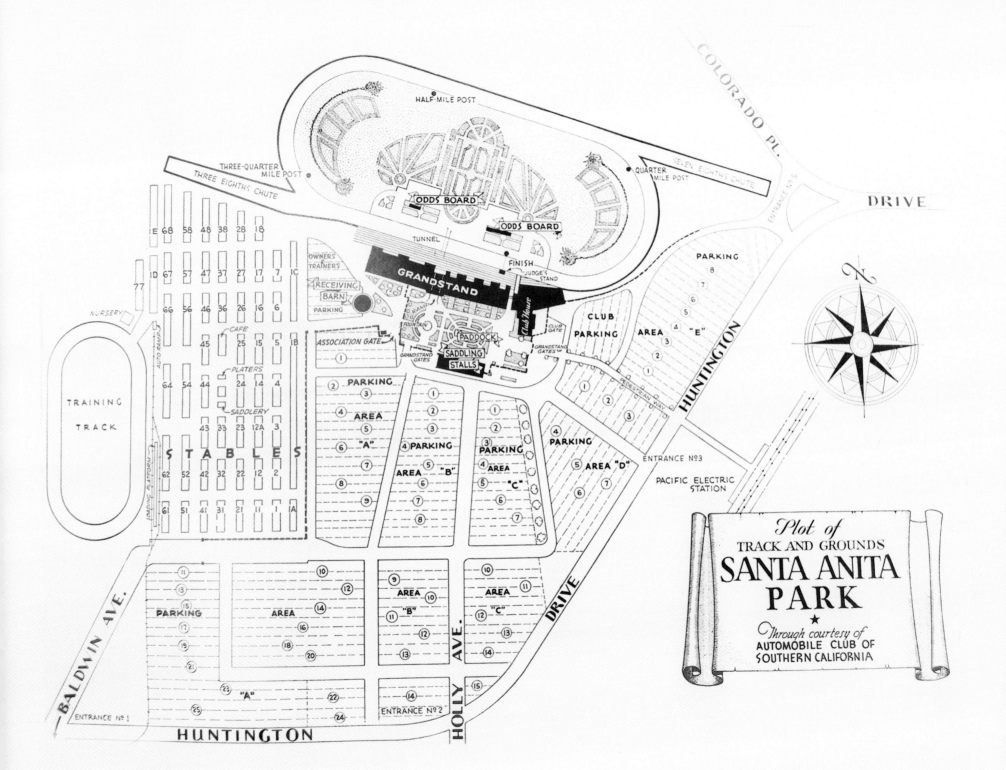

quality of the built environment was perceived as a vital
ingredient in its future and Strub was determined that his
racecourse needed to stand out for its architecture and
landscape. Conscious of the lingering stigma which had
led moral reformists to suppress the industry in 1909 and
mindful of competition from already-established venues
such as Agua Caliente in Tijuana, Tanforan near San
Francisco and Hialeah in Florida, Santa Anita had to be
more than a place to gamble; it had to be a spectacle. And
so, Strub set about with the aim of building the world's most
luxurious racecourse (Figure 2.49). To realise this, he spent
lavishly. Lore has it that he spent so profusely, in fact, that
by opening day no money was available for the ticket sellers
to make change.

Leading Los Angeles architect Gordon B. Kaufmann
(1888-1949) was engaged as architect of the scheme. By the
1930s, Kaufmann was a noted member of the architectural
establishment and creator of several high-profile projects,
including Scripps College in Claremont (1926), California
Institute of Technology (1928) and the Hoover Dam (1935).
Reflecting the stylistic tenor of southern California, his
work embodied Mission Revival, Art Deco, Streamline
Moderne and the International styles across his career.
Kaufmann was a 'conservative modernist' and, as such, the
ideal architect to create for Santa Anita a sophisticated yet
uncontroversial image.[6]

Never before had Kaufmann been commissioned
to design a racecourse, and he undertook a tour of racing

clubs across North America. He was left dismayed. All,
he observed, 'were very much alike and reflected more or
less stereotyped methods of planning and treatment'.[7] He
resolved to create at Santa Anita an architecture 'expressive
of the colourful aspects of the sport'. The result was in many
ways characteristic of his oeuvre at this time in its skillful
combination of the traditional and modern. Whilst Strub was
insistent upon high design quality, he did not impose stylistic
prescriptions upon his architect. Kaufmann chose to fuse
stripped classical revival accents with a principally modern
Art Deco scheme, the former expressed in the clubhouse and
the latter in the grandstand.

Opposite **2.49** Santa Anita Park
was comprehensively planned by
architect Gordon B. Kaufmann.
Provision was made for car parking
on an unprecedentedly large scale

Above **2.50** Trackside elevation
of clubhouse and grandstand,
photographed in 1942

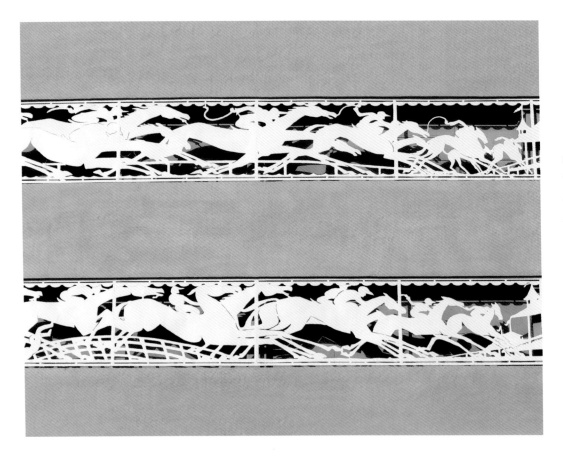

conveyed the spirit of modernism specific to 1930s Los Angeles. The Streamline Moderne, as its style was known, articulated the speed and image of the Machine Age. The image of speed was a particularly apt one for a racecourse, and Kaufmann's façade gave Santa Anita a distinct identity. This was made more pronounced by its distinctive blue-green colour and beige metal cutouts, the chromatic scheme which remains today.

In the years that followed, the building grew and grew. In 1937 a small, stand-alone grandstand was built to the west of the original structure, and the following year the two stands were conjoined, more than doubling its original seating capacity to 20,000.[9] Designed by Kaufmann, the new work reproduced the colouration and distinctive metal panels of the original stand. It was during this phase of work that the grandstand acquired perhaps its most idiosyncratic feature, a tall entrance pavilion topped with celebratory flags. Exuding Art Deco flair, the pavilion created the sole vertical accent on Santa Anita's horizontal façade. Four streamlined, engaged pilasters framed vertically-fluted panels, above which emblazoned letters spelling 'Santa Anita Park'. Further additions followed in 1948 and 1953.

The sleek Deco lines of the grandstand were not, though, replicated in the clubhouse. This had a stripped Georgian and Colonial Revival aesthetic not unlike some of Kaufmann's residential commissions. The clubhouse was designed as an independent and freestanding structure, joined to the grandstand by a bridge. It was a two-storey building with a curving entrance portico supported by paired slender columns

The steel-framed grandstand epitomised Los Angeles's architecture of entertainment in the 1930s. The 1934 stand was roughly a third of the length of the present building. Its trackside, or north, elevation adopted the conventional format of tiered seating upon simple concrete bleachers sheltered by a cantilevered roof (Figure 2.50). Its south exterior expressed the spirit of Moderne. The façade was vertically split into five bays and each bay was further divided horizontally by two strips of banding, 15 metres wide by nearly 2 metres in height (50 feet by six feet), alternately containing a punched metal frieze of racing horses and louvers (Figure 2.51).[8] With its emphatic horizontal direction, the building

projecting from its eastern elevation. Its symmetrically-arranged shuttered windows, the beltcourse trim, and classical urns crowning the building 'might well grace an old southern mansion', conjectured one contemporary commentator.[10] Like the grandstand, the clubhouse was soon enlarged. In 1937, Kaufmann added a three-storey wing to the north, espousing the same aesthetic as the original wing (Figure 2.52). Its stucco façade was regimentally symmetrical, and coursed by emphatic horizontal cordons and cornice lines. Pilasters split the elevation into bays, and wrought-iron balcony columns and railings shaped as palm trees made for fanciful motifs. Successive westward additions in the 1940s, 50s and 60s connected it to the grandstand, creating an uninterrupted line of building the full length of the homestretch, and yet the clubhouse's architectonic autonomy was preserved throughout.

Undertones of the clubhouse's stripped Georgian and Colonial features were echoed in the saddling barn and the east and south gateway buildings, all completed in 1938. Built to the south of the paddock, the saddling barn was a long, gable-roofed space with a protruding central pavilion with a stylised temple-like entrance framed by fluted pilasters.[11] The entrance gates, one adjoining the west of the saddling barn and the other directly south of the clubhouse, were rectangular, hipped-roof structures housing ticket booths and also bearing fluted pilasters on their exterior walls.

Tomson planted the 14-hectare (34-acre) infield with flowers in tightly-organised decorative patterns.

The box hedge-lined walkways and avenues of trees were not solely beautifying devices, but also reflected the importance given within the master plan to accommodating and directing the movement of crowds. To Kaufmann, planning an effective circulation system was key to designing a successful racecourse. 'The chief planning problem in such an establishment, obviously is one of circulation,' he explained to *Architectural Forum* in 1937. Large crowds moved quickly from the confines of the homestretch through the grounds to restaurants, services, betting rings and so forth. A broad pathway was laid out across the infield to a tunnel which connected to the grandstand and paddock area. A contemporary critic lauded that the 'park was so designed and developed as to provide egress to large crowds without confusion. Walks, promenades and terraces afford views of the exciting pre-race ceremonies of saddling and parading the mounts before they pass out to the track.'[12] Kaufmann planned exhaustively not only for the movement of pedestrians within the grounds, but also for car access to the grounds. Strub's research into North American courses led him to the conclusion that a major failing of these venues was their lack of adequate parking facilities. He and Kaufmann were determined this problem should not mar their enterprise. Upon opening, Santa Anita possessed a 10,000-car park adjacent to the paddock and three years later a northern car park was added with direct access to the infield via a tunnel.[13] It ranked amongst the first complexes to make comprehensive arrangements for the increasing use of cars.

2.53 The paddock was formally landscaped by landscape architect Tommy Tomson in 1934

The stylised classicism of the paddock buildings was paralleled by the formal landscaping of the paddock itself (Figure 2.53). Designed by Tommy Tomson in 1934, the parade ring was set within two and a half hectares (six acres) of park-like gardens, with French-inspired parterres, and manicured hedges and allées of trees delineating pathways and bounding compartments of lawn. Within the paddock, he designed a walking circle as the focal point of a rectangular garden outlined by parterres edged by neatly clipped box hedge. Brazilian pepper trees delineated the elliptical pathway around the walking circle, while allées of olive trees bounded the east and south of the garden.

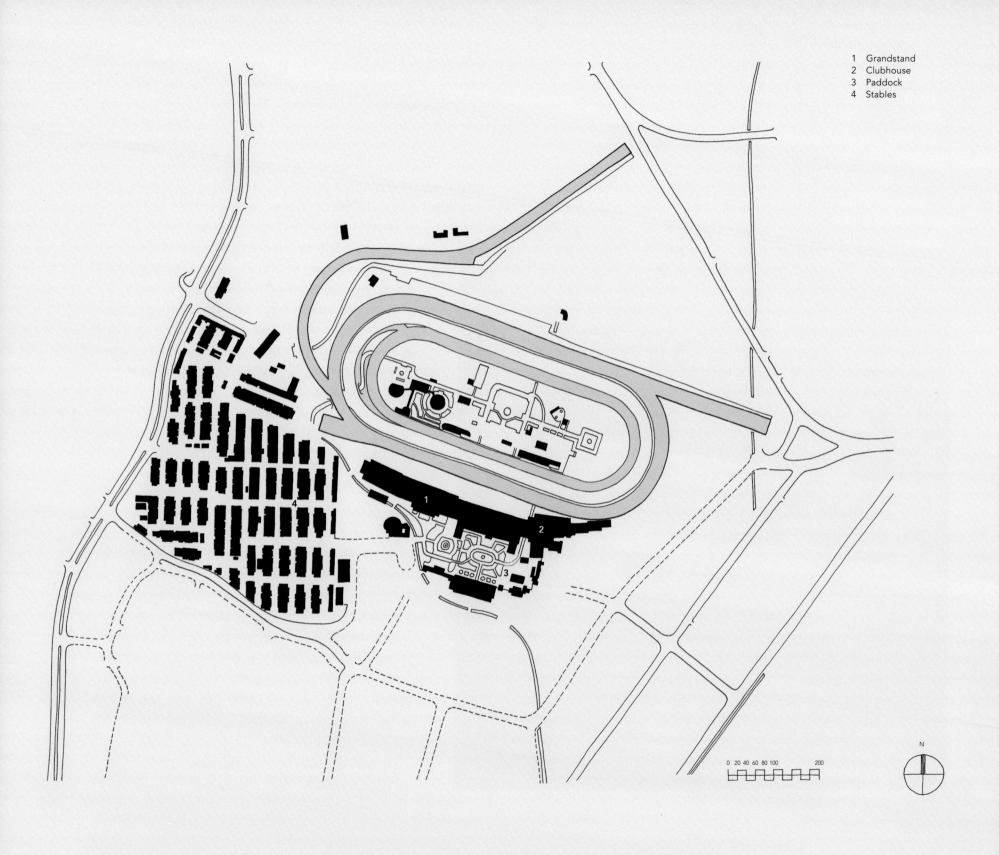

1 Grandstand
2 Clubhouse
3 Paddock
4 Stables

0 20 40 60 80 100   200

N

The care and attention lavished upon the master plan, architecture and landscape was not squandered. By the close of its first year of trading, investors had received a dividend of 100 per cent of their initial investment. Quickly it was noted for the Hollywood stars that were often spotted there, stars such as Clark Gable, Marlene Dietrich, Betty Grable, and Erol Flynn. Moreover, Santa Anita was immediately recognised for the quality of its physical setting. Called a 'smashing architectural triumph' by *California Arts and Architecture*, it was saluted for elevating the aspirations traditionally ascribed to the building type, 'giving architectural expression to structures which are not treated with any aesthetic consideration'.[14]

After a 25-year ban, the course had brought legalised racing back to California with a level of glamour unparalleled in America. Architecture and landscape had been harnessed to instill an image of sophistication, éclat and propriety to the sport, distancing Santa Anita from horse racing's disreputable past. Kaufmann's blend of Streamline Moderne and period revival adroitly expressed both the dynamism of modernity and an established conservatism. His vision is still pronounced today. Almost continual expansions in the 1930s, 40s and 50s (guided by Kaufman until his death in 1949) and again in the 1980s and 90s preserved the spirit of the original design. It was a spirit of elegance and quality which augmented forever the image and experience of thoroughbred racing in California and, indeed, across the whole of the nation.

ROBERT W. McMEEL
ARCHITECT
·LEXINGTON· ·KENTUCKY·

·CLUB·HOUSE·

Keeneland Race Course
Kentucky, USA

Keeneland Race Course was built to a comprehensive master plan and to a stringent set of design guidelines, informed by the beauty of the surrounding countryside and the local building material, limestone. For the past seven decades, new development has upheld these guidelines, resulting in an unparalleled degree of visual integrity.

The sport of racing is the heritage of Kentuckians, especially of those Kentuckians who live in the midst of the region where the majority of the champions of the American Turf have been bred. These words are addressed to those who would have that heritage restored and made permanent through the agency of a model racetrack dedicated solely to the perpetuation and improvement of the sport and specifically committed never to seek profits...

(A Proposal for the Establishment of a Model Race Track at Keeneland, 1935)

On 15 October 1936, a few minutes before two o'clock in the afternoon, a silence of anticipation descended upon an 8,000-strong crowd. A spotted pony stepped onto a freshly-ploughed dirt track, in whose wake followed eight impatient thoroughbreds. The crowd erupted as racing returned to the town of Lexington with the first ever meeting at Keeneland Race Course.

When the Kentucky Association racecourse in Lexington shut its gates for the last time in 1933, for the first time in over a century the city was without a track. A group of forward-thinking horsemen quickly set about establishing a replacement - the course which was to become Keeneland. From the outset this was to be no ordinary course; this was to be a 'model racetrack'. It was boldly envisioned as a place where thoroughbred racing was showcased at the highest level on a non-profit basis, which fed earnings back into its purses, its facilities and local charities rather than line shareholders pockets. And this unique doctrine was reflected in a unique setting. Characterised by rustic limestone surfaces, groves of trees and uninterrupted views over the rolling hills of Bluegrass Country, Keeneland's environment was the physical expression of its heritage and values. This

environment, however, began to be shaped much earlier than Keeneland's 1936 genesis.

Keeneland's story began two decades earlier, with the Lexington-born horseman, John Oliver 'Jack' Keene. Blunt, gruff and exacting he may have been, but it was Keene's indefatigable vision which laid the foundation for what would become Keeneland. By turns a thoroughbred breeder, trainer and track manager, Keene was a hands-on horseman with a driving passion for the turf. The state of his local course in Lexington, though, frustrated him. Built at the north-eastern outskirts of the town in 1828 by the Kentucky Association, the Lexington racecourse hosted spring and autumn meetings for over a century. By the opening of the twentieth century, its facilities were declining, its prestige was falling and financial difficulties pressed. To the boon of horse racing posterity, Keene was not a man content merely to bemoan the failings of the Lexington track. Instead, he set about building his own. Beginning in 1916, on land belonging to the Keene family farm, his dream of creating a private training and racing club for himself and his friends slowly began to take shape (Figure 2.57).

Keene's racecourse was part training centre, part country estate. As befitting any noble estate, Keene decided upon endowing his with a distinguished entrance. Possibly no other decision had such a bearing upon the architectural character that Keeneland was to assume. He engaged local stonemasons to build a low mortared stone wall, based upon

Page 236 **2.56** View of the clubhouse, by Keeneland's long-standing architect Robert McMeekin. Keeneland Race Course opened its doors on 15 October 1936

Opposite above **2.57** Aerial photograph 1935. Jack Keene's track, barn and training track

Opposite below **2.58** Keene's castle-like limestone barn, subsequently transformed into Keeneland's clubhouse

his own sketches and using limestone quarried from his own farm. It was Kentucky's ancient limestone bedrock that created its renowned fertile soils, and quarried limestone fences had long been a quintessential feature of the Bluegrass landscape. However, Keene's sketches showed a 'two-to-one' building pattern, inspired perhaps by his travels in England or Russia, which was unknown in central Kentucky. It was this wall, legend has it, that sparked the biggest project of Keene's racecourse – the 'barn'.[1]

When it came to his building projects, Keene was not only ambitious he was also exacting. His masons were forced to blast huge piles of limestone in search for a pair of large slabs to cap the posts of his new entrance before they found anything that satisfied their indefatigable employer. Unsurprisingly a huge stockpile of rejected rock was left over. This pile, however, prompted a new idea; it was to be put to use building a vast structure alongside the track. The structure was called a barn, but its scope far exceeded this epithet. It epitomised what Keene envisioned his facility to be. Housing living quarters, dining room, ballroom as well as stalls, it was built not merely to stable horses but as a place for Keene and his friends to eat, dance, sleep and watch their horses race around the 1700-metre (mile-and-sixteenth) track in the morning with the sun warming their backs. (This intention explains many of Keeneland's more individual features, notably why it has the only west-facing clubhouse standing at the head of the stretch of any racecourse in the country.) The barn was no less idiosyncratic in its architecture.

Constructed from hand-chiselled limestone personally superintended by Keene, it was a fortress-like landmark with crenelated walls (Figure 2.58). It comprised a square, two-storey central section linked by stone arcades to flanking three-storey wings. To the rear was another limestone structure, almost as eccentric as the barn. This was an enclosed training track, 40 metres (one quarter of a mile) in circumference, based upon Keene's experiences as a thoroughbred trainer in Russia. Naturally, there was not a blueprint in sight.[2]

The track was a labour of love for Keene that he wrestled with for nearly 20 years. He was never a tremendously rich man, though, and his limited coffers and perfectionist nature spelt downfall for the project when the Great Depression hit. After investing two decades and $400,000, his aspirational complex was not even halfway to completion and he had no means to complete it.[3]

The old Kentucky Association course was also in crisis. It had 'served its full term of usefulness... The buildings are in poor condition, the roadways in worse. The whole plant is such an unlovely affair that its reclamation is highly impractical.'[4] After years of neglect, Lexington's racecourse finally closed its doors in 1933 and a committee-led search began for a new home for racing in the town. Out of a potential 20 sites, Jack Keene's half-finished facility emerged as the forerunner. Not only were the ready-made circuit and stone barn categorical advantages in its favour, but also, recognising in the committee a shared purpose, Keene had offered the land at a price far less than market value. With that, the Keeneland Association was born.

For a price of $130,000, in 1935 the foundling Keeneland Association secured 60 hectares (148 acres) of land, a weed-ridden racing circuit, a stone building measuring 80

2.59 Trackside elevation of the clubhouse, with triple-height timber porch overlooking the track

Opposite **2.60** The grandstand, here photographed in 1939, shared the same limestone, timber and slate palette of materials as the clubhouse

by 18 metres (258 by 58 feet), an incomplete indoor training track and 'an irreplaceable accumulation of planting and shrubbery'.[5] Much still remained to be done though before the facility was ready for public use. At a time when the nation was plunged in financial depression, this was an almost herculean task. Keene's original unbounded plans for the site were immediately reigned in. Keene's stone barn was to be remodelled as a clubhouse; a grandstand was planned between the main track and enclosed training track; new roads and parking space were necessary; and, much to Keene's distress – he openly wept as he watched it happening – the stone walls of the enclosed training circuit were to be knocked down to chest height to create a picturesque outdoor paddock. To achieve all this, the nascent Keeneland Association quickly launched a design competition.

On 1 October 1935, Lexington architect Robert McMeekin (1898-1983) was announced as the winner. He was perhaps an unlikely choice. He had never before designed a racecourse nor any other sporting venue, but in his short career designing houses and barns in the Bluegrass Country he had evidenced a commitment to local materials and traditional techniques, the bedrock of which was a life-long love of Kentucky limestone. He turned to the material again and again as a seamless method of rooting his buildings to their native soil. It was this empathy, no doubt, which distinguished him amidst the other entrants of Keeneland's architectural competition and which continues to characterise the facility's buildings in the twenty-first century.[6]

McMeekin took Keene's rough diamond and polished it into a genteel setting for southern thoroughbred racing. Keene's

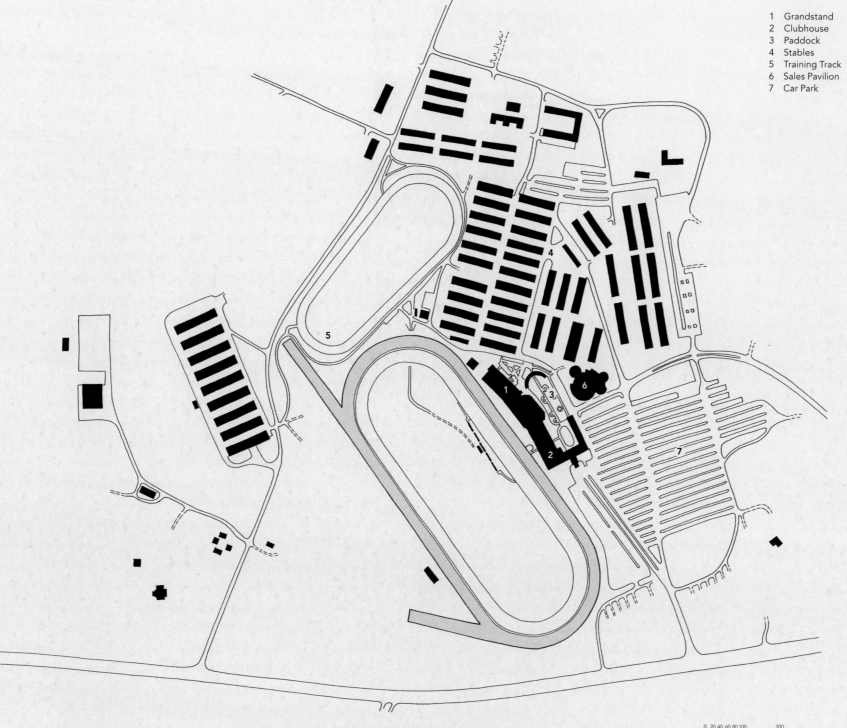

1 Grandstand
2 Clubhouse
3 Paddock
4 Stables
5 Training Track
6 Sales Pavilion
7 Car Park

0 20 40 60 80 100   200

N

2.62 The paddock, looking north. Saddling stalls were added to its northern boundary in 1984. Their repertoire of arches and limestone blended seamlessly with Keeneland's existing architecture

Opposite **2.63** Keenestone's famous limestone. Limestone has linked all stages of Keeneland's evolution from 1916 to the present day

stone barn – deemed 'bare, lifeless and forbidding' by McMeekin – was given new life as a clubhouse (Figure 2.56). Its central great hall, complete with a fireplace big enough for logs nearly two metres (six feet) long, became the club's main entry; its eastern wing became staff offices; and from its western wing, large wooden porches were built overlooking the track, one from each level (Figure 2.59). To the interior, McMeekin introduced the heavy panelled woodwork and huge fireplaces which characterised his residential work. The building's austere exterior was softened with cottage-like, low-sweeping slate eaves, burly chimney stack and wooden portico. All was unified by textured limestone walls. It was unlike any other racecourse clubhouse probably before or since.

Several hundred yards to the north, a grandstand was erected (Figures 2.60). An exceptionally simple design, it possessed a single storey of tiered seating upon a stone base and accommodated 2,500. McMeekin had envisaged it to be a steel grandstand, like that erected at Santa Anita Park a year earlier; Keeneland's co-founder Major Louie Beard, though, was determined it should be built of wood. 'So the stand I built had wood columns, wood beams and everything, even wood railings around the boxes,' McMeekin later recalled.[7] Although a wide open space separated it from the clubhouse, with its timber posts, slate roofs and limestone base punctuated by stout round arches, the grandstand made a harmonious pairing with Keene's remodelled fortress.

By opening day in October 1936, McMeekin had equipped the Keeneland Association with a highly singular complex. 'Both the grandstand and the clubhouse faced the wrong way,' the architect recalled years later. 'But we had that situation. The track was there and the clubhouse was at the head of the stretch and there was nothing to do but elaborate on it.' So conditioned as the facility was upon Jack Keene's legacy and the Kentucky locality, it does not slot easily into any chronological discussion about the history of racecourse design. Indeed, McMeekin purposefully did not study many other courses. 'I visited a track or two before I started on my plans,' he wrote in his memoirs. 'But they didn't affect my ideas very much. Most tracks are rather stark. There was an opportunity at Keeneland to build a plant in unusually pleasant surroundings.'[8]

A major component of Keeneland's 'pleasant surroundings' has, from its earliest days, been its commitment to landscaping. Beginning in the 1940s with the appointment of respected New York landscape architects, Innocenti and Webel, the racecourse's acreage of parkland has been a mainstay of its reputation. The duo transformed the vocabulary of the Bluegrass Country – its rolling pastures, soaring trees, hedges, rock fences and bountiful roads – to the scale of Keeneland itself. From the parade ground to the parking lot, the whole site was unified by Innocenti and Webel's guiding vision.[9]

Amongst their most important legacies was the tradition of planting to coincide with the spring and autumn meetings. The flowering dogwoods and redbuds in spring or the colourful oak and maple in autumn added festal colour for which the seasonal meetings soon became renowned. Trees rank amongst the most memorable features of the Keeneland experience. Across almost 1,000 acres, species range from the aristocratic pear trees along the track rail, to the white pines lining the clubhouse lawn, the Autumn Blaze maples framing its driveway, and the infield's manicured evergreens trimmed to spell out 'Keeneland' in bold lettering (Figure 2.61). The row after row of vertiginous pin oaks and long grassy strips planted by Innocenti and Webel created what must be America's must beautiful parking lot.[10] Within the shell of Keene's old training track, a tree-shaded paddock grew up around a majestic sycamore, one of the few trees that predated the Keeneland Association (Figures 2.62). Today bordered by a low hedge, limestone wall and, at its northern end, a curving

row of limestone saddling stalls, the paddock is probably the most distinctive and certainly the most intimate spot of the entire racecourse.

The sixteen saddling stalls were added to the paddock in 1984, but they blended seamlessly with Keeneland's venerable limestone and landscape aesthetic. The racecourse has seen several phases of expansion since its 1936 opening, but, with each drawing heavily on Keene and McMeekin's repertoire of limestone (Figure 2.63), stout round arches and meticulous attention to detail, the physical growth has largely remained seamless. Beginning in 1953 with an extension by McMeekin, the grandstand slowly edged towards the clubhouse and ten years later, the gap was closed. By 1976 the original timber grandstand was succeeded by a concrete and steel replacement designed by the leading racecourse architects of the day, Arthur Froehlich and Associates, who by that time had realised a portfolio which included Saratoga Race Course in New York, Hollywood Park in California and La Rinconada in Caracas (Figure 2.64). In 1984, a further swell in attendances gave rise to a 3,700 square-metres (40,000 square-feet) addition to the rear of this stand, featuring balconies giving elevated views across the paddock. Lead architect of the Froehlich firm, Morio Kow, singled out the original clubhouse as the model for the work. Limestone covered the exterior of the extension with round arches on its ground floor in homage to Keeneland's architectural heritage. 'The concept has always been pretty simple,' Kow

has said of his work at Keeneland. 'We have always tried to make everything fit together. We wanted to carry the tradition of the old clubhouse throughout the rest of the facility.'[11] When Kow designed a 930 square-metre (10,000 square-feet) library building for Keeneland (2002), it was intended to appear as though it had always belonged to the landscape. Each slab of the 325 tons of limestone which clad the building was individually hand chiselled.[12]

Keeneland's relationship with limestone has framed the racegoer's experience since the days of Jack Keene. Its physical setting is intimately entwined with the heritage of the Bluegrass – with its landscape, its limestone bedrock and its horse-raising traditions. Keeneland is a product of this heritage, and of the exceptional ambitions of its founders. Much of the original vision outlined in the 1930s has remained intact and while expansion has occurred to keep pace with the track's success, this has taken its impetus from Keene's and McMeekin's foundations. The apollonian Keeneland experience has consistently been conveyed not by conspicuous or ultramodern architecture but by a commitment to the Kentucky landscape and the thoroughbred. The Association's motto – 'racing as it was meant to be' – resounds throughout the facility. McMeekin wrote of Keeneland in later life, 'I consider it one of my most important jobs, not only for my own small contribution, but also for what it has meant to this area. With its beautiful setting and its air of graciousness, it seems to give an invitation to come in and enjoy.'[13]

Singapore Racecourse

Kranji, Singapore

The Kranji racecourse is a racecourse of its time. This wholly new complex, built on an empty site from 1994-99, palpably demonstrates the architectonic that has shaped racing venues in Asia since the latter decades of the twentieth century.

In the 1990s, Singapore Turf Club was presented with a rare chance: to build itself a wholly new course on a virgin site. This was not merely an especial case for the city-state of Singapore, whose highly urbanised island offers little scope for fresh development, but was a rarity in the racing world the globe across. The instances of wholesale construction of racecourses in recent decades are few and far between. From grandstand, to parade ring, to multi-storey car park and stables for over 1,000 horses, the club had the scope to build in bricks and mortar (or in this case steel and glass) an expression of the modernity of the Asian racing industry. How the club interpreted this opportunity is the subject of this case study.

The seeds of thoroughbred racing in Singapore were first sown in the mid-nineteenth century. The early British who arrived to colonise the island quickly ensconced an ebullient whirl of social engagements, promenading and sporting activities. The colony was less than 20 years old when, in October 1842, a band of racing enthusiasts, with memories of Ascot and Epsom still fresh in their hearts, established the Singapore Sporting Club (later to become the Singapore Turf Club). A mere five months later, Singapore's first racecourse had opened. The Club was a haven of social as well as sporting life for the wealthy expatriates, and soon wealthy Chinese immigrants were also drawn to the course. By the twentieth century, the racecourse's popularity had outgrown its cramped original site and in 1933 the club relocated to Bukit Timah. Heralded as the finest track in the East, the Bukit Timah course was much loved for its architectural blend of European classicism and south-east Asian detailing set within a lush, tropical plantation. Mingled feelings were thus generated when the government decreed that the Bukit Timah

city-centre land would be better utilised as housing and that the 60-year old racecourse would have a new home in the suburb of Kranji, 22 kilometres (15 miles) from the city centre.[1]

In 1994 a design competition was launched for the new course. From six proposals, the successful entrant was a Singapore-United States partnership between local firm Indeco Consultants and American architects Ewing Cole Cherry Brott. The partnership was a pragmatic one; no Singapore practice had ever been called to design a racecourse while Ewing Cole Cherry Brott had amassed considerable expertise in the field, having worked for numerous US tracks including Meadowlands, Emerald Downs and Garden State Park. The firm was not, however, known for innovative design approaches in its racecourse work. Five years later, in August 1999, the Singapore Turf Club's new facility at Kranji held its first meeting.

The Indeco-Ewing Cole Cherry Brott master plan was shaped by a brief which dictated provision for three tracks, a grandstand with a 30,000-person capacity, stabling for 1,000 horses residing at the facility year-round, a multi-storey car park and entryway leading from a planned railway station; everything that was considered necessary to a vanguard Asian racing complex. The site, though undeveloped, was less than ideal for the master planners and architects. The 80-hectare (200-acre) property assigned to the club had as yet none of the botanical beauty associated with the Bukit Timah site.[2] Situated at the northwest of the island, it was a water catchment area – that is, a drainage basin collecting rainwater for the densely populated island. It was, moreover, uneven terrain featuring two 40-metre (130-feet) hills alongside swampy ground. Adding to the challenge of locale was that of climate. Singapore's demanding weather system of year-round downpours and extreme heat had to be considered within the design. Such challenges were brought to bear in the master plan, and indeed in the final product.[3]

From the outset, the design of the complex was shaped by functional rather than aesthetic priorities. Architectural distinction was not a driving force. In its architectural character the grandstand symbolised the archetypal grandstand model that has prevailed in Asia since the final decades of the twentieth century. During these years, the Asian racing industry boomed and a natural repercussion was a steady period of grandstand construction. Overwhelmingly, this construction was dominated by a single architectural typology, a typology characterised by utility, vast size, but not, unfortunately, by innovative architecture. Examples at Sha-Tin (1978), Nakayama (1990) and Tokyo (2007) demonstrated that in this generation, grandstands were not designed to be beautiful objects in themselves but to be rational structures built to high technological specifications and capable of holding high-capacity crowds year-round.

With racing at its facility being held twice weekly throughout the year, the Singapore Turf Club's priorities lay in securing a low-maintenance grandstand which delivered air-conditioned accommodation to large numbers of spectators overlooking the finishing post. The solution that Indeco and Ewing Cole Cherry Brott provided was a glass-fronted, stacked configuration, 250 metres (820 feet) in length (Figures 2.65, 2.66). This was by now a familiar formula for the firm. The building was arranged over five levels, in which services were confined to the basement leaving the remaining four storeys primarily devoted to spectator facilities.

In relocating to its new site, the Turf Club sought not only to bring with it Bukit Timah's veteran racing patrons but also to attract two new audience groups of covetable spending power: corporate clientele and Singapore's affluent younger generations. To this end, it was crucial to create a facility that was as much about the social elements of going to the races as about the sport itself and the grandstand had to provide a mixture of facilities to support a range of objectives. The ground floor was designed as a space where Singapore's seasoned racing and betting enthusiasts could get the best live race experience. Unlike the upper storeys, this level was open to the track generating a sense of immediacy and intimacy with the action of the turf that was cherished by seasoned racegoers, not withstanding the disadvantages of Singapore's oppressive heat and risk of downpours (Figure 2.67). With no air conditioning, stadium-style plastic seating and limited refreshment facilities, it offered basic

Page 248 **2.65** Singapore Turf Club, a rare opportunity to design a complete racecourse on empty land

Above **2.66** The grandstand, opened in 1999, was designed by local firm Indeco Consultants in partnership with American architects Ewing Cole Cherry Brott

amenities for the lowest entrance price. Conversely, the top three storeys overlooked the track and parade ring from air-conditioned comfort behind an uninterrupted glass frontage. The higher the level, the more commodious the spaces became, with increasingly generous seating and dining provisions. Differing from the attitude of many sporting clubs in the late twentieth century, the Turf Club never intended to capitalise on using its facilities for hospitality on non-race days. The design of the grandstand was thus purely intended to function for its race-going patrons.

Glass and steel characterised the grandstand building. Giant steel trusses supported an undulating steel roof, whose curving surface covered in the region of 22,000 square metres (240,000 square feet) (Figure 2.68). Stainless steel – non-porous and stain-resistant – was the obvious choice for durability and minimum upkeep. Of the 19 transverse steel trusses that make up the building's robust frame, nearly half of their 56-metre (184 feet) length cantilevered over the trackside, supporting from above the overhanging viewing galleries on the second and third floors. The result was a column-free trackside façade indicative of the value placed on clear sightlines within twentieth- and twenty-first-century grandstand construction at large. The two highest levels were formed from a concrete slab and metal deck suspended from solid steel tension bars which meant that the view from the lower levels was not obstructed by columnar supports. The upper three air-conditioned storeys were encased with a glazed frontage offering a floor-to-ceiling vista over the 2,000-metre (one-and-one-quarter mile) track along most of the grandstand's length. The glazed viewing galleries are a symptom of the necessity of air conditioning for patron comfort in the humid climate. On the ground floor, however, where seating was unenclosed specific adaptations were introduced to promote air circulation. Tall ceiling heights (over six metres or 20 feet) and large openings on both sides of the grandstand encouraged cross-ventilation, whilst the configuration of tote offices and internal walls was carefully conceived to benefit from prevailing winds.[4]

Functionality was the governing dictate of the scheme. There was no romance to the stand's design; this building meant business and business alone. In describing the grandstand's design, its architects were keen to stress that inspiration for its silhouette came from the dramatic image of a horse in full gallop, an image replicated in the building's cross section. The success with which this imagery has been translated is, however, a matter of debate. The Kranji grandstand never aspired to being a beautiful building. The Turf Club was not a client with aspirations to architectural iconicism but instead sustained the habitual Singaporean psychology which valued fast-paced development with short expected lifespans.[5] The very idea of Singapore has long rested on its claim to archetypal newness, and it was to this philosophy that the club subscribed. Its glass and steel aesthetic, of stacked and stocky proportions, could be seen at any racecourse across Asia; it made no attempt at individualism but rather sought to replicate what was perceived as the most modern essentials of an end-of-century racing facility.

If the architecture did not seek to express its Singaporean context, though, this is not the case with the green landscape beyond it. The landscaping is the most dynamic, notable aspect of the racecourse's physical environment. From its earliest planning stages, the master plan had been structured around a theme of 'racing in

the tropics' – that is to say, that the garden city identity of the island as a whole was to be replicated at the racecourse. If the grandstand was perceived as a vehicle to establish the Turf Club as a state-of-the-art venue, then in many ways its landscape setting was a vehicle of nostalgia. Bukit Timah's verdant surroundings ranked amongst the most beloved aspects of the old track, and landscape architects Belt Collins were charged with creating at the club's new home a mature landscape that echoed its old one. Similar species of trees, shrubs and flowers that had flourished at Bukit Timah were planted extensively throughout the Kranji site, both in the public grounds and private stabling areas. The lush setting, large in scale and tropical in ambiance, was evocative of the Singapore of long ago.[6]

From the moment that the visitor enters the grounds, either by road or by the adjoining rail station, he is greeted by immaculately maintained surroundings of hard and soft

Opposite **2.67** Column-free hanging decks allow unobstructed viewing for the grandstand patrons, and provide shelter for those in the unenclosed seating below

Above **2.68** The grandstand's undulating, stainless steel roof covering 22,000 square metres

1 Grandstand
2 Parade Ring
3 Stables
4 Multi-Storey Car Park
5 Railway Station

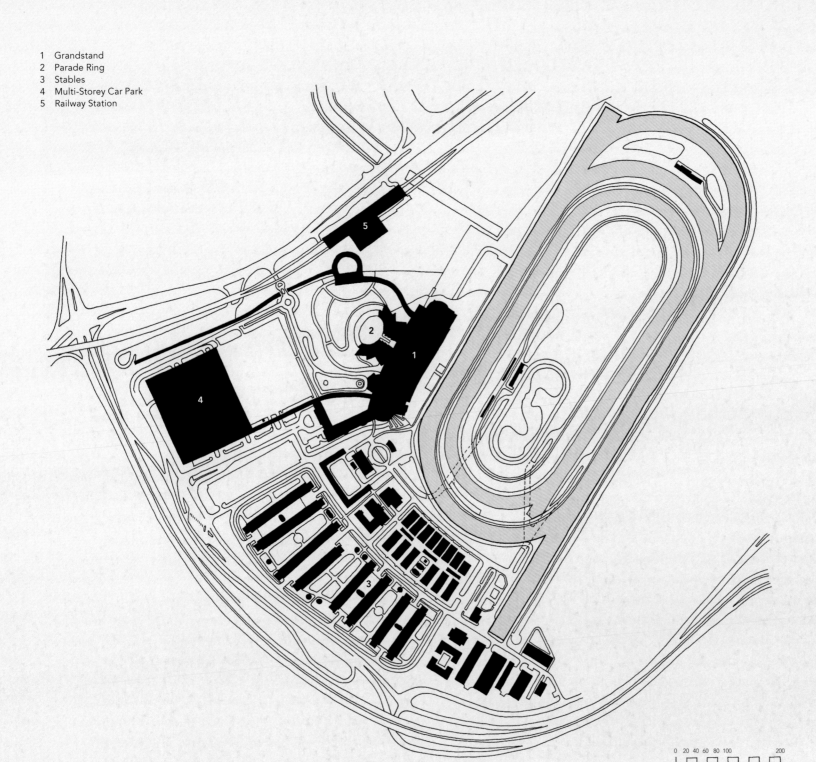

0 20 40 60 80 100   200

landscaping (Figure 2.69). Mature trees were planted from the outset to ensure that even the racecourse's earliest visitors received this impression. Their canopies provided welcome shading for both the two- and four-legged attendees of the course while cascading flora, such as bougainvillaea, softened the lines and materials of the built fabric. Planting was used to define and rationalise the site's comprehensive circulation network, with a spacious paved courtyard geometrically studded by flowering trees and ringed by a sheltered walkway, greeting patrons upon approach. For those arriving by rail, a covered walkway led to a tropical entrance garden and from there to the grandstand, sheltering racegoers from sun and rain.

The centrepiece of the four-hectare (10-acre) entrance garden was the parade ring, on the north side of the grandstand (Figure 2.70). While the trackside frontage of the grandstand is characterised by expansive translucency, this area had a different persona. It was a hub of movement and colour. Timber-lined saddling stalls framed one half of the ring, whilst the opposite side was lined by tiered concrete platforms from which racegoers observed the pre-race parade ritual. The platforms were covered by what is the most architecturally distinct feature of the complex, 60 white sun canopies held aloft by a bright yellow frame (Figures 2.71). The white panels, Teflon-coated for low maintenance, fanned out in different directions like the wings of birds. It was a joyous motif which complemented well the ceremonial nature of the parade ring. The unusual canopies were conceived not solely upon an aesthetic plane but also for pragmatic reasons. Designed to shield those watching the parade from equatorial showers and the powerful sun, the canopies were

Opposite **2.70** The parade ring, as seen from the horse walk

Above **2.71** The Teflon-coated fabric canopies of the parade ring

another of the racecourse's climate-specific features. At the design stage, studies were undertaken to ascertain the angles of the sun at different times of the day and months of the year to ensure that the canopies were positioned exactly so as to shield from the sun when used for racing. They have proved, however, one of the least practical components of the complex. With the designers underestimating the extent of the area's downpours, spectators often find themselves getting wet and the horses are allotted no protection at all. During heavy rainfall, water runs off the canopies and deluges the parade ring circuit. Discussions are underway to replace the canopies with a roof fully covering the ring, including both horses and patrons alike.

The vibrant atmosphere of the parade ring was continued through a highly successful design feature: a glass-sided horse-walk running from the ring, through the grandstand and to the track. The horse-walk allowed the patron to watch from the sidelines each stage of racing's rituals. The glass-fronted weighing room and official's room that line the horse-walk enhanced the degree of public participation.

As mentioned at the opening of the study, the opportunity to build a new racecourse from scratch is a rare and exciting one. The path taken by the Singapore Turf Club gave the island one of Asia's leading racing venues, but it was a venue that conformed wholly to the typology of racecourse building prevalent within the continent. In terms of its architecture, it was a racecourse of its time. The site has none of the history of Ascot, for example, nor the grand charm of Santiago. What it represents is a hugely important pattern of racecourse design that has, almost without exception, shaped Asian racing in recent decades. Within this creed, it is one of the best. Architecturally it may be undistinguished, but its tropical landscape has gone a long way to redeeming this. In creating such a setting, the Turf Club has demonstrated the advantages that can be accrued from starting afresh on empty land. The club's directors harboured few aesthetic sensibilities; what was important was creating a vast, glass and steel cohesive complex that performed functionally well as a home for Singapore's thriving racing industry and as an expression of its modernity. In this, it was a resolute success.

Glossary

Adobe: Sun-dried, unburnt brick of clay and straw.

Anglo-Normand: Style popular in late nineteenth- and early twentieth-century France originating in the seaside resorts of Normandy and based on vernacular rural architecture of the Pays d'Auge. Typified by half-timbering (pan-de-bois), patterned brickwork and overhanging tiled roofs.

Arts and Crafts: Widely influential late nineteenth-century movement initiated in England, which promoted the traditional forms of design and craftsmanship threatened by mass production and industrialisation. Its architectural expression is seen in the use of traditional materials and vernacular decoration.

Ashlar: Finely worked masonry with a smooth finish.

Balustrade: Small columns joined together by a rail, found on tops of buildings, balconies and staircases.

Baroque: Seventeenth- and early eighteenth-century style, which developed the classical architecture of the Renaissance towards greater extravagance, theatricality and stylistic levity.

Bas-relief: Sculpture in low relief.

Beaux-Arts: Denotes the academic neo-classical style taught at the École des Beaux-Arts in Paris.

Belt-course: Horizontal band on façade marking subdivisions of a building.

Carpenter Gothic: Mid to late-nineteenth-century American architectural style which applied Gothic Revival architectural detailing traditionally carved in stone to modest wooden structures built by house carpenters. An improvisational style, emphasising quaintness rather than fidelity to authentic Gothic models. Characterised by its profusion of jig-sawn details.

Cartouche: Decorative classical tablet with ornate frame.

Colonial Georgian: Style widely disseminated in English colonies in America, used widely for residential architecture. Characterised by symmetry, central porch, clapboard and classical proportions.

Console: S-shaped ornamental bracket.

Corbel: Block projecting from an elevation and supporting a structure above such as parapet, beam or arch.

Cornice: The top course of a wall or architectural member which is sometimes moulded and/or projects from the wall.

Cornucopia: Ornamentation in the form of a horn filled with fruit etc.

Cupola: A domed structure on the roof.

Eaves: The lower, overhanging section of a pitched roof, intended to throw rain water away from the wall below.

Entablature: In Classical architecture, the horizontal member carried on columns and pilasters. A term to cover all the horizontal mass resting on a row of columns, including the architrave, frieze and cornice.

Eyebrow dormer: Low dormer with curved top.

Fascia board: Horizontal band capping the end of rafters below the roof edge.

Finial: Crowning ornamental feature, usually above a spire, gable or cupola.

Fluted pilaster: Pilaster decorated with vertical channels.

Gable roof: A roof with two sloping surfaces from the ridge.

Gable: The vertical part of the end wall of a building contained within the roof slope, usually triangular.

Gingerbread: Heavily, gaudily, and superfluously ornamented. Commonly used in reference to late-nineteenth-century American architecture.

Googie Style: Architecture originating in Southern California between 1940s and 60s. Influenced by car design and Space Age motifs, it was characterised by upswept roofs, neon, glass and geometric shapes and was popular for motel and gas station design.

Greek Revival: See neo-classical.

Hipped roof: A roof with sloping sides and ends.

International Style: Design style dating from the 1930s characterised by clean lines and minimal decoration and the use of materials such as steel, concrete, and glass.

Japonisme: Term referring to the European and American vogue for Japanese art and culture in the late nineteenth century after Japan opened trade links in 1853. In the USA, Japanese displays at the 1876 Centennial Exposition in Philadelphia initiated a wave of enthusiasm for its architectural and artistic production.

Jugendstil: Late nineteenth- and early twentieth-century style in Germany and Austria which paralleled Art Nouveau.

Keystone: Central stone in arch or vault.

Louver: A framed opening, as in a wall, door, or window, fitted with fixed or movable horizontal slats for admitting air and light and shedding rain.

Mansard roof: A roof of two pitches, the lower one being more steeply pitched than the upper.

Mascaron: Representation of a face, commonly carved in relief.

Mission Revival: Popular in Florida, south west United States and elsewhere circa 1890-1930 and suggestive of eighteenth-century Spanish Mission architecture in the Americas. It was characterised by white stucco walls, red tile roofs, semi-circular arches and overhanging eaves.

Neo-classical: Architectural style inspired by the architecture of Classical Greece. Stimulated by the archaeological rediscovery of Greek architecture which gathered momentum from the eighteenth century onwards. Buildings have a regular, formal appearance and symmetrical facades and incorporate Classical details such as an entablature at the wall top or pilasters dividing bays.

Off-track Betting (OTB): In New York State, wagering at legalised betting outlets run by independent companies chartered by the state. Wagers at OTBs are usually commingled with on-track betting pools.

Ogee: Two S-shaped curves joined at the top with their concave sections at the top.

Paddock: Enclosure of racecourse where horses are paraded prior to a race.

Palladian: Derived from the buildings and publications of the classical architect Andrea Palladio (1508-80), and based on proportion, rules and symmetry.

Pari-mutuel System: System of wagering in which odds are determined by the amount of money bet on each horse. In essence, bettors are competing against each other not against the track, which acts as an agent, taking a commission on each bet to cover purses, taxes and operating expenses.

Parterre: Ornamental garden with flower beds, lawns and pathways arranged to form a pattern.

Pediment: Triangular space at the top of a wall contained between the sloping eaves of a pitched roof and a horizontal cornice. Sometimes contains decoration.

Pilaster: Flat version of a column, consisting of a slim rectangle projecting from a wall.

Quatrefoil: A four-lobed opening, similar to a four-leaf clover.

Queen Anne style: Architectural style which evolved from the 1860s first in England then in USA. Essentially an eclectic style drawing on a wide range of motifs from various periods and regions typified by irregular and unsymmetrical facades. Key characteristics include bay windows, wrap-around porches, steeply sloping roofs, prominent gables, turrets, and an abundance of decorative details combined in unexpected ways.

Quoin: Emphasised stone at the angles of a building, or their imitation in brick or other materials.

Racino: A racecourse at which slot machines are permanently installed.

Rococo: Eighteenth-century decorative style typified by light, highly elaborate detail.

Roof plate: Horizontal structural element that supports the lower ends of roof rafters.

Rustication: Masonry prepared in such as way as to give a rough, rugged surface and cut in large blocks.

Salomonic column: A column whose shaft is sculpted to give it a twisted appearance, sometimes referred to as a spiral or barley-twist column.

Shingle: Thin timber slab cut to standard sizes, used instead of slates or tiles to cover roofs or clad walls.

Spanish Colonial: See Mission Revival.

Streamline Moderne: Late phase of Art Deco with emphasis on horizontal contours. Characterised by rounded corners, flush windows and white or light-coloured stucco walls.

Stripped classical: Classical architecture in which mouldings, ornament and details have been removed, leaving only structural and proportional systems.

Truss: Rigid structural framework of timbers or steel bridging a space, designed to support a structure, such as a roof.

Volutes: Spiralled scrolls.

Voussoir: Wedge-shaped stones forming an arch.

Notes

PART I: A Chronology of Racecourse Architecture

Introduction
1 International match races had taken place as early as the 1920s, but these were one-off occasions with a field of two.

Chapter I – Racing Begins
1 In Greek times, racing tended to be spontaneous and informal, with no permanent setting. Some evidence exists that the Etruscans did provide limited facilities to accompany horse and chariot racing. A fifth-century BC painting from the Tomba delle Bighe at Tarquinia, for example, shows an arena bounded by wooden spectator stands. Continuous wooden benches were elevated upon wooden uprights and sheltered by an awning or curtain. But it was the Romans that developed the hippodrome into a sophisticated architectural construct. Humphrey, *Roman Circuses*, London: Batsford, 1986, pp. 6, 12-3.

2 Humphrey, op. cit., pp. 33, 47, 50.

3 D. Langmead and C. Garnaut, *Encyclopedia of architectural and engineering feats*, Santa Barbara: ABC-CLIO, 2001, p. 70.

4 S. Turner, *The History of the Anglo-Saxons from the Earliest Period to the Norman Conquest*, vol. 3, London: Longman, Rees, Orme, Brown and Green, 1828, p. 17.

5 The precise date is debated. The years 1539 and 1540 are both cited. For example, see D. Birley, *Sport and the Making of Britain*, Manchester: University of Manchester Press, 1993, p. 62 and J. Hemingway, *History of the City of Chester, from its Foundation to the Present Time*, Chester: J. Fletcher, 1831, p. 208.

6 L. Thompson, *Newmarket. From James I to the Present Day*, London: Virgin Publishing, 2000, pp. 17-8.

7 Thompson, 2000, op. cit., p. 17.

8 Thompson, 2000, op. cit., pp. 26, 35; T. Collins, J. Martin, W. Vamplew, *Encyclopedia of Traditional British Rural Sports*, London: Routledge, 2005, p. 153.

9 A later engraving of a race near Windsor shows a stand of this nature.
T. Gibson, 'Horse-racing, architecture and society: the emergence and development of the racecourse grandstand in Britain 1753-1851', unpublished thesis, Courtauld Institute of Art, 1997, p. 2.
C. Knight's *Old England*, (vol. 1, London: Charles Knight & Co., 1845) features an engraving professedly of the seventeenth-century course showing a two-storey structure. It is likely, however, that the print is no earlier in date than the mid-eighteenth century. The structure featured within the illustration is most probably a mid-eighteenth-century viewing platform containing stables on the ground floor for which the plans still survive (British Library K TOP.8.76b). The authors are indebted to Timothy Cox for his guidance on this point.

10 Peter Tillemans, *View of Newmarket Heath*, Government Art Collection 2364.

11 Gibson, 1997, op. cit., pp. 3-5.

12 J. Freeman, 'The Grandstand at Stamford: its history, repair and reuse', *Association for Studies in the Conservation of Historic Buildings*, vol. 23, 1998, pp. 15-6.

Chapter II – York: The First Grandstand
1 The social melange of racedays is evoked in this 1735 description of Epsom in the *Bath, Bristol, Tunbridge and Epsom Miscellany*:
  On Epsom Downs when Racing does begin,
  Large companies from every part come in,
  Tag rag and Bob-tail, Lords and Ladies meet,
  And, Squires without Estates, each other greet....
G. Home, *Epsom: Its History and its Surroundings*, Wakefield: S. R. Publishers Ltd, 1971, p. 109.

2 Gibson, 1997, op. cit., p. 9; T. Gibson, 'The Designs for the Knavesmire Grandstand, York', *Georgian Group Journal*, vol. 8, 1998, p. 76.

3 Freeman, op. cit., p. 15; Gibson, 1998, op. cit., p.76.

4 York's grandstand was not only the first of its kind, but it still partly survives to this day, albeit in radically truncated form. Given the survival rate of racecourse buildings, this is nothing short of miraculous. The stand exists today as the façade of its ground-floor veranda, which was transplanted in 1908 to its present location in the paddock.

5 Sir Thomas Robinson, who also submitted a design for the York grandstand, associated the building with the new Assembly Rooms in terms of finance, direction and clientele, underlining his conception of the raison d'être of the new building.

6 Gibson, 1997, op. cit., pp. 16-7.

7 Gibson, 1998, op. cit., p. 83.

8 Freeman, op. cit., pp. 16-7.

9 Gibson, 1997, op. cit., pp. 22-3.

Chapter III – The Nineteenth Century
1 Gibson, 1997, op. cit., pp. 24-8.

2 J. Kay and W. Vramplew, *Encyclopaedia of British Horseracing*, Oxford: Routledge, 2003, p. 113.

3 D. Hunn, *Goodwood*, London: Davis-Poynter, 1975, pp. 97, 104, 117.

4 See J. Beavis, *The History of Bath Racecourse*, Beckenham: Jim Beavis, 2011, pp. 190-1.

5 Gibson, 1997, op. cit., p. 25.

6 G. Tattersall, *Sporting Architecture*, London: R. Ackermann, 1841, p. 95.

7 S. Magee with S. Aird, *Ascot The History*, London: Methuen, 2002, pp. 67, 69, 78-80; Tattersall, op. cit., p. 95; G. Cawthorne and R. Herod, *Royal Ascot: Its History and Its Associations*, London: A. Treherne and Co., 1902, p. 79.

8 Gibson, 1997, op. cit., p. 30.

9 J. Walvin, *Leisure and Society 1830-1950*, London: Longman, 1978, pp. 16, 21.

10 M. Huggins, *Flat Racing and British Society 1790-1914*, London: Frank Cass, 2000, p. 121; Walvin, op. cit., p. 21.

11 Gibson, 1997, op. cit., p. 30.

12 J. P. L. Luchet, *Les Contemporains de 1789 et 1790*, I, p. 56. Quoted in J. Hayward, *Fragmented France: Two centuries of disputed identity*, Oxford: Oxford University Press, 2007, p. 4.

13 Hayward, op. cit., p. 4.

14 Ascot did have a royal stand. The first was erected in 1807, followed by a larger replacement in 1822. However, this was an isolated happening amongst English courses and reflected Ascot's close royal links. See case study for further detail.

15 The authors are grateful to Guy Thibault for explaining this point.

16 J. Bagnell-Bury, *History of the Later Roman Empire*, vol. 1, New York: Courier Dover Publications, 1958, pp. 81-2.

17 R. Herbert, *Impressionism: Art, Leisure and Parisian Society*, New Haven: Yale University Press, 1991, p. 154; G. Thibault, *Une Autre Regard sur les Courses*, Menton: Castelet, 2007, pp. 38, 78; A. Alphand, *Les Promenades de Paris*, New York: Princeton Architectural Press, 1984, pp. 97-8; R. Hopkins, 'From Place to Espace: Napoleon III's transformation of the Bois de Boulogne', *Proceedings of the Western Society for French History*, vol. 31, 2003, p. 204.

18 Hopkins, op. cit., p. 206.

19 R. Romanet-Riondet and G. Thibault, *Centenaire de la Société d'Encouragement 1833-1933 et Les Heures Mouvementées de la Société d'Encouragement 1993-1991*, Boulogne: Castelet, 1993, p. 38.

20 *Photographs of Paris Life by Chroniqueuse*, London: Tinsley Brothers, 1862, p. 300.

21 R. Hopkins, *Engineering Nature: Public Green Spaces in Nineteenth-Century Paris*, unpublished dissertation, Arizona State University, 2008, p. 335.

22 V. Thompson, 'The Art of Racing in Paris', *Outing*, vol. 42, August 1903, p. 564.

23 E. Reynolds-Ball, *Paris in its Splendour*, vol. 2, Boston: D. Estes & Co., 1900, p. 268.

24 K. Reinbothe, *Internationale Rennen zu Baden-Baden: 150 Jahre Rennbahn Iffezheim*, Baden-Baden: Wesel Kommunikation, 2008, p. 5.

25 The total cost was 300,000 francs.
O. Christ, *Die Rennen in Iffezheim seit 1858 und 80 Jahre Rennen des Internationalen Clubs 1873-1953*, Baden-Baden: Koelblin, 1953, p. 14.

26 E. Hotaling, *They're Off!: Racing at Saratoga*, Syracuse, NY: Syracuse University Press, 1995, p. 9; W. Robertson, *The History of Thoroughbred Racing in America*, Englewood Cliffs: Prentice-Hall, 1964, p. 15.

27 C. C. Smith, 'Splendid Survivors: Horse Racing Stable Construction Saratoga Springs, New York 1840-1913', unpublished thesis, Cornell University, 1987, p. 44; T. Underwood, *Thoroughbred Racing and Breeding: The Story of the Sport and Background of the Horse Industry*, Whitefish: Kessinger Publishing, 2005, p. 137.

28 J. Dizikes, *Yankee Doodle Dandy: The Life and Times of Tod Sloan*, New Haven: Yale University Press, 2000, p. 14.

29 W. S. Vosburgh, 'The Passing of Jerome Park', *Outing*, vol. 38, August 1901, p. 513.

30 Dizikes, op. cit., pp. 15-6.

31 K. Raitz, (ed.), *The Theater of Sport*, Baltimore: Johns Hopkins University Press, 1995, p. 325.

32 *New York Times*, 22 September 1866.

33 Vosburgh, op. cit., p. 514.

34 Vosburgh, op. cit., p. 513.

35 M. Adelman, *A Sporting Time: New York City and the Rise of Modern Athletics, 1820-70*, Urbana: University of Illinois Press, 1986, pp. 80-1, 87-8.

36 D. Black, *The King of Fifth Avenue: The Fortunes of August Belmont*, New York: The Dial Press, 1981, p. 283.

37 *New York Times*, 26 September 1866.

38 Dizikes, op. cit., p. 71.

39 It closed in 1904. However, the Clubhouse was still intact as late as 1921 when it was sold to a company who converted it for use as a factory. *New York Times*, 21 July 1921.

40 F. Trevelyan, 'The American Turf: The Race Courses of the East', *Outing*, vol. 20, no. 2, p. 130.

41 N. Di Brino, *The History Of The Morris Park Racecourse and Morris Family*, New York: Nicholas di Brino, 1977, p. 3.

42 Di Brino, op. cit., p. 3.

43 *New York Times*, 12 May 1889.

44 Trevelyan, op. cit., p. 132.

45 *New York Times*, 12 May 1889.

46 In Britain, the Jockey Club set a 10 per cent limit on dividends. S. Reiss, 'From Pitch to Putt: Sport and Class in Anglo-American Sport', *Journal of Sport History*, vol. 21, no. 2, 1994, p. 143.

47 P. Roberts and I. Taylor, *The Spa: Saratoga's Legendary Race Course*, London: Turnberry Consulting, 2011, p. 47.

48 K. Gatto, *Churchill Downs: America's Most Historic Racetrack*, Charleston: The History Press, 2010, p. 31.

49 E. C. Buley, *Australian Life in Town and Country*, New York: G.P. Putnam, 1905, p. 143.

50 J. Pisani, Report on Early Randwick Racecourse, unpublished report, University of Sydney, 1984, p. 6; G. Partington, *The Australian Nation: Its British and Irish Roots*, Melbourne: Australian Scholarly Publishing, 1994, p. 253.

51 M. Twain, *Following the Equator*, Rockville: Wildside Press LLC, 2003, p. 145.

52 W. Peake, 'Unregistered Proprietary Horse Racing in Sydney 1888-1942', unpublished thesis, University of Western Sydney, 2004, p. 100.

53 *Hamilton Spectator*, 3 December 1873.

54 *Hamilton Spectator*, 3 December 1873.

55 E. G. Robertson, *Decorative Cast Iron in Australia*, South Yarra: Currey O'Neil, 1984, pp. 24.

56 This was seemingly a feeble one. An 1850 edition of the *Mercury and Sporting Chronicle* noted that the annual meeting was dampened by the collapse of parts of the flimsily-erected stand 'precipitating upwards of 40 persons into the lower portion'. *Victoria Park, Adelaide, South Australia: the course of natural beauty; centenary, 1871-1971*, Adelaide: Adelaide Racing Club Inc, 1971, p. 2.

57 Following enlargements made some time after World War I, the stand is no longer symmetrical.

58 *South Australian Advertiser*, 18 February 1882.

59 This was not an automatic totalisator, which was a twentieth-century development. See following chapter for more information. This instance was an early experimentation with manual totalisator machinery. Totalisator betting had been introduced to Adelaide in 1879, based upon the French pari-mutuel system. State legislation banned both the 'tote' and bookmakers a mere four years later, but the debilitating effect this had on the local racing industry led to the repeal of the law in 1888.

60 E. Thomson and A. Minnaard, *Heritage Assessment Eagle Farm Racecourse*, unpublished report, December 2001, p. 8; *Australian Town and Country Journal*, 7 May 1887.

61 The Eagle Farm totalisator building was an early experiment with manual totalisator machinery, installed in 1898. It was perhaps the first instance in which the staff operating the machine were all inside the building with the machinery itself.

62 The grandstand accommodation at Eagle Farm was, arguably, less architecturally distinguished than these ancillary structures. The Paddock grandstand, built in 1890, was a large brick building with an unusually-shaped curved corrugated iron roof. The roof was supported upon 7.6-metre (25-feet) high, cast-iron columns with huge cast-iron brackets, whilst cast-iron balustrades railed the front of the stand. It was designed by local firm Hunter and Corrie in partnership with the prominent John Buckeridge, Diocesan Architect to the Church of England, yet its decorative repertoire and basic form were far more modest than Victoria Park's earlier grandstand, especially in terms of the inventiveness of its cast-iron ornament.

63 *Brisbane Courier*, 9 November 1899.

Chapter IV – The Gilded Age

1 W. Adamson, *Embattled Avant-Gardes: Modernism's resistance to commodity culture in Europe*, Berkeley, CA: University of California Press, 2007, p. 117.

2 Quoted in D. Heddon, 'Given by God, Sport of Kings, or A Mug's Game: Horse Racing in Australian Literature', in *Journal of the Australian Society for Sports History*, vol. 5, no. 1, Nov 1988, p. 30.

3 The Tea House was restored by Fulton Ross Team Architecture and reopened in 2008 thanks to funding from a Charitable Trust.

4 'Races Against Time', *Heritage New Zealand*, Summer 2006, p. 7.

5 *Wairarapa Daily Times*, 2 February 1910.

6 *Feilding Star*, 29 November 1906.

7 The Tea House burned down in 1917 but was immediately rebuilt to the same design.

8 N. Foley, 'Background notes: Robertson and Marks, Architects', unpublished research, 1985, p. 3.

9 Another was also built in the infield; this does not survive.

10 *Sydney Morning Herald*, 28 September 1917.

11 J. Pacini, *A Century Galloped By*, Melbourne: Victoria Racing Club, 1988, p. 240.

12 A. Lemon and H. Freedman, *The History of Australian Thoroughbred Racing*, vol. 2, Port Melbourne: Southbank Communications Group, 1990, p. 471.

13 *The Times*, 21 June 1902.

14 *The Times*, 17 June 1903.

15 Divorcees, notably, were blacklisted from entering, a stricture which stood in place until 1955.

16 *The Star*, 31 January 1915.

17 *The Times*, 9 July 1913.

18 *The Standard*, 22 May 1911.

19 *The Times*, 16 April 1914.

20 W. H. P. Phyfe, *Five Thousand Facts and Fancies*, New York: G. P. Putnam, 1901, p. 456.

21 G. Thibault, *Un Siècle de Galop 1900-2000*, Levallois-Perret: Filipacchi, 2001, p. 9.

22 S. Cueille, *Maisons-Laffitte: Parc, Paysage et Villégiature 1630-1930*, Paris: Cahiers du Patrimoine, 53, 1999, p. 145.

23 Thibault, 1993, op. cit., pp. 45-8.

24 The racecourse is no longer extant. It held its last race in 1967.

25 'L'Hippodrome du Tremblay', *Construction Moderne*, vol. 22, November 1906, p. 89.

26 J. Schopter, 'A New Race Course for Parisians', *Architectural Record*, vol. 21, 1907, p. 345.

27 A. le Bas, *Architecture du Sport: Val de Marne – Hauts de Seine*, Paris: Cahiers de l'Inventaire, 1991, p. 107.

28 *Evening Post*, 6 February 1933.

29 K. Dutta, *Calcutta: A Cultural and Literary History*, Oxford: Signal Books, 2003

30 For further reading see T. Metcalf, *An Imperial Vision: Indian Architecture and Britain's Raj*, Berkeley: University of California Press, 1989 and J. Morris, *Stones of Empire*, Oxford: Oxford University Press, 1983.

31 W. G. C. Frith, *The Royal Calcutta Turf Club*, Calcutta: Royal Calcutta Turf Club, 1976, pp. 103-4.

32 B. Bach, *Calcutta's Edifice: The Buildings of a Great City*, New Delhi: Rupa & Co, 2006, p. 485.

33 G. Tillotson, 'Vincent J. Esch and the Architecture of Hyderabad, 1914-36', *South Asian Studies*, vol. 9, 1993, p. 30.

34 Tillotson, op. cit., p. 31.

35 *The Worker*, 15 December 1921.

36 D. Bayon, 'Latin American Architecture, c.1920-c.1980', in Bethell, L., (ed.), *The Cambridge History of Latin America*, vol. 10, Cambridge: Cambridge University Press, 1995, p. 365.

37 *Casabella*, March 1964, p. 6.

38 In 1953, it was renamed Hipódromo Argentino de Palermo.

39 V. Salgueiro, 'Visual Culture in Brazil's First Republic (1889-1930): allegories and elite discourse', *Nations and Nationalism*, vol. 12, no. 2, April 2006, pp. 245-6.

40 *Club Hipico de Santiago: Society, architecture and spectacle*, Santiago: Ocho Libros, 2010, pp. 46-7; F. Letamendi Urcelay, 'La Arquitectura del Club Hipico de Santiago y la Contribucion de Josue Smith Solar', unpublished research, n.p.

Chapter V – Modernity

1 The design of the hippodrome is commonly ascribed to Paul Furiet and Georges-Henri Pingusson, who worked in partnership from November 1925. Simon Texier, however, has pointed out that since the hippodrome was completed in August of that year, it is unlikely that Pingusson's involvement was anything more than informal.
S. Texier, *Georges-Henri Pingusson. Architecte (1894-1978)*, Paris: Verdier, 2006, p. 22.

2 E. R. Bill, 'Racecourse Stands', *Architects' Journal*, 3 August 1927, pp. 163-7

3 'New Stands, Epsom Racecourse', *The Builder*, 27 May 1927, p. 859

4 Bill, op. cit., pp. 171.

5 Despite these examples, the buildings at many UK racecourses became increasingly outdated between the wars. Mounting concern was expressed in the press that the standard of accommodation for general patrons was far lower than in other countries, and that the Jockey Club and racecourse companies were interested only in providing facilities for higher-paying spectators. When it was rebuilt in 1924, Thirsk Racecourse was heralded as affording state-of-the-art facilities. Perhaps this was true for the racing insiders, but its ordinary stand was relatively basic, being roofless with 26 cemented steps.
M. Huggins, *Horse-Racing and the British, 1919-39*, Manchester: Manchester University Press, 2003, pp. 140-1.

6 Construction began in 1935, and the complex was largely finished in 1936 when the Civil War broke out. The grandstand was badly damaged during the conflict, but from 1940-1 the damage was restored and the rest of the complex was brought to completion.

7 'Madrid Hippodrome', *Architectural Forum*, vol. 92, May 1950, p. 130

8 A. Lapunzina, *Architecture of Spain*, Westport: Greenwood Publishing Group, 2005, pp. 110-2; D de Witt and E de Witt, *Modern Architecture in Europe: A Guide to Buildings Since the Industrial Revolution*, London: Weidenfeld and Nicolson, 1987, p. 130.

9 W. N. Thompson, *Gambling in America: an encyclopedia of history, issues and society*, Santa Barbara: ABC-Clio, 2001, p. 169; Raitz, op. cit., pp. 329-331.

10 C. Nichols, *The Leisure Architecture of Wayne McAllister*, Layton: Gibbs Smith, 2007, p. 38.

11 McAllister referred to the influence of the Exposition in an interview with the Tijuana Historical Society. T. D. Proffitt III, *Tijuana: The History of a Mexican Metropolis*, San Diego: San Diego State University Press, 1994, p. 196; D. Beltran, *The Agua Caliente Story: Remembering Mexico's Legendary Racetrack*, Lexington: Eclipse Press, 2004, p. 37.

12 C. Johnson, *Florida Thoroughbred*, Gainesville: University Press of Florida, 1993, pp. 16-7; J. Crittenden, *Hialeah Park: A Racing Legend*, Miami: Pickering Press, 1989, p. 58; N. Stout, *Great American Thoroughbred Racetracks*, New York: Rizzoli, 1991, p. 95.

13 Its small size was to prove its undoing though, as in 1948 it was deemed too modest in scale to accommodate Hialeah's rapid pace of expansion and was demolished to make room for a larger replacement.

14 Stout, 1991, op. cit., p. 96.

15 Quoted in R. Reeves, *Crown Jewels of Thoroughbred Racing*, Lexington: The Blood-Horse, Inc., 1997, p. 56.

16 The complex has been listed on the National Register of Historic Places since 1979. It has changed greatly since its 1932 opening, however. Extensive construction took place between 1948 and 1952 under Geisler's hand, greatly expanding its facilities in line with its popularity. A new wing was added to the north of the grandstand, while a replacement clubhouse was erected. Again, French Provincial Architecture was the starting point. The entrance façade of the clubhouse was dominated by a sweeping double staircase leading to the first floor boxes, while a three-storey elliptical bay projected from the rear façade. This long, curving, arcaded bay created terraces overlooking the paddock.

17 Stout, 1991, op. cit., p. 63; E. Read, 'Bing's Baby', *San Diego Magazine*, July 1967, p. 57.

18 'The Hollywood Turf Club at Inglewood California. Stiles O. Clements: Architect', *California Arts and Architecture*, June 1938, pp. 22-3

19 *Architect and Engineer*, December 1938, p. 7.

Chapter VI – Post-War

1 Fobert was later succeeded by Georges Boutelier and Pierre Vanbeginne.

2 C. Croft, *Concrete Architecture*, London: Laurence King Publishing, 2004, p. 18.

3 J. K. Hession and D. Pickrel, *Frank Lloyd Wright in New York: The Plaza Years, 1954-1959*, Salt Lake City: Gibbs Smith, 2007, p. 103.

4 E. L. Bowen and R. S. Reeves, *Belmont Park: A Century of Champions*, Lexington: Eclipse Press, 2005, p. 18.

5 Letter from Povlika to Frank Lloyd Wright, February 26, 1956. Quoted in Hession and Pickrel, op. cit., p. 103.

6 Bowen and Reeves, op. cit., p. 18.

7 A. Berrizbeitia, *Roberto Burle Marx in Caracas: Parque del Este, 1956-1961*, Philadelphia: University of Pennsylvania Press, 2005, p. 4.

8 'Three-Inch Shell Cantilevers 90 Feet', *Architectural Record*, vol. 123, May 1958, p. 252.

9 P. Koch, 'Winning Streak', *World of Interiors*, January 2009, p. 126.

10 J. Murray, 'Dreamland For The $2 Bettor', *Sports Illustrated*, 10 August 1959, p. 44.

11 J. Bobrowski, B. K. Bardhan-Roy, T. Maciag, 'The Design and Analysis of Grandstand Structures', *The Structural Engineer*, vol. 52, no. 2, February 1974, p. 48.

12 M. Gaillard, *Hippodromes*, Paris: La Palatine, 1984, p. 148.

13 R. Coopey and P. Lyth, *Business in Britain in the Twentieth Century*, Oxford: Oxford University Press, 2009, p. 338.

14 *The Windsor, Slough and Eton Express*, 16 June 1961, p.11

15 *Sporting Life*, 12 June 1961, p. 3.

16 Magee, 2002, op. cit., p. 267.

17 *Concrete Quarterly*, Spring 1970, pp. 11-2; *Building*, 26 September 1969, pp. 75-6.

18 *Concrete Quarterly*, Spring 1970, p. 14; *Concrete*, July 1969, p. 258.

19 Bobrowski et al, op. cit., pp. 49 and 52.

Chapter VII – To the Present

1 Blood Horse Publications, *Horse Racing's Top 100 Moments*, Lexington, KY: Eclipse Press, 2006, pp. 74-7.

2 'Race Course Complex, Perak Turf Club, Ipoh, Malaysia', *Architecture in Australia*, vol. 61, no. 4, August 1972, p. 443.

3 'Perak Turf Club grandstand, Ipoh racecourse, Malaysia; Architects: J. Nankivell Associates', *Asian Building and Construction*, December 1971, pp. 25-27; *The Straits Times*, 26 February, 1971.

4 J. Bedford, *The World Atlas of Horse Racing*, London: Hamlyn, 1989, p. 198.

5 B. Shelton, J. Karakiewicz, T. Kvan, *The Making of Hong Kong: from vertical to volumetric*, New York: Routledge, 2011, p. 149.

6 Bedford, op. cit., p. 202.

7 N. Nobuhiro, 'The Cult of Oguricap: Or, how women changed the social value of Japanese horse-racing', in D. Martinez, (ed.), *The Worlds of Japanese Popular Culture*, Cambridge: Cambridge University Press, 1998, p. 168.

8 S. Buckley (ed.), *Encyclopedia of Contemporary Japanese Culture*, London: Routledge, 2002, pp. 199, 220.

9 International Federation of Horseracing Authorities Annual Report 2010, p. 42.

10 Kay and Vamplew, op. cit., p. 121.

11 Kay and Vamplew, op. cit., p. 146.

12 *Bloodhorse*, 18 October 2002.

13 'Racino Concept May Create "Destination Entertainment Venues"', *Northeast Pennsylvania Business Journal*, September 2003, pp. 1, 30.

14 H. Kruse, 'Social Interaction, the Arrangement of Interior Space, and Racetrack Renovation,' *Journal of Sport and Social Issues*, vol. 27, no. 4, November 2003, p. 338.

15 A. Beyer, 'Stronach's vision bumps up against reality', *Daily Racing Form*, 16 September 2011.

16 K. Powell, 'Racecourses Under Starter's Orders', *Country Life*, vol. 196, November 21, 2002, p. 67.

17 S. Dawson, 'Metalworks: Racing Times', *Architects' Journal*, vol. 216, December 19, 2002, p. 8.

18 British Horseracing Authority, 'Economic Impact of British Racing', 2009 report, p. 39.

19 'Nad Al Sheba to unveil new Millennium Grandstand', *Thoroughbred Times*, 18 March 2001.

20 *Gulf News*, 6 October 2009.

21 A hotel was included within an aborted scheme for the redevelopment of Ascot's grandstand which took place in 2003-6.

22 *The National*, 28 January 2010.

23 R. Sheard, *The Stadium: Architecture for the New Global Culture*, Singapore: Periplus Editions, 2005, p. 20.

24 R. Horden and W. Blaser (eds), *Light Tech: Towards a Light Architecture*, Basel: Birkhauser, 1995, p. 65.

25 A. Brookes and D. Poole, (eds), *Innovation in Architecture*, London and New York: Spon Press, 2004, p. 90; D. Walker, 'Plane Sailing: The Queen's Stand at Epsom', *Architecture Today*, no. 36, March 1993, p. 26; Horden and Blaser, op. cit., pp. 60-5.

26 R. Bennetts, 'Rational and Romantic: Arup Associates at Goodwood', *Architecture Today*, no. 11, September 1990, pp. 66-8; 'Sussex Grandstand Goodwood Racecourse', *The Arup Journal*, vol. 27, Summer 1992, pp. 21-2.

27 C. Donati, *Michael Hopkins*, Milan: Skira, 2006, p. 152; M. Summerfield, 'Glorious Goodwood', *The Architectural Review*, vol. 211, February 2002, p. 56.

28 C. Lycett Green, 'Towcester Boasts a Winner', *Country Life*, 23 October 1997, p. 70.

29 Interview with Frank Roberts, June 30, 2010; G. Worsley, 'Towcester's Winning Streak', *Perspectives on Architecture*, Feb/March 1998, p. 48.

30 M. Spring, 'A Different Beast', *Building*, no. 12, March 2007, p. 41.

31 Spring, op. cit., pp. 42-3; 'BDP's redevelopment of Aintree', *Architecture Today*, no. 178, May 2007, p. 83.

32 Interview with Tony McGuirk of BDP, 21 May 2010.

33 Both the AELTC at Wimbledon and Lords have invested heavily in their architectural fabric in the past 15 years. At Wimbledon, works include Centre Court (2009, Populous) and the Millennium Building (2000, BDP); at Lords, they include the Media Stand (1999, Future Systems) and the refurbishment of its Grade II*-listed Pavilion Stand (2005).

34 If the prime interest of patrons in visiting a racecourse is to bet – as in Japan for example where horse racing is one of the very few legal outlets for gambling – then this philosophy is irrelevant. Architecture in these cases carries far less importance to the financial success of a racecourse.

PART II: Case Studies

Ascot Racecourse

1 S. Magee, *Ascot: The History*, London, Methlien, 2002, p. 44.

2 G. Cawthorne and R. Herod, *Royal Ascot: Its History and Its Associations*, London: A. Treherne and Co., 1902, p. 52.

3 S. David, *Prince of Pleasure*, London: Little, Brown & Co, 1998, p. 136.

4 D. Laird, *Royal Ascot*, London: Hodder and Stoughton, 1976, p. 59; Cawthorne and Herod, op. cit., p. 64; Magee, 2002, op. cit., p. 52.

5 *Windsor and Eton Express*, 20 June 1829.

6 K. Baker, *George IV: A Life in Caricature*, London: Thames and Hudson, 2006, p. 12.

7 Magee, 2002, op. cit., pp. 55-7.

8 *Mirror*, 8 June 1839.

9 Ascot's grandstand was indicative of a significant change that affected the development of stands in the 1830s and 1840s, namely that it was owned by a private company. These companies, by their nature, intended to generate a profit and stands of this era grew in size and capacity to ensure that good financial returns were gained. Epsom's new grandstand (1829-30) for instance was the work of the Epsom Grand Stand Association, founded in 1828 specifically to fund a new stand, and it accommodated 5,000 spectators. Ascot's new building was the venture of the Grand Stand Trust.

T. Gibson, 'Horse-racing, architecture and society: the emergence and development of the racecourse grandstand in Britain 1753-1851', unpublished thesis, Courtauld Institute of Art, 1997, p. 26.

10 Cawthorne and Herod, op. cit., p. 79.

11 Magee, 2002, op. cit., p. 78.

12 Magee, 2002, op. cit., p. 97.

13 G. St Aubyn, *Edward VII: Prince and King*, London: Collins, 1979, p. 132.

14 *The British Turf and the Men Who Have Made It*, 1906. Quoted in Magee, 2002, op. cit., p. 99.

15 A red-brick Stewards' House was also built in 1903 adjoining the Victorian entrance buildings.

16 When the Royal Stand was remodelled in the 1930s, this façade was replaced with a neo-Georgian, yellow stock brick and stone dressed elevation featuring a much larger porte-cochere decorated with sculpted masks.

17 *The Times*, 17 June 1903.

18 *The Star*, 31 January 1915.

19 *The Sporting Life*, 13 June 1908.

20 *The Sporting Life*, 13 June 1908.

21 Its architects were by Hunt and Steward. Its stepped parapet and clock were added in 1939.

22 *London Illustrated News*, 9 May 1931.

23 *Windsor and Eton Express*, 16 June 1961.

24 *The Sporting Life*, 25 May 1961.

25 *The Sporting Life*, 20 June 1963.

26 *The Sporting Life*, 14 June 1961.

27 *Windsor and Eton Express*, 16 June 1961.

28 *The Guardian*, 12 October 2005.

29 R. Sheard, *The Stadium: Architecture for the New Global Culture*, Singapore: Periplus Editions, 2005, p. 71.

30 *Daily Telegraph*, 21 June 2006.

31 *Daily Telegraph*, 14 December 2006

Goodwood Racecourse

1 Quoted in J. Kent, *Records and reminiscences of Goodwood and the dukes of Richmond*, London: Sampson Low, Marston & Co., 1896, p. 100.

2 C. Cecil, G. Ennor, and R. Onslow, *Glorious Goodwood*, Westbourne: Kenneth Mason Publications, 2002, p. 16.

3 R. Baird, *Goodwood: Art and Architecture, Sport and Family*, London: Frances Lincoln, 2007, pp. 152-3; Cecil et al., op. cit., pp. 16-17.

4 W. H. Mason, *Goodwood Its House Park And Grounds*, London: Smith, Elder and Co. Cornhill, 1839, p. 183.

5 Cecil et al., op. cit., pp. 24, 29, 67-8, 146.

6 Mason, op. cit., p. 183

7 'Goodwood Races', *American Turf Register and Sporting Magazine*, October 1840, p. 534.

8 Cecil et al., op. cit., p. 33.

9 C. Richardson, *The English Turf: A Record of Horses and Courses*, London: Methuen, 1901, p. 77.

10 Baird, op. cit., p. 197.

11 G. Plumptre, *The Fast Set: the World of Edwardian Racing*, London: André Deutsch, 1985, pp. 11, 13.

12 E. Moorhouse, *The Racing Year*, 1903. Quoted in Baird, op. cit., p. 197.

13 The authors thank Rosemary Baird for this information.

14 Cecil et al., op. cit, p. 72.

15 Cecil et al., op. cit, pp. 77, 80.

16 Cecil et al., op. cit, p. 184.

17 *Daily Mail*, 20 January 1970.

18 Cecil et al., op. cit, p. 12.

19 The Sussex Stand was the culmination of the second phase of the master plan. The first phase was realized with the erection of the Charlton Stand in 1989, a curving brick building at the head of the track housing dining facilities.

20 'Rational and Romantic: Arup Associates', *Architecture Today*, no. 11, September 1990, p. 68.

21 P. Murray and R. Maxwell (eds), *Contemporary British Architects*, Munich and New York: Prestel, 1994, p. 39.

22 M. Summerfield, 'Leisure Time: Goodwood', *Architectural Review*, vol. 211, February 2002, p. 56.

Hippodrome de Chantilly

1 Quoted in O. Prud'homme Farges, A. Vayron de la Moureyre, G. Boiselle, *Stables: Majestic Spaces for Horses*, New York: Rizzoli, 2006, p. 146.

2 R. Black, *Horse Racing in France*, London: Sampson Low, Marston, Searle & Rivington, 1886, pp. 50-1.

3 Black, 1886, op. cit., p. 51.

4 J. G. Janin, *The American in Paris during the Summer*, London: Longman, Brown, Green and Longmans, 1844, p. 107.

5 D. Montauroux, 'Hippodromes', *Monuments Historiques*, no. 167, January/February 1990, p. 115.

6 G. Thibault, *Une Autre Regard sur les Courses*, Menton: Castelet, 2007, p. 121; R. Romanet-Riondet and G. Thibault, *Centenaire de la Société d'Encouragement 1833-1933 et Les Heures Mouvementées de la Société d'Encouragement 1993-1991*, Boulogne: Castelet, 1993, p. 45.

7 Romanet-Riondet and Thibault, op. cit, p. 178.

8 See for example, an article in *Sports Illustrated* entitled 'The Most Beautiful Racetrack in the World', 8 June 1964, pp. 44-51.

9 P. Jodidio, *A Racing and Breeding Tradition. The Horses of the Aga Khan*, Munich: Prestel, 2010, p. 190.

10 S. Montgomery, 'Fading Glories in a Grand Setting', *The Independent*, 5 June 1994.

11 G. Wood, 'Chantilly all set for the coup de grace', *The Independent*, 20 January 1994.

12 Jodidio, op. cit., pp. 190-2.

13 'Dining Room with a View', *The Daily Telegraph*, 7 June 2007.

14 *The Mercury*, 24 July 1934.

Saratoga Race Course

1 J. Sterngass, *First Resorts: Pursuing Pleasures at Saratoga Springs, Newport and Coney Island*, Baltimore, MD: Johns Hopkins University Press, 2001, p. 146.

2 *New York Herald*, 10 August 1847

3 *New York Times*, 4 August 1864.

4 *New York Times*, 4 August 1864.

5 J. Bartels, *Saratoga Stories: Gangsters, Gamblers and Racing Legends*, Lexington: Eclipse Press, 2007, p. 108.

6 The practice was finally ended in 1986 when the paddock was enclosed by fencing. The Saddling Shed had been filled in 23 years earlier as a betting and office facility.

7 'Field Stand and Betting Ring are among many Improvements', *This Week in Saratoga Life*, 12-19 August, 1938, p. 4.

Club Hipico de Santiago

1 F. Letamendi Urcelay, 'La Arquitectura del Club Hipico de Santiago y la Contribucion de Josue Smith Solar', unpublished research, 2000, n. pag.; L. Bethell (ed.), *The Cambridge History of Latin America*, vol. 10, Cambridge: Cambridge University Press, 1995, pp. 365-6; *Club Hipico de Santiago: Society, architecture, spectacle*, Santiago: Ocho Libros, 2010, p. 18.

2 *Club Hipico de Santiago*, op. cit., pp. 21, 25; Urcelay, op. cit.

3 *Club Hipico de Santiago*, op. cit., pp. 44-7.

Santa Anita Park

1 'Santa Anita Track Ranks Amongst World's Best', *Los Angeles Times*, 2 January 1935.

2 *Los Angeles Times*, 4 February 1909.

3 P. McAdam and S. Snyder, *Arcadia: Where Ranch and City Meet*, Arcadia: Friends of the Arcadia Public Library, 1981, p. 125.

4 McAdam and Snyder, op. cit., p. 126.

5 The Santa Anita Handicap was first run on 23 February 1935 with a $100,000 purse.

R. Reeves, *Crown Jewels of Thoroughbred Racing*, Lexington: The Blood-Horse, Inc., 1997, p. 102.

6 R. G. Wilson, 'Gordon B. Kaufmann and Modernism', p. 71, in J. Belloli et al, *Johnson, Kaufmann, Coate: Partners in the California Style*, Capra Press, California, 1992.

7 'Architectural Treatment of Racing Plant at Arcadia is Pleasing', *Southwest Builder and Contractor*, 25 January, 1935, 13.

8 Kaplan Chen Kaplan, 'Santa Anita Park Racetrack, Historic Resources Evaluation', Appendix DI Cultural Resources Technical Report, August 2006, p. 17; N. Stout, *Great American Thoroughbred Racetracks*, New York: Rizzoli, 1991, p. 196.

9 Kaplan Chen Kaplan, op. cit., pp. 17-8.

10 'The King of Sports Comes Back to California with a Smashing Architectural Triumph', *California Arts and Architecture*, vol. 47, February 1935, p. 24.

11 The footprint of the building was dramatically enlarged in 1948 when Roland Coate added a Jockeys' Room.

12 'King of Sports Comes Back to California with a Smashing Architectural Triumph', *California Arts and Architecture*, vol. 47, February 1935, p. 25.

13 Stout, 1991, op. cit., p. 194.

14 Gordon B. Kaufmann FAIA Nomination, February 3, 1937, American Institute of Architects Archives, Washington DC, p. 5.

Keeneland Race Course

1 *Keeneland: A Thoroughbred Legacy*, Lexington: Blood Horse Publications/Keeneland Association, 2010, p. 21; C. Murray-Wooley and K. Raitz, *Rock Fences of the Bluegrass*, Lexington: University Press of Kentucky, 1992, p. 1, 51.

2 *Keeneland: A Thoroughbred Legacy*, op. cit., pp. 20-2.

3 *Keeneland: A Thoroughbred Legacy*, op. cit., pp. 25-6.

4 *A Proposal for the Establishment of a Model Race Track at Keeneland*, unpublished report, nd. [1935]

5 *Keeneland Opening Souvenir*, 1936, p. 51; *A Proposal for the Establishment of a Model Race Track at Keeneland*, op. cit., p. 14.

6 *Discovering Robert Ward McMeekin (1898-1983): Bluegrass Architect*, University of Kentucky College of Architecture, exhib. cat., 1988, pp. 3, 47.

7 C. R. Koch, 'Brass Rings and Leather Bindings', n.d., p. 51.

8 V. Mitchell, 'Set in Stone', *Keeneland Magazine*, Spring 2011, p. 46.

9 G. Hilderbrand, *Making a Landscape of Continuity: The Practice of Innocenti and Webel*, New York: Princeton Architectural Press, 1997, p. 80.

10 D. Liebman, 'The Prettiest Race Course', *Keeneland Magazine*, Spring Summer 1992, p. 73.

11 G. McLean, 'It started with a shiver', *Keeneland Magazine*, 1999, p. 18.

12 *Keeneland: A Thoroughbred Legacy*, op. cit., pp. 158-9.

13 Mitchell, op. cit., p. 51.

Singapore Racecourse

1 N. Loh, *Star Track: Designing and Building the Singapore Racecourse*, Singapore: Epigram Books, 2000, pp. 3-4.

2 Interview with Peter Chua, Singapore Turf Club, 2 November 2010.

3 Loh, op. cit., p. 10.

4 Loh, op. cit., pp. 16, 26, 29.

5 Interview with Peter Chua.

6 Belt Collins, *Belt Collins*, Mulgrave: Images Publishing, 2003, p. 111.

Bibliography

Adamson, W., *Embattled Avant-Gardes: Modernism's resistance to commodity culture in Europe*, Berkeley: University of California Press, 2007

Adelman, M., *A Sporting Time: New York City and the Rise of Modern Athletics, 1820-70*, Urbana: University of Illinois Press, 1986

Alphand, A., *Les Promenades de Paris*, New York: Princeton Architectural Press, 1984

Architects' Journal, 'Roof, Sussex Grandstand', 26 February 1992, pp. 36-9

Architectural Design, 'Racecourse "Guanabara", Rio de Janeiro', May 1964, p. 251

Architectural Forum, 'Hollywood Turf Club', October 1938, p. 261

Architectural Forum, 'Madrid Hippodrome', May 1950, pp. 130-1

Architectural Forum, 'Racing Club, Arcadia, California', June 1937, pp. 527-31

Architectural Record, 'Three-Inch Shell Cantilevers 90 Feet', vol. 123, May 1958, p. 252

Architecture and Arts, 'Moonee Valley Grandstand', February 1959, p. 38

Architecture in Australia, 'Perak Turf Club Grandstand', vol. 61, August 1972, p. 442

Architecture Today, 'Rational and Romantic: Arup Associates', no. 11, September 1990, pp. 66-73

Architecture Today, 'BDP's redevelopment of Aintree', no. 178, May 2007, pp.83-4

Arup Journal, 'Happy Valley', vol. 23, 1988, p. 91

Arup Journal, 'Sussex Grandstand, Goodwood Racecourse', vol. 27, no. 2, 1992, pp. 21-3

Bach, B., *Calcutta's Edifice: The Buildings of a Great City*, New Delhi: Rupa & Co, 2006

Bagnell-Bury, J., *History of the Later Roman Empire*, vol. 1, New York: Courier Dover Publications, 1958

Baird, R., *Goodwood: Art and Architecture, Sport and Family*, London: Frances Lincoln, 2007

Baker, K., *George IV: A Life in Caricature*, London: Thames and Hudson, 2006

Bardham Roy, B., 'The new grandstand for the Sandown Park Racecourse', *Concrete*, vol. 8, April 1974, pp. 57-8

Bartels, J., *Saratoga Stories: Gangsters, Gamblers and Racing Legends*, Lexington: Eclipse Press, 2007

Bayon, D., 'Latin American Architecture, c.1920-c.1980', in Bethell, L., (ed.), *The Cambridge History of Latin America*, vol. 10, Cambridge: Cambridge University Press, 1995, pp. 365-392

Beavis, J., *The History of Bath Racecourse*, Beckenham: Jim Beavis, 2011

Bedford, J., *The World Atlas of Horse Racing*, London: Hamlyn, 1989

Belt Collins, *Belt Collins*, Mulgrave: Images Publishing, 2003

Beltran, D., *Agua Caliente Story: Remembering Mexico's Legendary Racetrack*, Lexington: Eclipse Press, 2004

Berrizbeitia, A., *Roberto Burle Marx in Caracas: Parque del Este, 1956-1961*, Philadelphia: University of Pennsylvania Press, 2005

Bethell, L., (ed.), *The Cambridge History of Latin America*, vol. 10, Cambridge: Cambridge University Press, 1995

Beyer, A., 'Stronach's vision bumps up against reality', *Daily Racing Form*, 16 September 2011

Bill, E. R., 'Race-course Stands', *Architects' Journal*, 3 August 1927, pp. 163-74

Binney, 'The Deauville Phenomenon', *Country Life*, vol. 184, no. 4, 25 January 1990, pp. 76-9

Black, D., *The King of Fifth Avenue: The Fortunes of August Belmont*, New York: The Dial Press, 1981

Black, R., Horse Racing in France, London: Sampson Low, Marston, Searle & Rivington, 1886

Blood Horse Publications, *Horse Racing's Top 100 Moments*, Lexington: Eclipse Press, 2006

Boronat, J. Yolanda and Risso, M., *Roman Fresnedo Siri. Un Arquitecto Uruguayo*, Montevideo: Universidad de la Republica, 1984

Bowen, E., and Reeves, R., *Belmont Park: A Century of Champions*, Lexington: Eclipse Press, 2005

Bramson, S., *Curtiss-Bright Cities: Hialeah, Miami Springs & Opa Locka*, Charleston: History Press, 2008

Bobrowski, J., Bardhan-Roy, B. K., and Maciag, T., 'The Design and Analysis of Grandstand Structures', *The Structural Engineer*, vol. 52, no. 2, February 1974, pp. 37-52.

Brookes, A., and Poole, D., (eds) *Innovation in Architecture*, London and New York: Spon Press, 2004

Buckley, S., (ed.) *Encyclopedia of Contemporary Japanese Culture*, London: Routledge, 2002

Builder, 'New Stands, Epsom Race Course', 27 May 1927, p. 859

Builder, 'Queen Elizabeth II Grandstand, Ascot', 13 October 1961, p. 672

Building Design, 'Courses for Horses', no. 875, 4 March 1988, p. 28

Buley, E. C., *Australian Life in Town and Country*, New York: G.P. Putnam, 1905

Byrne, F., 'New Stand for an Old Course', *Country Life*, 30 August 1973, p. 549

Byrne, F., 'Racing Notes', *Country Life*, vol. 166, 9 August 1979, p. 393

California Arts and Architecture, 'The Hollywood Turf Club, Inglewood', vol. 53, June 1938, pp. 22-3

California Arts and Architecture, 'The King of Sports comes Back to California with a Smashing Architectural Triumph', vol. 47, February 1935, pp. 24-6

Casabella, 'Argentina', vol. 285, March 1964, pp. 4-5

Casabella, 'Introduzione Storica alla Architettura di Buenos Aires', vol. 285, March 1964, pp. 6-11

Cawthorne, G., and Herod, R., *Royal Ascot: Its History and Its Associations*, London: A. Treherne and Co., 1902

Cecil, C., Ennor, G., and Onslow, R., *Glorious Goodwood*, Westbourne: Kenneth Mason Publications, 2002

Christ, O., *Die Rennen in Iffezheim seit 1858 und 80 Jahre Rennen des Internationalen Clubs 1873-1953*, Baden-Baden: Koelblin, 1953

Club Hipico de Santiago: Society, Architecture and Spectacle, Santiago: Ocho Libros, 2010

Collins, T., Martin, J., Vamplew, W., *Encyclopedia of Traditional British Rural Sports*, London: Routledge, 2005

Concrete, 'Grandstand At Doncaster', July 1969, pp. 257-9

Concrete Quarterly, 'Race Against Time: Sandown Park Grandstand, Esher, Surrey', 98, July-September 1973, pp. 36-40

Construction Moderne, 'Saint Cloud Racecourse', April 1955, p. 127-33

Coopey, R., and Lyth, P., *Business in Britain in the Twentieth Century*, Oxford: Oxford University Press, 2009

Crittenden, J., *Hialeah Park: A Racing Legend*, Miami: Pickering Press, 1989

Croft, C., *Concrete Architecture*, London: Laurence King Publishing, 2004

Cueille, S., *Maisons-Laffitte: Parc, Paysage et Villégiature 1630-1930*, Paris: Cahiers du Patrimoine, 53, 1999

David, S., *Prince of Pleasure*, London: Little, Brown & Co, 1998

Davies, C., *Hopkins 2: Work of Michael Hopkins and Partners*, London: Phaidon, 2001

Dawson, S., 'Metalworks: Racing Times', *Architects' Journal*, vol. 216, December 2002, pp. 8-9.

De Witt, D., and De Witt, E., *Modern Architecture in Europe: à Guide to Building since the Industrial Revolution*, London: Weidenfeld and Nicolson, 1987

Di Brino, N., *The History Of The Morris Park Racecourse and Morris Family*, New York: Nicholas di Brino, 1977

Dizikes, J., Yankee Doodle Dandy: The Life and Times of Tod Sloan, New Haven: Yale University Press, 2000

Docomomo Journal, 'Brazil: Mainstream Modern and Parallel Modernities', no. 36, March 2007, pp. 19-21

Donati, C., *Michael Hopkins*, Milan: Skira, 2006

Dutta, K., *Calcutta: A Cultural and Literary History*, Oxford: Signal Books, 2003

Fairs, M., 'Racing Builds New Image', *Building Design*, 21 January 2000, p. 4

Foley, N., 'Background notes: Robertson and Marks, Architects', unpublished research, 1985

Frampton, K., (ed.) *World Architecture 1900-2000: A Critical Mosaic*, vol. 4, Vienna and New York: Springer, 2002

Freeman, J., 'The Grandstand at Stamford: its history, repair and reuse', *Association for Studies in the Conservation of Historic Buildings*, vol. 23, 1998, pp. 15-24

Frith, W. G. C., The Royal Calcutta Turf Club, Calcutta: Royal Calcutta Turf Club, 1976

Gaillard, M., *Hippodromes*, Paris: La Palatine, 1984

Gaillard, M., 'Grand Ecuries de Chantilly et muse vivant du Cheval', *Monuments Historiques*, no. 167, January/February 1990, pp. 49-53

Gatto, K., *Churchill Downs: America's Most Historic Racetrack*, Charleston: The History Press, 2010

Gebhard, D., and Breton, H. von, *L.A. in the Thirties*, Layton: Peregrine Smith, 1975

Gibson, T., 'Horse-racing, architecture and society: the emergence and development of the racecourse grandstand in Britain 1753-1851', unpublished thesis, Courtauld Institute of Art, 1997

Gibson, T., 'The Designs for the Knavesmire Grandstand, York', *Georgian Group Journal*, vol. 8, 1998, pp. 76-87

Girault, C., *Notes sur la vie et les oeuvres de Honore Daumet*, Paris: Jacquemin, 1919

Heritage New Zealand, 'Races Against Time', Summer 2006, pp. 4-7

Hayward, J., *Fragmented France: Two centuries of disputed identity*, Oxford: Oxford University Press, 2007

Herbert, R., *Impressionism: Art, Leisure and Parisian Society*, New Haven: Yale University Press, 1991

Hession, J. K., and Pickrel, D., *Frank Lloyd Wright in New York: The Plaza Years, 1954-1959*, Layton: Gibbs Smith, 2007

Hilderbrand, G., *Making a Landscape of Continuity: The Practice of Innocenti and Webel*, New York: Princeton Architectural Press, 1997

Home, G., *Epsom: Its History and Surroundings*, Wakefield: S. R. Publishers Ltd, 1971

R. Hopkins, 'From Place to Espace: Napoleon III's transformation of the Bois de Boulogne', *Proceedings of the Western Society for French History*, vol. 31, 2003, pp. 197-211

Hopkins, R., 'Engineering Nature: Public Green Spaces in Nineteenth-Century Paris', unpublished thesis, Arizona State University, 2008

Horden, R., and Blaser, W., (eds) *Light Tech: Towards a Light Architecture*, Basel: Birkhauser, 1995

Hotaling, E., 'They're Off!: Horse Racing at Saratoga', Syracuse: Syracuse University Press, 1995

Huggins, M., *Flat Racing and British Society 1790-1914*, London: Frank Cass, 2000

Huggins, M., *Horse-Racing and the British, 1919-39*, Manchester: Manchester University Press, 2003

Humphrey, J., *Roman Circuses: Arenas for Chariot Racing*, London: Batsford, 1986

Hunn, D., *Epsom Racecourse, its story and its people*, London: Davis-Poynter, 1973

Hunn, D., *Goodwood*, London: Davis-Poynter, 1975

Kay, J., and Vamplew, W., *Encyclopaedia of British Horseracing*, London: Routledge, 2003

Koch, P., 'Winning Streak', *World of Interiors*, January 2009, pp. 120-127

Janin, J. G., *The American in Paris during the Summer*, London: Longman, Brown, Green and Longmans, 1844

Jodidio, P., *A Racing and Breeding Tradition. The Horses of the Aga Khan*, Munich: Prestel, 2010

Johnson, C., *Florida Thoroughbred*, Gainesville: University Press of Florida, 1993

Jones, K., 'A Day at the Races: A Brief History of Horse Racing in France', in Sutherland Boggs, J., (ed.), *Degas at the Races*, New Haven and London: Yale University Press, 1998, pp. 208-224.

Kain, 'Deauville-Trouville', *Connoisseur*, vol. 204, January 1980, pp. 140-7

Kay, J., and Vamplew, W., *Encyclopedia of British Horseracing*, London: Routledge, 2003

Keeneland: A Thoroughbred Legacy, Lexington: Blood Horse Publications/Keeneland Association, 2010

Klein, R., Le Touquet-Paris-Plage, Paris: Norma Editions, 1994

Koch, C. R., 'Brass Rings and Leather Bindings', [n.d.]

Kruse, H., 'Social Interaction, the Arrangement of Interior Space, and Racetrack Renovation,' *Journal of Sport and Social Issues*, vol. 27, no. 4, November 2003, pp. 330-345

Construction Moderne, 'L'Hippodrome du Tremblay', vol. 22, November 1906, pp. 77-9, 89-91

Laird, D., *Royal Ascot*, London: Hodder and Stoughton, 1976

Langmead, D., and Garnaut, C., *Encyclopedia of architectural and engineering feats*, Santa Barbara: ABC-CLIO, 2001

Lapunzina, A., *Architecture of Spain*, Westport: Greenwood Publishing Group, 2005

Lemon, A., and Freedman, H., *The History of Australian Thoroughbred Racing*, vol. 1, Melbourne: Classic Reproductions, 1987

Lemon, A., and Freedman, H., *The History of Australian Thoroughbred Racing*, vol. 2, Port Melbourne: Southbank Communications Group, 1990

Lemon, A., and Freedman, H., *The History of Australian Thoroughbred Racing*, vol. 3, Prahran: Hardie Grant Books, 2008

Le-shi Li, *Sha-Tin Racecourse*, Hong Kong: Royal Hong Kong Jockey Club, 1979

Letamendi Urcelay, F., 'La Arquitectura del Club Hipico de Santiago y la Contribucion de Josue Smith Solar', unpublished research, 2000

Lewin, R., and Gill, B., 'Happy Crowds', *The New Yorker*, 8 October 1955, p. 38

Loh, N., *Star Track: Designing and Building the Singapore Racecourse*, Singapore: Epigram Books, 2000

Lycett Green, C., 'Towcester Boasts a Winner', *Country Life*, 23 October 1997, p. 70

McAdam, P., and Snyder, S., *Arcadia: Where Ranch and City Meet*, Arcadia: Friends of the Arcadia Public Library, 1981

Magee, S., *The Channel 4 Racing Guide to Racecourses*, London: Hamlyn, 1998

Magee, S., with Aird, S., *Ascot The History*, London: Methuen, 2002

Mason, W. H., *Goodwood Its House Park And Grounds*, London: Smith, Elder and Co. Cornhill, 1839

Metcalf, T., *An Imperial Vision: Indian Architecture and Britain's Raj*, Berkeley: University of California Press, 1989

Mitchell, V., 'Set in Stone', *Keeneland*, Spring 2011, pp. 40-51

Montauroux, D., 'Hippodromes', *Monuments Historiques*, no. 167, January/February 1990, pp. 113-17

Monuments Historiques, 'Trouville-Deauville 1910-1940', no. 189, September/October 1993, pp. 68-71

Morris, J., *Stones of Empire: The Buildings of the Raj*, Oxford: Oxford University Press, 1983

Muntz, J. Furey, 'Gordon B. Kaufman: California Classicism', in Belloli, J., (ed.), *Johnson, Kaufman, Coate: Partners in the California Style*, Claremont: Scripps College; Santa Barbara: Capra Press, 1992, pp. 29-41

Murray, J., 'Dreamland for the $2 Bettor', *Sports Illustrated*, 10 August 1959, pp. 44-5.

Murray, P., and Maxwell, R., *Contemporary British Architects*, Munich and New York: Prestel, 1994

Murray-Wooley, C., and Raitz, K., *Rock Fences of the Bluegrass*, Lexington: University Press of Kentucky, 1992

Ngiom, 'Selangor Turf Club, Sungei Besi', *Majalah Arkitek*, vol. 5, no. 2, March/April, pp. 20-5

Nichols, C., *The Leisure Architecture of Wayne McAllister*, Layton: Gibbs Smith, 2007

Nobuhiro, N., 'The Cult of Oguricap: Or, how women changed the social value of Japanese horse-racing', in Martinez, D., (ed.), *The Worlds of Japanese Popular Culture*, Cambridge: Cambridge University Press, 1998, pp. 167-80

Northeast Pennsylvania Business Journal, 'Racino Concept May Create "Destination Entertainment Venues"', September 2003, pp. 1, 30

Oliver, P., (ed.), *Encyclopedia of Vernacular Architecture of the World*, vol. 2, Cambridge: Cambridge University Press, 1997

Pacini, J., *A Century Galloped By*, Melbourne: Victoria Racing Club, 1988

Partington, G., *The Australian Nation: Its British and Irish Roots*, Melbourne: Australian Scholarly Publishing, 1994

Peake, W., 'Unregistered Proprietary Horse Racing in Sydney 1888-1942', unpublished thesis, University of Western Sydney, 2004

Phyfe, W., *Five Thousand Facts and Fancies*, New York: G. P. Putnam, 1901

Pisani, J., 'Report on Early Randwick Racecourse', unpublished report, University of Sydney, 1984

Plumptre, G., *The Fast Set: the World of Edwardian Racing*, London: André Deutsch, 1985

Powell, K., 'Race Courses Under Starters Orders', *Country Life*, vol. 196, 21 November 2002, pp. 64-7

Powell, R., *Rethinking the Skyscraper: The Complete Architecture of Ken Yeang*, London: Thames and Hudson, 1989

Proffitt, T. D., *Tijuana: the history of a Mexican Metropolis*, San Diego: San Diego State University Press, 1994

Prud'homme Farges, O., Vayron de la Moureyre, A., and Boiselle, G., *Stables: Majestic Spaces for Horses*, New York: Rizzoli, 2006

Raitz, K., (ed.), *The Theater of Sport*, Baltimore: Johns Hopkins University Press, 1995

Read, E., 'Bing's Baby: The Del Mar Story', *San Diego Magazine*, July 1967, pp. 54-79

Reeves, R., *Crown Jewels of Thoroughbred Racing*, Lexington: The Blood-Horse, Inc., 1997

Reinbothe, K., *Internationale Rennen zu Baden-Baden: 150 Jahre Rennbahn Iffezheim*, Baden-Baden: Wesel Kommunikation, 2008

Revue De L'Architecture et des Travaux Publics, 'Nouvelles Tribunes pour les Courses, à Chantilly (Oise)', vol. 10, 1883, pp. 218-221

Reynolds-Ball, E., *Paris in its Splendour*, vol. 2, Boston: D. Estes & Co., 1900

Richardson, C., *The English Turf: A Record of Horses and Courses*, London: Methuen, 1901

Riess, S., 'From Pitch to Putt: Sport and Class in Anglo-American Sport', *Journal of Sport History*, vol. 21, no. 2, 1994, pp. 138-84

Rispa, R., (ed.), *Birkhäuser Architectural Guide: Spain 1920-1999*, Basel: Birkhäuser, 1998

Roberts, P., and Taylor, I., *The Spa: Saratoga's Legendary Race Course*, London: Turnberry Consulting, 2011

Robertson, E., *Decorative Cast Iron in Australia*, South Yarra: Currey O'Neil, 1984

Robertson, W., *The History of Thoroughbred Racing in America*, Englewood Cliffs: Prentice-Hall, 1964

Romanet-Riondet, R., and Thibault, G., *Centenaire de la Société d'Encouragement 1833-1933 et Les Heures Mouvementées de la Société d'Encouragement 1993-1991*, Boulogne: Castelet, 1993

Ryall, G., 'The Race Track', *The New Yorker*, 12 September 1959, p. 120

St Aubyn, G., *Edward VII: Prince and King*, London: Collins, 1979

Salgueiro, V., 'Visual Culture in Brazil's First Republic (1889-1930): allegories and elite discourse', *Nations and Nationalism*, vol. 12, no. 2, April 2006, pp. 241-60

Sampson, A., *Courses of Action: the homes of horse racing*, London: Robert Hale, 1984

Schopfer, J., 'A New Race Course for Parisians', *Architectural Record*, vol. 21, 1907, pp. 353-9

Sheard, R., *Sports Architecture*, London: Spon Press, 2001

Sheard, R., *The Stadium: Architecture for the New Global Culture*, Singapore: Periplus Editions, 2005

Smith, C. C., 'Splendid Survivors: Horse Racing Stable Construction Saratoga Springs, New York 1840-1913', unpublished thesis, Cornell University, 1987

Spring, M. 'A Different Beast', *Building*, no. 12, March 2007, pp. 40-4

Steiner, D., and Gsteu, J., *Architecture in Vienna*, Vienna: Prachner, 1990

Sterngass, J., *First Resorts: Pursuing Pleasures at Saratoga Springs, Newport and Coney Island*, Baltimore, MD: Johns Hopkins University Press, 2001

Stevens, J., *Knavesmire: York's Great Racecourse and its Stories*, London: Pelham Books, 1984

Stout, N., *Great American Thoroughbred Racetracks*, New York: Rizzoli, 1991

Stout, N., *Homestretch*, Philadelphia: Courage Books, 2000

Summerfield, M., 'Leisure Time: Goodwood', *Architectural Review*, vol. 211, February 2002, pp. 56-9

Tattersall, G., *Sporting Architecture*, London: R. Ackermann, 1841

Teague, M., 'Metalworks. Sports Architecture', *Architects' Journal*, vol. 216, December 2002, pp. 1-16

Texier, S., *Georges-Henri Pingusson. Architecte (1894-1978)*, Paris: Verdier, 2006

Thibault, G., *Un Siècle de Galop 1900-2000*, Levallois-Perret: Filipacchi, 2001

Thibault, G., *Une Autre Regard sur les Courses*, Menton: Castelet, 2007

Thomson, E., and Minnaard, A., *Heritage Assessment Eagle Farm Racecourse*, unpublished report, December 2001

Thompson, L., *Newmarket. From James I to the Present Day*, London: Virgin Publishing, 2000

Thompson, W. N., *Gambling in America: an encyclopedia of history, issues and society*, Santa Barbara: ABC-Clio, 2001

Tillotson, G., 'Vincent J. Esch and the Architecture of Hyderabad, 1914-36', *South Asian Studies*, vol. 9, 1993, pp. 29-46

Trevelyan, F., 'The American Turf: The Race Courses of the East', *Outing*, vol. 20, no. 2, pp. 129-40

Turner, S., *The History of the Anglo-Saxons from the Earliest Period to the Norman Conquest*, vol. 3, London: Longman, Rees, Orme, Brown and Green, 1828

Twain, M., *Following the Equator*, Rockville: Wildside Press LLC, 2003

Underwood, T., *Thoroughbred Racing and Breeding: The Story of the Sport and Background of the Horse Industry*, Whitefish: Kessinger Publishing, 2005

University of Kentucky College of Architecture, *Discovering Robert Ward McMeekin (1898-1983): Bluegrass Architect*, exhib. cat., 1988

Victoria Park, Adelaide, South Australia: the course of natural beauty; centenary, 1871-1971, Adelaide: Adelaide Racing Club Inc, 1971

Vosburgh, W. S., 'The Passing of Jerome Park', *Outing*, vol. 38, August 1901, pp. 513-20

Walker, D., 'Plane Sailing: The Queen's Stand at Epsom', *Architecture Today*, March 1993, no.36, pp. 24-30

Walvin, J., *Leisure and Society 1830-1950*, London: Longman, 1978

Wilkinson, R., 'Sandown Park grandstand, Esher', *Architects' Journal*, vol. 160, 27 November 1974, pp. 1261-77

Wilson, R. G., 'Gordon B. Kaufmann and Modernism', in Belloli, J., (ed.), *Johnson, Kaufman, Coate: Partners in the California Style*, Claremont: Scripps College; Santa Barbara: Capra Press, 1992, pp. 71-81

Wragg, B., *The Life and Works of John Carr of York*, York: Oblong, 2000

Worsley, G., 'Towcester's Winning Streak', *Perspectives on Architecture*, February/March 1998, pp. 48-9

Year Book Australia, issue 87, Canberra: Australian Bureau of Statistics, 2005

Index

Page numbers in italics denote an illustration

Picture Credits

Acknowledgements

The authors are indebted to the help of many people in the preparation of this book. Many racecourses and individuals offered invaluable assistance in compiling the information and photographs necessary for its completion, and to all those we extend our thanks.

Thanks go to Timothy Cox, Tony McQuirk, Julianne McAtarsney, Francis Roberts, Richard Horden, the Australian Turf Club, Andrew Lemon, Luis Molina, Peter Chua, Guy Thibault, Sophie Cueille, Matthieu Vincent, Marilyn Charlton, Jim Beavis, Roger Cave, Lesley Keast, Rosemary Baird, Seamus Buckley, Keeneland Library, staff of the Saratoga Room at the Saratoga Springs Public Library, James Parillo at the Saratoga Springs History Museum, and to our colleague McKenzie O'Neill.

Special acknowledgements go to Brendan Phelan of Phelan Architects for preparing the plans that feature within each of the case studies and Dave Gibson of Draught Associates for designing the book.

Acanthus Press, 1133 Broadway, Ste.1229, New York, NY, 10010, USA
www.acanthuspress.com (+1) 212-414-0108

Turnberry Consulting Ltd, 41-43 Maddox Street, London, W1S 2PD, UK
www.turnberryuk.com (+44) 020 7493 6693

Designed by Draught Associates. Printed by Blackmore Ltd

Every effort has been made to contact and acknowledge the copyright
holders, but if any have been inadvertently overlooked the authors will be
pleased to make the necessary arrangements at the first opportunity.

British Library Cataloguing in Publication Data.
A catalogue record for this book is available from the British Library

Library of Congress Cataloguing in Publication Data.
A catalogue record for this book is available from the Library of Congress

ISBN 978-0-926494-83-1